THE BLACK PRINCE AND
THE SEA DEVILS

THE BLACK PRINCE
AND THE SEA DEVILS

The Story of Valerio Borghese and
the Elite Units of the Decima MAS

JACK GREENE

ALESSANDRO MASSIGNANI

DA CAPO PRESS
A Member of the Perseus Books Group

Library of Congress Cataloging-in-Publication Data
Greene, Jack.
    The Black Prince and the Sea Devils : the story of Prince Valerio Borghese and the elite commandos of the Decima MAS / Jack Greene and Alessandro Massignani.—1st Da Capo Press ed.
        p.   cm.
    Includes bibliographical references and index.
    ISBN 0–306–81311–4
    1. World War, 1939–1945—Commando operations—Italy.   2. World War, 1939–1945—Naval operations, Italian.   3. Borghese, Iunio Valerio, 1907–1974. 4. Italy, Marina. Flottiglia M.A.S., 10.   I. Massignani, Alessandro.   II. Title.
D794.5.G74   2004
940.54'5'092—dc22

                                                                2003025385

First Da Capo Press edition 2004

Published by Da Capo Press
A Member of the Perseus Books Group
http://www.dacapopress.com

Da Capo Press books are available at special discounts for bulk purchases in the U.S. by corporations, institutions, and other organizations. For more information, please contact the Special Markets Department at the Perseus Books Group, 11 Cambridge Center, Cambridge, MA 02142, or call (800) 255-1514 or (617) 252–5298, or e-mail special.markets@perseusbooks.com.

1 2 3 4 5 6 7 8 9 10 / 07 06 05 04

To the memory of
Richard L. Blanco, Professor of History at
State University of New York at Brockport, 1968 to 1992—
Friend and mentor to our first co-authored book

and

The eminent Italian historian and friend
Dr. Paolo Ferrari

CONTENTS

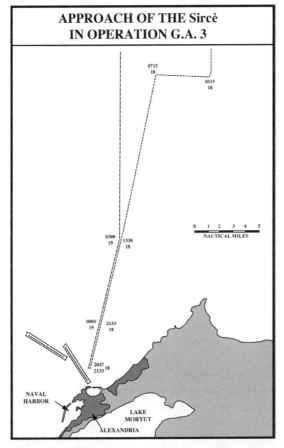

APPROACH OF THE Sircè
IN OPERATION G.A. 3

0715
18

0515
18

0 1 2 3 4 5
NAUTICAL MILES

0300
19

1330
18

0005
19

2133
18

2047 18
2133

NAVAL
HARBOR

LAKE
MORYUT

ALEXANDRIA

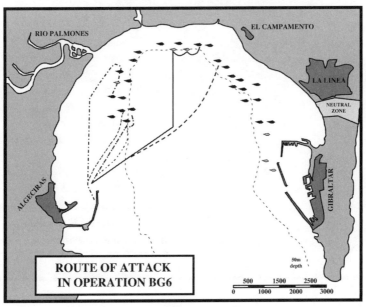

RIO PALMONES

EL CAMPAMENTO

LA LINEA

NEUTRAL
ZONE

ALGECIRAS

GIBRALTAR

50m
depth

ROUTE OF ATTACK
IN OPERATION BG6

500 1500 2500
0 1000 2000 3000

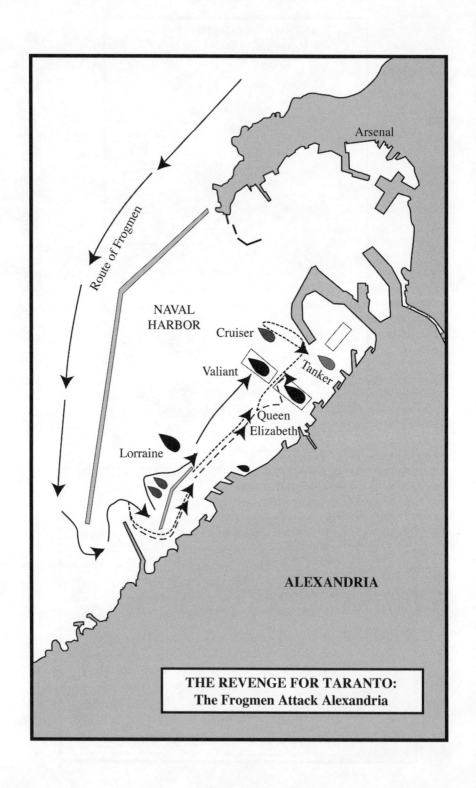

Route of Frogmen

Arsenal

NAVAL
HARBOR

Cruiser

Valiant

Tanker

Queen
Elizabeth

Lorraine

ALEXANDRIA

THE REVENGE FOR TARANTO:
The Frogmen Attack Alexandria

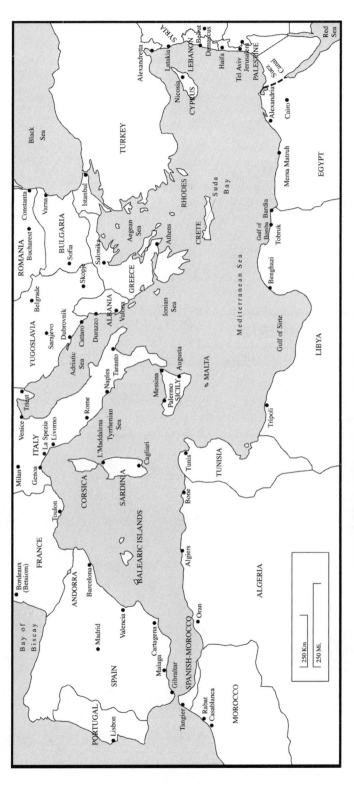

MEDITERRANEAN THEATER OF OPERATIONS

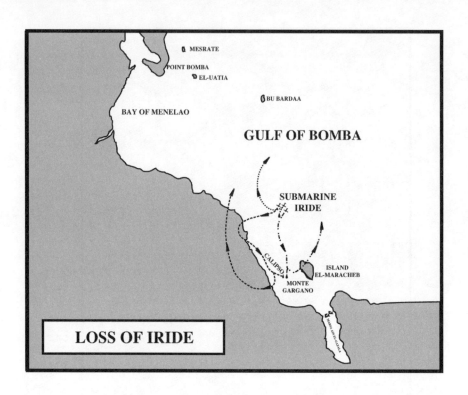

MESRATE

POINT BOMBA
EL-UATIA

BU BARDAA

BAY OF MENELAO

GULF OF BOMBA

SUBMARINE
IRIDE

CALIPSO

ISLAND
EL-MARACHEB

MONTE
GARGANO

LOSS OF IRIDE

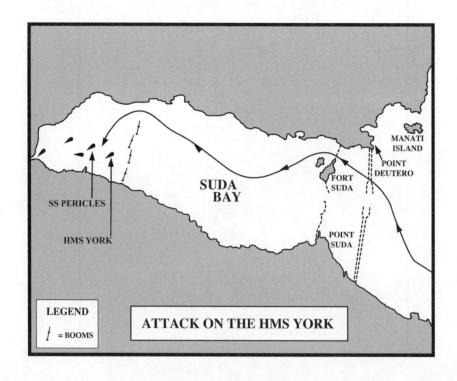

MANATI
ISLAND

POINT
DEUTERO

SUDA
BAY

FORT
SUDA

SS PERICLES

HMS YORK

POINT
SUDA

LEGEND

= BOOMS

ATTACK ON THE HMS YORK

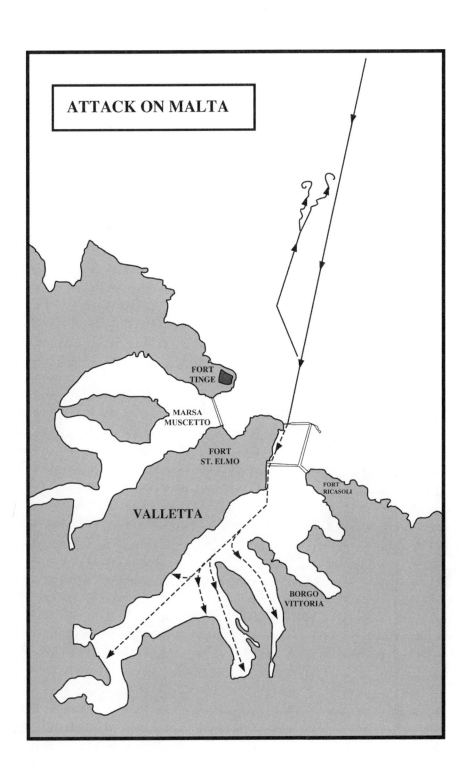

ATTACK ON MALTA

FORT TINGE

MARSA MUSCETTO

FORT ST. ELMO

FORT RICASOLI

VALLETTA

BORGO VITTORIA

OPERATION BG3 - Route of Scirè

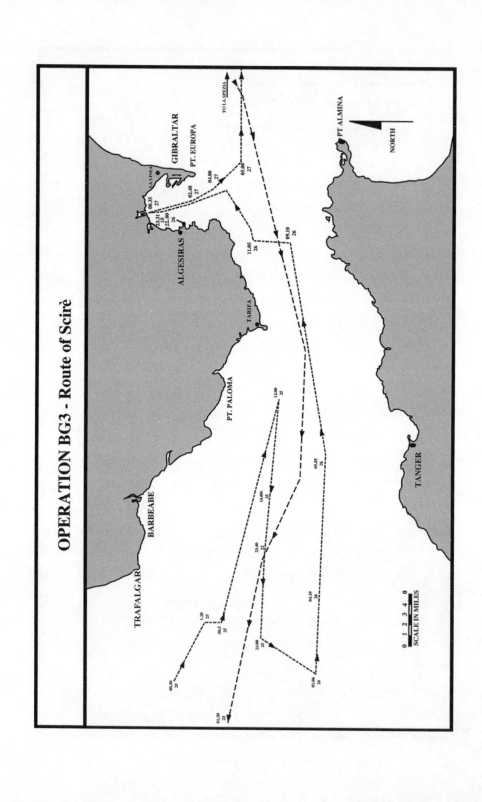

TRAFALGAR

BARBEABE

PT. PALOMA

TARIFA

ALGESIRAS

GIBRALTAR

PT. EUROPA

LA LINEA

TO LA SPEZIA

PT. ALMINA

TANGER

NORTH

0 1 2 3 4
SCALE IN MILES

ACKNOWLEDGMENTS

We would like to express our gratitude to a number of individuals whose assistance made this work possible. First, we would like to extend our special thanks to Andrew Smith for his scholarship and thoughtful critiques. Several times he was able to correct details and offer insights concerning key events in Borghese's life. We would also like to thank Professor Brian R. Sullivan, who was especially helpful with a cache of contemporary newspaper articles; Paolo Ferrari for his advice and assistance with documents and pictures; and Ken Gallagher of Combined Publishing for his learned guidance. We also appreciate the kind assistance offered by Carlos Mari of Venezuela, whose grandfather served in the Decima MAS; Lawrence H. McDonald at the National Archives for supplying documents; and Dave Sagor for his help in researching the Repubblica Sociale Italiana (RSI). Several noted scholars of the period have generously contributed their expertise to this project, including Professors David Alvarez and Richard Drake.

We cannot forget the friendly help of Mario Bordogna, who served as Borghese's aide-de-camp during the 1943–1945 Italian Civil War; and Christina Huemer of the American Academy in Rome, who confirmed to us that the Borghese family papers have been entrusted to the Vatican and that virtually all papers after 1922—to our temporary detriment but potentially to the benefit of future historians—are still under lock and key.

Thanks also to Carlo Alfredo Panzarasa and Sergio Nesi; Antonella Furlan for his help at the Archive of the Italian Navy; Achille Rastelli for his advice and assistance with photographs; Mario Del Pero, whose competence in the realm of secret services was as enlightening as it was helpful; Filippo Sinagra for his advice in the field of secret communications; Paolo Battistelli, who helped obtain documents on the X MAS; Renzo Brugnolli of the Museo della Guerra di Rovereto for his suggestions; Captain Christopher Page, head of the British Ministry of Defence Naval Historical Branch; and Dana Lombardy. We appreciate, too, the friendly assistance of Major of the Carabinieri Stefano Toscano, Antonio Semg, lieutenant colonel of the general staff to Fabrizio Stivoli.

Robert Pigeon, our senior editor who husbanded this project along for eight years. Richard Lane as project editor for Da Capo has been helpful, and if our tome sounds more robust than many, we must thank the copy editor Kathy Streckfus. Thanks also to Beth Queman for her maps and charts. Finally, special thanks go to the South Bay County Library and its helpful staff for filling the vast majority of our many book requests. To the many other individuals who have provided advice, expertise, and moral support to this project, our appreciation is sincerely offered.

Jack Greene
Baywood Park, California

Alessandro Massignani
Valdagno, Vicenza

INTRODUCTION

Prince Junio Valerio Borghese was born to a noble family that traced its lineage back to Imperial Rome and that over the centuries had held a prominent place among the Italian aristocracy. Born at the beginning of the twentieth century, Borghese came of age during the dictatorship of Benito Mussolini and became a Fascist. But he was more fundamentally a man of action. He began his career as an enterprising submarine commander and went on to lead the most successful Italian special operations raids of World War II.

Through these successes, Borghese rose to command the Decima MAS, or X MAS, the Italian naval unit devoted to clandestine naval operations. The attacks of the Decima MAS ranged from frogmen walking on the seafloor or riding manned torpedoes into enemy harbors to the employment of midget submarines and speedboats. The latter were modified to carry explosive charges—from which the rider would eject just before contact with an enemy target. Although Italian conventional forces gradually succumbed to Allied power in World War II, the Decima MAS continued to counterattack, often with devastating results.

After the Royal Italian government withdrew from the war in September 1943, Borghese moved his operation to the north, making a pact with both Hitler and Mussolini, and fought on—both on sea and also now the land. He would become a modern-day condottiere, commanding his own private army like the captains of medieval times, fighting for his own ambitions rather than a government's. After Italy's capitulation to the Allies, the Royal flag came down at its main naval base at La Spezia, and up went the flag of the Decima MAS. And thousands of new recruits flocked to that banner. In the ensuing civil war, having gained the sobriquet the "Black Prince," Borghese was briefly arrested by Mussolini, who was afraid of his growing power, and went on to lead vicious antipartisan raids in northern Italy and Yugoslavia, primarily against Communist partisans. In the bloody chaos that ensued after the collapse of the Axis, he and his wife would be the only Italian Fascists to be rescued by the American Office of Strategic Services (OSS).

Though sentenced to jail for war crimes, Borghese would serve but a short time because the Anglo-American secret services suddenly desired his help—for here was a Fascist who was also an anti-Communist, and after the destruction of the Axis the West now faced its next menace. In 1955, Borghese may have played a shadowy role in the sinking of the Soviet battleship *Novorossiysk,* the former Italian *Giulio Cesare,* which had been given to the Soviet Union as a spoil of war.

It was in the postwar period that Borghese became a leader of Italy's extreme political right wing. His adventures would ultimately culminate in a coup attempt against the legitimate government of Italy in 1970, after which he would flee to Franco's Spain to live out the remainder of his life.

Borghese is one of the most interesting personalities to emerge from World War II onto the world stage. And whether launching combat missions against the might of the British Royal Navy, commanding his private army in the north of Italy, or launching a coup attempt against the Italian government in the postwar era, he always played for major stakes.

Because of the many twists and turns in his career, and perhaps primarily because he fought on the wrong side of history, Borghese has become a "non-person" in Italy. We were regularly faced with governmental blocks in our attempts to find out all the facts about this remarkable man. This might have been expected from Italian governments, both Left and Right, but we would also be denied information about Borghese from U.S. government files that are still classified—or to use a CIA term, "sanitized"—despite the Freedom of Information Act. The British Public Records Office still seals its files on Borghese from public view, and of course the Vatican continues to privately hold the Borghese family papers, which are unlikely to be opened for many years to come. Unraveling the course of Borghese's life, particularly after 1945, has thus been like wandering through a maze with many locked doors.

Nevertheless, the amount of information that is available is considerable, and we have tried to present as complete a picture as possible of Borghese's life and the events in which he was involved. As Vietnam Medal of Honor winner James Elliot Williams once said, when asked why he would not sign away movie rights to his story, "If you're not going to tell the truth about that battle, then it ain't worth telling." We have tried to live up to this ethos throughout this work.

Because of Borghese's actions, actions he sanctioned (especially in 1944–1945 in northern Italy against the Resistance), and actions he has been credited with, though may have been opposed to or unaware of, the political Left in Italy has come to hate the man. As for the political Right, he is either mentioned in passing (if at all) or, in the case of the extreme Right, lionized as a hero.

So this life, wrapped in mystery, is one that we now bring before the English-language audience for the first time in a full-length work. But we also know that further research needs to done on this Black Prince of the Commandos. If we can be a starting point for some future historian, then we have succeeded in both our missions—telling the story of a man's life, and pointing the way for others to follow.

As the following chapters will attest, however, this book is not just the story of one man but the story of an organization, the Decima MAS. After commanding the unit during the conflagration of World War II, Borghese led it to even more prominence as a rallying point for

Italians (perhaps in the Prince's mind, "Romans") to continue the struggle against the tide of geopolitical events. Once the dust had finally settled from the world war, the Decima MAS would persist as a fertile ground for recruitment into the "Black International," the neo-Fascist paramilitary network that extended across national boundaries and other continents and took many forms, often violent.

In purely military terms, Italy's armed forces did not emerge from the greatest war in history covered with glory. The major (though not only) exception was the nation's innovative naval commandos, who inspired imitation by the British at the time, and whose conceptual descendants can now be found in American services such as the U.S. SEALs. Borghese and the courageous, innovative men with whom he served not only set an example but created a legacy for future naval special operations.

In today's world, and in the aftermath of September 11, 2001, where secret organizations employing unconventional means of attack are perhaps a greater threat than ever, the story of the Black Prince and the Decima MAS retains a special relevance. Dynamic leadership, skill, and imagination can often trump superior numbers and hardware, even if to the detriment of progressive civilization. Individuals, as always, remain the key, and the story of Prince Borghese's Decima MAS, in the final analysis, constitutes an important lesson in what pure daring can achieve in the face of great odds.

CHAPTER 1

To the Eve of War

He seemed a born leader, a condottiere, a captain, in the great tradition of the ancient republics.

Rear Admiral Franco Maugeri[1]

T HE STRUGGLE FOR THE SEA HAS ALWAYS SEEN the employment of great fleets and powerful warships, but at times countries unable to match their opponents in pure power have turned to developing a special naval assault capability. The successful employment of small units at sea generally involves innovation, creativity, and elite personnel with a high degree of training. And this kind of naval offense became the specialty of Junio Valerio Borghese, a twentieth-century soldier whose skill and audacity would have marked him a great warrior in any era.[2]

Prince Junio Valerio Borghese was born in Rome on June 6, 1906. The second son of Livio Borghese and Valeria Keun, he was raised at the small family castle of Artena, south of Rome near Anzio. His family tree ostensibly stretched back to the Rome of the Caesars, though in medieval lists the family name first appears in 1513. Among the Prince's ancestors were Camillo Borghese, better known in the early 1600s as Pope Paul V, and the family also produced several cardinals. In 1803, the Borgheses added an illustrious in-law when another

1

Prince Camillo Borghese married Pauline Bonaparte, Napoleon's favorite sibling. This marriage, which took place after twenty-three-year-old Pauline's first husband died while commanding Napoleon's expeditionary force to Haiti, was not a happy one. The beautiful Pauline became as renowned for being an exhibitionist as her brother was for military skill, and in the fabulous Borghese palace in Rome, she and Camillo occupied separate wings, closed off for mutual isolation. After a number of tempestuous years, Camillo declared a truce with Pauline, who today is viewed with much respect as the only one of Napoleon's siblings to visit him in exile.

By the time he was born, Junio Valerio's branch of the family was no longer extremely rich, having lost much of its wealth in the previous century, but it was still well connected, and his father was a diplomat and later plenipotentiary minister for the Italian government. Borghese lived in Great Britain for a few years as a boy, and later in Lisbon, owing to his father's career. He mainly grew up in Rome, where he studied for a career in the navy. He went to the Leghorn Naval Academy, Italy's Annapolis, and became a *guardiamarina* (midshipman) in 1928.

It was in 1922, when Borghese was sixteen, that Benito Mussolini accomplished his "March on Rome," and by the time the Prince emerged from school as an officer, the Duce and his new Fascist philosophy were fully in control of Italy. Aside from making trains run on time, the charismatic Mussolini was determined to reestablish Italian greatness—invoking the glory of Rome—with his principal instrument, the young Italian armed forces.

Borghese was most interested in submarine combat and at Leghorn specialized in that field. Among various appointments in the navy after graduation, he served on the cruiser *Trento* in voyages to Spain and South America and on the royal ship *Colombo* to North America. In 1930, he served a stint on torpedo boats in the Special Adriatic Division, and the following year he found time to marry Countess Daria Wassiliewria Olsonfieff. They went on to have four children: Elena, Paolo, Livio, and Andrea Scirè. His youngest was named in tribute to the submarine with which Borghese achieved some of his most daring successes in World War II.

Borghese also obtained his underwater diving certificate in his early years and was interested in the kind of unconventional naval combat actions at which his country had already demonstrated proficiency. During the Great War, after Italy joined the Allies against the Central Powers, the Italian Navy had excelled at special operations, sinking two Austro-Hungarian battleships by clandestine or special means.

The development of special assault units occurred in World War I when the stalemate of the war at sea in the Adriatic led the Italians to attempt to besiege enemy bases by other means. The Italians developed— as later happened in other navies, including the British, German, and Japanese—what had been one of the main war devices in the Russo-Turkish war: the very small and fast boat armed with torpedoes, better known by Americans after World War II as the PT boat. To the Italians, they were known as MAS, that is, *Motoscafi Anti Sommergibili* (antisubmarine motorboats), or in some early documents of the time, *Motoscafi Armati Siluranti* (armed motor torpedo boats). The name SVAN was also used occasionally, since the craft were built by the SVAN company. Despite specific prewar intentions for Italy's agile torpedo boats, the term MAS eventually entered idiom as a catchall for light craft or sub-fleet operations. (*Decima Flottiglia MAS* is often translated into English as "10th Light Flotilla.") Finally, it should be noted that MAS is also the abbreviation for the motto *Memento Audere Semper* (Remember Always to Dare) used by the MAS sailors.[3] The men of the Decima MAS personified this credo until the end of Italy's participation in the war—and beyond.

The early small torpedo boats were studied in several countries, including France and Britain, and Italy produced the first model around 1906. They were later built during World War I by an American company, Elco, as submarine chasers for Italy and Great Britain. For the Italian Navy, their main duty was to operate in the northern Adriatic Sea, where the waters were shallow, and the Adriatic coast of Austria required small vessels to operate because it was rocky and had many islands. The western, Italian, side of the Adriatic is mainly sandy coast. So to engage the Austro-Hungarian warships, the Italians developed special assault techniques.[4]

At the beginning of 1915, the first SVAN design was presented according to specifications requiring the motorboats to be armed with torpedoes and able to hunt submarines. The first orders to the yards of SVAN, to Orlando in Leghorn, and to Elco in the United States were issued in 1916, and by the beginning of 1917, 50 vessels, out of the 102 ordered, were available for action. The increasing rate of shipping lost to Austrian and German submarines caused the employment of some of the MAS armed with guns as submarine hunters.

In 1917, an additional 100 MAS were ordered, and these were also used for attacks against Austro-Hungarian bases. Of the 244 MAS employed during the war by the Italians, 38 were equipped with electrical engines that allowed them to be more silent and stealthy. Only 12 were fitted to launch two torpedoes. The armament of the boats varied and would be changed from time to time from torpedo to antisubmarine use. It included machine guns, 47 mm, 57 mm, and 76 mm guns, one or two towed torpedoes, and ship-mounted torpedoes.[5]

Of course, light craft were not the only menace from the sea, as submarines had in the meantime enjoyed great strides in development and were operating on both sides. The submarines of the Central Powers were quite active and dangerous to Mediterranean shipping, and French submarines displayed great courage by entering Austrian ports. On their side, the Austrian Navy began to study the defensive requirements necessary to counter the new motorboat threat. Booms and nets were deployed, and therefore the Italians were compelled to develop new assault tactics able to overcome such static defenses. In any case, the MAS vessels proved themselves an important weapon when they performed the considerable feat of sinking, on June 10, 1918, the Austro-Hungarian dreadnought *Szent Istvan*.

Other attacks had been planned but many failed for various reasons. By the end of the war, 244 MAS were in operation and 178 were under construction. But Austrian countermeasures compelled the Italian Navy to study some other means of assault, and a new design resulted from this endeavor. Of the four light boats produced, only one of them, the *Grillo,* was actually employed. The others were named the *Cavalletta,* the *Locusta,* and the *Pulce.* These boats were designed with tank tracks in order to overcome the nets placed at port entrances as protection for the warships by literally climbing *over* them. On May 13, 1918, the *Grillo* tried to penetrate the naval base of Pola, overcoming four of the first five obstacles, but the action failed. The *Grillo* was hit while being scuttled and its crew was captured. Two more boats of this kind were scuttled because, after a canceled action, they delayed the return to base of the towing boats. Only the *Locusta* survived the war, but it was probably demolished in 1921.[6] These attempts were the forerunners of what would be the surface assault craft of the Italian Navy in World War II.

But the most interesting light assault weapon was based on the work of two naval officers. One of them, Major of the Naval Engineers Raffaele Rossetti, designed a *mignatta* (leech), or a long, 14-inch torpedo, from the regular Italian B57 model, where the warhead could be detached, brought near the target, and left with a timer to explode. Physician Sublieutenant Raffaele Paolucci designed a mignatta that could be carried by a frogman walking on the bottom of the sea close to the ship being targeted. He volunteered to carry out the action and did much training, walking for miles on the bottom of the sea in a diving suit while towing a piece of iron that simulated the explosive charge. Although Paolucci's idea dated from 1915, work on the weapon went on in secret at Italy's naval base at La Spezia and the weapon began tests only on January 18, 1918. By March, it was considered ready for action. In the last months of 1918, Captain Costanzo Ciano, inspector of the MAS and father of the famous Count Galeazzo Ciano, Mussolini's son-in-law and onetime foreign minister, developed a new weapon merging these two ideas. The arm was christened *Torpedine Semovente Rossetti* (T.S.R.) (self-propelled torpedo Rossetti).

The chief of staff of the navy, Admiral Thaon di Revel, wanted the mines in operation, and on October 30 Ciano issued orders for their employment against the enemy naval base at Pola after aerial reconnaissance had gathered intelligence about the Austrian ships stationed there. Therefore, on the night of October 31, 1918, two torpedo boats towed two MAS piloted torpedoes to Pola, one of them carrying two T.S.R.s, under the command of Ciano.

The device had compressed air inside to propel it and had a range of 10 miles at 1 mph. It could carry two or three men and two warheads, which could be detached from the torpedo and fixed with a magnetic clamp to the keel of the warship the frogmen wanted to sink. In this case, the charge used against the *Viribus Unitis* had to be connected with ropes, because the keel of the Austrian battleship was too uneven due to fouling by barnacles.

The piloted torpedo was 8 meters long and had a diameter of 600 mm (24 inches). The personnel had little control over it, as they could only regulate the flow of the compressed air, and to turn, they had to extend their arms and legs on one side. The torpedoes were generally uncomfortable to drive: Operators preferred to stay on the sides instead of over the torpedo, as the craft was navigating stern down and the stern operator had the water at his throat. (The T.S.R. did not really navigate under water.)

At 2200, Paolucci and Rossetti were 1 km from the outer obstacles after being released by a MAS and proceeded onward with their rudimentary weapon. It took 32 minutes to reach Pola's outer boom. The seven booms of the Pola base were all overcome by 0300 on the morning of November 1. They fixed the charges, but at 0525 they were discovered and captured. The war was only days from being over, and on board, the Italians "acknowledged with surprise the new Yugoslavian badges on the caps of the sailors. Someone asked us in Venetian dialect how we reached the place and we replied that a seaplane brought us, as suggested by our commander Ciano."[7]

Confused by the friendly attitude of the sailors, the two discussed what to do. They asked for the ship's commander, Janko Vukovic de Podkapelski, and warned him about the approaching explosion. The ship was abandoned, but later all the crew and the two Italians went back on board. The crew was angry with Paolucci and Rossetti. There was considerable confusion on board, as the day before the sailors had formed seamen councils, which challenged the authority of the officers. But at 0630 on November 1, the charge exploded. Paolucci reported "a muffled noise, a deep rumble, not great and terrible, rather light, but a pillar of warm water." He wrote, "I felt under our feet the deck vibrating, tossing, staggering."[8]

In a short time, the *Viribus Unitis* capsized. A similar situation would occur many years later at Alexandria for other frogmen on board at the moment of an explosion. In any case, the commander saved Rossetti and Paolucci. In the ensuing chaos caused by the explosion, they were picked up by a boat from the dreadnought Austro-Hungarian *Tegetthoff* and freed on November 5 after the armistice between Italy and Austria-Hungary. The other explosive charge went off near the transport ship *Wien*, which sunk. Awkwardly for the Italians, the *Viribus Unitis* had already been turned over to the Southern Slav National Council (the future Yugoslavia); it had been renamed *Jugoslavija* and the harbor was undefended! However, it has been claimed by most Italian sources, and some non-Italian ones, that it was still Austro-Hungarian when sunk.[9]

It should be stressed that "an important factor of the building of these devices was the extreme security measures with which all the operations concerning production, tests and experiments were carried out."[10]

The Italian Navy's main strategic problem after World War I was the command of the Adriatic Sea, as the new Yugoslavia partly replaced the old threat of the Imperial Austro-Hungarian Navy. But the Yugoslavian Navy would be much smaller than the old Austro-Hungarian one. Further, this sea would be choked off again on the eve of

World War II, when Albania was invaded by Italy and the Otranto Strait at the head of the Adriatic would be closed again.

But before this could happen, the Italian Navy was thinking beyond the Adriatic Sea. After his Fascist takeover, the Duce considered the Mediterranean a *Mare Nostrum* (Our Sea) that should be ruled by Italy, and for this task the fleet needed to have new, large battleships. The admirals, of course, wanted many large warships, but at the same time they did not overlook the necessity of building minor vessels, especially submarines. Quite different was the continuation of the tradition of the motorboats. Little was added to them while seven heavy cruisers were built by Italian yards, in many cases in order to give commissions to hungry companies such as Ansaldo (the same company that would be involved in the early 1930s in a scandal over supplying defective armor plates to the Italian Navy).

The real problem for the Italian Navy, however, was that Mussolini's dreams of empire were about to be challenged by a greater power that had historically—since the ruin of the Spanish Armada—"ruled the waves." Italy had come down, after some hesitation, on the right side during the Great War, but the actions of Mussolini's revolutionary Fascist regime threatened to reverse its geopolitical relationships. In 1935, the British home fleet decided to take a tour through the Mediterranean just to "check on" developments. This sudden appearance of Britannia in the Mare Nostrum caused some consternation among the Italian naval command, and especially in the yards, where Italian industrial output was hardly able to keep pace with that of Great Britain and other major powers.

Yet, although the Italian Navy struggled to create new capital ships, it also possessed young officers such as Junio Valerio Borghese, who were less impressed by tonnage and firepower than by the concepts of innovation, small-unit actions, and bravery. As Mussolini began his attempt to found a new Italian empire, he counted very much on officers such as the young Prince, who would not be intimidated by the apparent strength of his rivals.

CHAPTER 2

Crises in Ethiopia and Spain

The swiftness with which the war in Africa terminated in a victory . . . caused the responsible military commanders to believe . . . that the situation had improved and the threat of a European conflict was less imminent. Accordingly, the small special weapons department had no sooner been set up than it was casually dissolved. This was a grave error.

Prince Junio Valerio Borghese[1]

I T WAS IN JULY 1933—AFTER MUSSOLINI HAD been in power for a decade in Rome and Hitler had just taken power in Germany—that Borghese became a lieutenant. Shortly afterward, he embarked as second in command on the submarine *Tricheco,* which sailed from Tobruk on September 10, 1935, toward the Red Sea. Together with four other submarines, the *Tricheco* had been assigned to support the Ethiopian (Abyssinian) campaign. Upon its return, the crew was awarded a citation by Undersecretary of the Navy Admiral Domenico Cavagnari.[2]

Italy's invasion of Ethiopia can probably best be explained by the fact that even though Italy (like Germany) had come to nationhood too late to fully engage in the Colonial Age, the Italians had nevertheless suffered the most devastating defeat in colonial history when their army

was wiped out by the Ethiopians at Adowa in 1896. This national hu-
miliation had been a burden to Italian leaders ever since, but it was only
Mussolini who dispatched new legions to avenge it. Exploiting a border
incident at Wal Wal (or Ual Ual), he took the occasion to mount a campaign against Ethiopia, and operations began on October 2, 1935, after
all attempts at mediation by the League of Nations had failed.

Italy's invasion of Ethiopia in 1935 caused tensions to mount with
other European powers, but Mussolini was certain that France and
Britain were not inclined to confront him and pressed the offensive,
hoping for a short campaign. He deployed every new method of warfare against the Ethiopian tribal armies, including poison gas, aircraft,
machine guns, and armor, and this time the Ethiopians did succumb.

His naked aggression, however—the first by a European power
since the "War to End All Wars"—did not sit well with the democracies. During the Ethiopian campaign there appeared for the first time
a serious possibility of war against the largest navy of the world,
Britain's Royal Navy. The Regia Marina (Royal Italian Navy) had
grown up in the British Royal Navy's shadow, and Britannia, like
Japan, had become a reference point, an example from which to learn
the art of naval combat. If one looks at *Rivista marittima,* Italy's naval
magazine, during all the years before World War I, this student/teacher
effect can be clearly seen. During the Great War, the Italian Navy did
not change its internal view and only strengthened its relationship
with Britain. Until 1935, Italy had prepared war plans against France,
Yugoslavia, and Germany; only after his African adventure did Mussolini request that his chief of staff plan for a possible war against
Britain.[3] The Italian Navy obviously lacked the resources to contest
command of the Mediterranean Sea with the Royal Navy, and much
faith was put in the Italian Royal Air Force, or Regia Aeronautica,
though its effectiveness was overrated.

Now that Mussolini had restirred the European stew, just as Hitler
was repudiating the Treaty of Versailles in Germany, all of Europe's
militaries began to reintensify their focus. As with many interesting

technical developments of World War I, Italy's special assault craft had been left aside for years. During the Italo-Ethiopian War, on November 27, 1935, Admiral Aimone D'Aosta proposed the use of explosive boats that could be transported some 10 miles from the target with the model Savoia Marchetti SM.55 seaplanes. This strategy had been suggested to him by his brother, Duke Amedeo D'Aosta. The resulting study was conducted by Commanders Giorgio Giorgis and Carlo Margottini and foresaw the employment of six boats, each with a torpedo warhead of 330 kg that would be launched against the enemy base.[4] When the base was reached, the first boat would have to run at maximum speed toward the enemy's boom defense, and at a distance of 50 to 100 yards the pilot would jump into the sea. After the first explosion opened a breach for the following boats, they would rush and attack any enemy warship found in the protected anchorage.[5]

A dummy wooden prototype was built in order to test its transportability by seaplane, but a March 1936 trial found that air transport was quite difficult. Meanwhile, on June 15, the Cantieri Baglietto yard (at the coastal town of Varazze lying between Genoa and Savona) was asked to produce the hulls for two MAS, and CABI Cattaneo of Milan was to produce the engine parts. For security reasons, the final assembly of the craft would be performed by the navy.

When tests were carried out in November 1936, one of the two boats reached a speed of more than 32 knots. Each boat weighed 950 kg and was propelled by a MAS 500-type Alfa Romeo engine of 2,500 cc, developing 90 hp, with which the boat had a range of some 80 km at maximum speed. The boat was not even 3 feet in height, a feature that helped make transport by seaplane possible.

The *barchino* (the first name—literally a small open boat) was not designed to explode at the moment of impact. Rather, it was built with a so-called "gun," that is, a series of little explosive charges placed behind the bow that would break the boat in two at the moment of impact. The main charge would not explode until well under the waterline near the target. This would inflict more damage than a surface explosion. A timer was also included to ensure the explosion of the charge; it was set for a minute and a half so that, at the very latest, the explosion would occur when the broken boat was resting on the bottom of the harbor.

But the old T.S.R. was also taken again into account, especially by Elios Toschi and Teseo Tesei, who each proposed a self-propelled craft based on the World War I assault device. Cavagnari accepted both proposals. Testing began on prototypes that would ultimately result in the two main attack craft used by the Italians during World War II. They were the SLC, or *Siluro a Lenta Corsa* (slow torpedo), nicknamed the *maiale* (pig), and the MT (*Motoscafo Turismo*, or touring motor-boat)—the official, somewhat deceptive name for the barchino.[6] Studies and experiments began and the first weapons were produced; meanwhile, the Ethiopian campaign concluded and the international situation began to relax. (See map on page xi.)

A third method was also developed. At the 1st Submarine Group near La Spezia, Italy's main naval base, training took place for divers who had to exit from surface units and walk on the bottom of the sea towing charges like Paolucci's leech. This training was carried out mainly at Port Santo Stefano, La Spezia, and later at Bocca di Serchio. The latter was at the mouth of the Serchio River, a lonely spot near the royal estate of San Rossore, well isolated from enemy eyes. At the same time, beginning in September 1935 the 1st Submarine Group began to produce prototypes of the SLCs developed by Toschi and Tesei.

These two naval engineers were assigned to the submarine arm, and when their design was ready and forwarded during the Mediterranean crisis, it was readily accepted. They were allowed to build an SLC employing thirty personnel of the submarine workshop. However, they could only devote their free time to the project after completing their regular duties. And, being engineers, they were not allowed to command their inventions.

In October 1935, the prototype was ready. Despite several small construction defects, it proved to work surprisingly well both in a swimming pool and at sea, so a second SLC was ordered. It was built quickly and was ready by January 1936. A demonstration of the new weapon was held for the inspector of naval construction, Vice Admiral Mario Falangola, who was quite impressed and ordered two more SLCs to be built. These SLCs, though built in a short time, were big improvements on the earlier Rossetti model. They were mainly drawn from torpedo parts but had a steering gear and a means of regulating the speed of the craft, and there were wind screens for the protection of the frogmen who rode them.

Secrecy again played a major role, and therefore steps were taken to avoid every breach of security. For Falangola's visit to La Spezia, security was cleared and controlled by the military police, the Carabinieri. Again, as the tests and training progressed, the Carabinieri, who also had the duty of counterintelligence, had to check every tourist coming to the area, especially foreign ones. Finally, the men of the assault craft were compelled to choose an out-of-the-way place. So they went to the Salviati estate at Bocca di Serchio, where they slept at first under tents, and then in primitive barracks, but the personnel had high morale and overcame these inconveniences.[7] It seems that although Italy's armed forces were routinely suspected of regular breaches in their security system—a trend that accelerated during World War II—in this case the secret was well protected and was the basis of the manned torpedoes' future success.

The work of Tesei and Toschi went on until the summer of 1936; the campaign in Ethiopia ended in the late spring and the international situation improved, although the League of Nations had inflicted economic sanctions on Italy. The fact is that the league and the Great Powers had been faced with a fait accompli and were still not fully ready to check the threat of Germany, Italy, and Japan. In any case, the prototypes were stored and forgotten until the Czechoslovakian crisis of 1938, although some documents show interest by officers in this assault weapon in 1937. Cavagnari's cavalier attitude toward the *Mezzi Insidiosi,* or naval guerrilla war, would be a crucial failure that would help ensure Italy's maritime defeat by the Allies in 1940.[8]

Of course, speculation has remained on the question of what a full-fledged war between Italy and Great Britain in the 1930s would have been like. According to some sources, the special assault means would have had to be available in great numbers and used during the first nights of such a war to exploit the element of surprise. However, with only a very few and still crude prototype models available, little, in reality, could have been done.

It was on September 10, 1935, that the British Home Fleet entered the Mediterranean, and the Italian Navy had little to oppose it. In fact, the only battleships available were two of the unmodernized *Duilio* class, armed with 12-inch guns, which would not be enough to check the Royal Navy. These old battleships would enter the yards for a complete facelift and reconstruction only in 1937. At this time, the old *Cavour* class battleships were undergoing a massive modernization. Finally, the two new *Littorio* class battleships were still in the yards, which proved rather slow in getting warships ready.[9]

The potential effectiveness of the Italian air arm was loudly trumpeted by Mussolini's regime at the time, and his boasting temporarily impressed the British. The Italians were said to be considering the employment of suicide aircraft, adopting proposals to make use of the old Fiat BR.5 bomber, but it was all just a bluff. Mussolini deliberately let the British know of this development, even though it was a sham.[10]

Meanwhile, Mussolini's foreign policy increasingly leaned toward Germany, and this trend would intensify during the international crisis in Europe that was next, the Spanish Civil War. But the feeling that the danger of a war at sea had eclipsed caused the tests on the SLCs to be suspended. The equipment was put aside in depots. The same happened with the explosive assault boats. After they were tested, they, too, ended up in storage, at the Cottrau proving ground near La Spezia. This happened not only because of the changed international situation but also because future developmental plans stressed the big ships and their powerful guns, which the navy thought would decide the war at sea.[11]

The war with Ethiopia was not completely over (Ethiopian guerrillas would fight on until the end of the Italian empire in East Africa) when on July 17, 1936, the Spanish crisis broke out. The young Spanish general, Francisco Franco, then governor of the Canary Islands, and other right-wing individuals revolted against the new republican, leftist government, and so began the Spanish Civil War between the Nationalists and the Loyalists (loyal to the government).[12]

On the Nationalist side, Italy and Germany intervened to help Franco, delivering weapons, supplies, and troops at an increasing rate. Already, at the beginning of August, as Tangier was in the Republican navy's hands, there was a need for planes to transport Franco's troops from Morocco to Spain. This need was filled by German Ju-52s and Italian SM-79s and supported by a handful of Spanish aircraft. Airplanes, land troops, and warships came to the Nationalists' aid, and the Italian Navy sent submarines to sink ships arriving with supplies for the Republican side. This contribution was particularly vital as the Republicans were able to control almost all the Spanish fleet, as the lower decks overthrew their officers.

The Italian Navy also employed secret operations, mainly with submarines. This is where Junio Valerio Borghese first walked onto the world stage. He was involved in the Italian naval support of the Nationalist side of the Spanish Civil War, receiving his first command in 1937 with the submarine *Iride* (which would later become the first submarine to begin an operation with the SLCs).

The *Iride* was one of a class of ten small submarines built during the Abyssinian crisis. They displaced 695 tons surfaced and 855 submerged, with a maximum dive depth of 80 meters, or about 260 feet. In an emergency they could go deeper. Their maximum speed was 14 knots surfaced and 7.5 knots submerged. They were armed with six 21-inch torpedo tubes and carried twelve torpedoes. Like most Italian submarines, they could also fire smaller, 17.7-inch torpedoes that were used on smaller targets to save money. This *gabbia di riduzione* (torpedo tube-reducing gear) was fitted on one bow and one stern tube.

Submerged, the subs could travel 74 miles at 4 knots. The *Iride* had a surface range of 5,200 miles at 8 knots, a crew of 45, and one 3.9-inch deck gun. It was delivered to the Italian Navy on November 6, 1936.[13]

Lieutenant Borghese was about to rendezvous with the first watershed event in his life when he sailed from Naples on August 24, 1937. He arrived in Sardinia, then sailed to Spain on the 26th for his assigned patrol area between the island of Ibiza and Cape St. Antonio. The *Iride* would commence attacks on a total of eight targets but did not fire on six of these. On the evening of the 29th, the submarine spotted a cargo ship steaming slowly toward the port of Valencia and attacked it twice but failed both times. At the target's estimated speed of 5 knots both torpedo salvos missed, the last launched at a distance of only 600 meters—four torpedoes wasted.

Disappointed, Borghese and his crew planned to try again the next night (August 30/31, 1937). Borghese intended to launch an attack from the surface. This would be the fifth time, to date, that an Italian submarine attacked a Loyalist destroyer. Four submarines had launched a total of six torpedoes; one had hit and severely damaged the *Churruca*. One submarine, the *Finzi*, had been depth-charged and slightly damaged in return.

At 2045 on the 30th, a dark silhouette of a ship was spotted and identified as a Loyalist Spanish destroyer of the *Sanchez Barzcaitegui* class—but the identification was mistaken. It was instead the British destroyer HMS *Havock*, which somewhat resembled the Spanish vessel. The *Havock* was steaming south from Valencia to Gibraltar at about 15 knots and had just made an alteration to its course to round Cape St. Antonio.

Borghese maneuvered for the attack at a speed of 5 knots and at 2052 launched a single 450 mm (17.7-inch) torpedo at 700 meters. The torpedo's wake was spotted by the HMS *Havock*, which turned toward the *Iride* "and narrowly missed" the torpedo, which passed astern at a depth of about 10 feet. *Havock* illuminated the submarine, which was on the surface about 400 yards distant. The crew of the *Havock* reported that the sub had broached after firing its torpedo, but in reality it was in the act of diving after having made a surface attack.[14]

The destroyer began to chase its unknown assailant, but the destroyer's sonar gave the location of the submarine as different from where it was sighted. So *Havock* pursued the sonar contact and launched depth charges on the sonar location. This did not damage the *Iride,* which in the meantime had crash-dived. This event would mark the first wartime use of sonar.[15]

Havock now circled the area, and at 0130 the ship made sonar contact again, this time about 3 miles from the original attack. The sonar contact was "as near 100% a submarine echo as it is possible to say." Depth charges were dropped but with no result. As Borghese maneuvered the *Iride* beneath the dark sea to evade the *Havock,* the hunt was joined by three other British destroyers, the *Hyperion,* the *Hotspur,* and the *Active* (the latter lacking sonar). These were supported by the light cruiser *Galatea,* hoisting Rear Admiral James Somerville's flag as commander of the Mediterranean Fleet's destroyers. By morning, the reinforcements were in position. The *Galatea* launched a seaplane at 0708 to aid in the search.[16]

Borghese escaped the nine-hour hunt, as he performed the "appropriate tactics," but also because the sonar procedure proved faulty. Somerville recommended changes that were later implemented.[17] Indeed, Somerville expressed frustration at Borghese's escape in his report to the Admiralty, stating, "I consider that the Commanding Officer, 'Havock' showed lack of judgement in not seizing the opportunity furnished by sighting a submarine only 400 yards away and carrying out an immediate full depth charge attack which I feel convinced would have sunk the submarine or brought her to the surface."[18]

Borghese was lucky enough to reach Naples again on September 5. There, the crew was placed in isolation to avoid the spread of gossip about the Spanish situation and the *Iride*'s episode. The Italian Navy was under fire because the incident had provoked international protests about "unidentified submarines" attacking the shipping that

supplied Republican Spain. This was the first scandal to involve Borghese. Coupled with the fact that the British merchant ship *Woodford* was
sunk in broad daylight by a surfaced submarine, the *Diaspro,* the event
had caused the British to become quite displeased with the Italians and
their pirate war. But the Russians and the French, especially, were
deeply angered with operations off North Africa that led to losses. The
Russians asked that those responsible be punished and that Italy pay
for the damages inflicted. The Italian foreign minister, Count Ciano,
was compelled to order Cavagnari to suspend naval actions in the
Spanish arena.[19]

The British were more restrained, but on September 4 Rear Admiral
Somerville visited the commander of the Italian force in Spain, Rear
Admiral Alberto Marenco di Moriondo, who hoisted his flag on the
old cruiser *Quarto.* Moriondo reported that Somerville was well aware
that submarines had launched both attacks, against the *Havock* and
the *Woodford,* and that they were certainly not Republican. "The attack
of the submarine was carried out so well," he said, "that it should be
excluded that it was a Red submarine." The British surmised that the
Iride was an Italian vessel because it did not retire toward a Spanish
Nationalist port. Somerville also told Moriondo that the British could
have sunk the submarine but chose to spare it. Borghese had expended
one of his nine lives.

One of the interesting things that surfaced at that meeting was the
fact that the British could detect and track the submerged Italian
submarine when their warships were at 20 knots—a previously unknown capability. After Somerville's visit, Moriondo received another officer of the Royal Navy, Captain D. W. Boyd, commander of
the 2nd Destroyer Flotilla on the *Hardy.* Boyd and the *Hardy* had arrived along with the *Hyperion* during the chase of the *Iride* early on
September 1. Boyd made it clear that Borghese's submarine had been
closely followed for ten hours, an achievement only possible with
some device other than hydrophones, which were only effective at
slow speeds.[20]

The tiny 334-ton submarine chaser *Albatross,* built in 1934, carried Italy's first experimental sonar set *(petiteo),* which was first being experimented with at the time of the Spanish Civil War. The Italians now suspected that the British had such a device because of their ability to track the *Iride.*[21] Another interesting point that emerged was that the British Admiralty's Operational Intelligence Centre (OIC), already operating from June 1936, knew at least some of the movements and missions of the Italian submarines. The OIC acted as a sort of clearinghouse for incoming combat information.

The Italian submarines used the SM 19/S manual code book, which was regularly read—according to historian Franco Bargoni—by the British Government Code & Cypher School (GC&CS). But if the British were aware of Italian submarine movements, it was more probably the result of interception of high-grade radio traffic from the services or perhaps at the diplomatic level. It appears that the manual codes generally used by the submarines were not penetrated at this time.[22] It is certain that the British often managed to intercept and locate submarine radio dispatches with range-finding stations, although not always. The 1937 submarine campaign also taught the OIC that the GC&CS needed to send the "raw" decrypts over, no matter how unclear. This issue arose because the GC&CS was making its own interpretations of signals without having access to all the data available to the OIC, and with corrupted signals.[23]

On September 1, 1937, the Nyon Conference was held to determine countermeasures against piracy in the Mediterranean, and at the end of the month Italy had to sign the Nyon Agreement. The country was even assigned an area to patrol for "pirate" submarines.

Borghese's quarantine when he arrived home was very brief, though he seemed in disgrace with Mussolini, who was angry about the international uproar caused by the attack. The Duce had to handle several difficulties at that moment. Thus the *Iride* had to berth at the end of a remote pier at Naples for a few hours and was then ordered to Taranto for repairs. The day Borghese arrived at Naples, a motorboat went immediately to confine the submarine far from the harbor. A car that was sent to pick up Borghese brought him first to the submarine base commander and then to Rome. From the attitude of the navy officers he saw, Borghese expected the worst consequences from the affair. He might not have been far from the truth, but as it turned out, a new turn of events changed all this.

After so much trouble created by Borghese, Mussolini then learned that the British had commented that the attack was carried out well. The Duce's attitude completely changed. Instead of being brought on the carpet for his actions, Borghese was instead awarded the Bronze Medal, and the crew was given the War Cross.[24] Borghese's Spanish activity was not finished. A few days later, he sailed from Cagliari and reached the Spanish Nationalist naval base of Soller, near Palma on Mallorca, on September 23, 1937. His *Iride,* also called *L3* (*L* was for *Legionaire*), hoisted the Nationalist flag and was renamed *Gonzales Lopez.* He also had a Spanish officer on board, Lieutenant Antonio Calin.

At first, the four Italian submarines at the base were inactive, but soon patrolling was resumed with heightened rules of engagement to avoid international incidents, as Italy had agreed to the antipiracy patrol decided at the Nyon Conference. Areas assigned to Italy were large but all very far from the Spanish coasts, so the "unknown" Italian submarines could only intercept shipping from the Aegean Sea to the western Mediterranean.

The Italian submarines made several missions, and Borghese's *Gonzales Lopez* took part in these during the four weeks the Prince was stationed at the Soller base. This is important for another incident involving a British destroyer, the HMS *Basilisk,* on October 3, 1937, near Cape St. Antonio. The commander of the warship reported a failed submarine attack, to which the destroyer reacted by launching depth charges. The nearby destroyer *Boreas* had not spotted the torpedo, so although newspapers made it into the stuff of another piracy scandal, the story soon petered out amid suggestions that it was not a torpedo but a dolphin that the *Basilisk* had detected. But in 1968, Borghese published a book in Spain recalling the story of the Italian submarines during the Spanish Civil War and declared that he had been there, had attacked the *Basilisk,* and had suffered two dead and four wounded in the subsequent depth charge attack. Although he altered times and names, he seemed to be referring to this same incident. The details of his account have not been verified, however.

Franco Bargoni wrote for the Italian historical naval office in that period, and he has claimed that, according to documents, Borghese was inactive at the Spanish base and could not have been involved in the attack on the *Basilisk.* In the opinion of noted naval historian Giorgio Giorgerini, who usually writes well-balanced accounts, some doubt remains. He commented that Borghese was quite accustomed to secret operations and that the absence of documents on his possible actions at the time would not necessarily mean they did not take place. "Summing up," Giorgerini wrote, "the case *Basilisk*-Borghese remains without solution." If Borghese lied here, then it casts doubt on some of his later claims, particularly about the attack on the Soviet battleship *Novorossiysk* in 1955. But as so much in his life, one can only conclude that the case is unproven but certainly possible.[25]

Borghese returned to Italy on November 11, 1937, because his echo sounder had jammed and could not be repaired on the spot. He returned to Spain with the *Gonzales Lopez* on January 5, 1938. The ensuing mission was unsuccessful, partly because the rules established about merchant hunting after the piracy campaign were rather difficult to maintain. Merchant ships could be attacked by night essentially only at a port's entrance because the submarine commanders had to be sure that the ship was in territorial waters and steaming to a Republican port.

The *Gonzales Lopez,* or *Iride,* sailed on January 14, 1938, and patrolled the coast, remaining mainly at periscope depth before Castellon de la Plana, Valencia, Cape St. Antonio, and Cape Oropesa. One day passed between Denia and Gandia and one between Valencia and

Sagunto. The record of the ambushes is disappointing: All the ports were busy with transports, and all of the ships observed by Borghese sailed under the British flag, and were only rarely suitable for attack. Moreover, Borghese had to attack within 3 km of the coast in shallow waters. But it should be noted that there were no antisubmarine escorts or other activity and Borghese did launch four torpedoes that failed to hit.

In general, the record of the Italian submarines in the Spanish Civil War was disappointing. Their performance should have drawn attention from the Italian Navy's "Admirals Committee," which might have made good use of it as a learning experience. The German naval attaché's report of June 16, 1937, noted that the operations in the Gulf of Naples were conducted well (resulting in the loss of several merchant ships). But he thought that the Italian Navy still had "much to learn in training" and was "too attached" to "rigid rules of conduct." He went on to state, "The training for war is still not carried out in the difficult situations we now are accustomed to."[26]

Borghese's report said that, in two cases, torpedoes did not launch owing to mechanical failure, and of the two launched successfully, one probably sank in the coastal sand and the other was evaded. Borghese later wrote that the "very calm sea, moonlight, and perfect visibility made surface attacks by night difficult." Nevertheless, the lack of opposition and antisubmarine actions were a dream come true for a submarine commander and the mission could not be considered a true war experience.[27] On January 23, Borghese returned to Soller, and on February 5, 1938, he left Spain and returned to Italy.

His performances were evaluated variously. The commander of the *Legionaries* submarines, Lieutenant Commander Francesco Baslini, justified two of Borghese's torpedo launch failures in his report. His opinion was shared by the Italian liaison officer with the Spanish Nationalist Navy, Lieutenant Commander Stefano Pugliese, the chief of the Missione Navale Italiana (MNI, or Italian Naval Mission). Captain Giovanni Ferretti, commander of the Italian Naval Mission in Spain, however, felt that Borghese's bad performances could only partly be due to the difficult circumstances. Ferretti acknowledged the "high of-fensive spirit of Commander Borghese," but he also wrote:

Launch of the 19th . . .
. . . Although I don't want to attribute the failure of the missed target to a launch error, in my opinion it was very probably that cause.

Launch of the 22nd—0100 p.m.
. . . The commander should have taken into account the shallow sea. But he had the attenuating circumstances that he was restricted to the coastal zone of the territorial waters.[28]

Borghese still had not entered the new dimension of special assault craft, but in the Spanish campaign he displayed the aggressive spirit necessary for the job. When total war burst upon the Mediterranean, the young submarine commander would find ample opportunity to demonstrate both his daring and his imagination.

CHAPTER 3

Preparing for the Secret War

Had the X MAS been fully operational in June 1940, when the British lacked ULTRA and good port security at Alexandria, Gibraltar, and La Valletta, the war might have gone very differently.

James J. Sadkovich[1]

BORGHESE WAS NOW A COMBAT VETERAN, EVEN as all the major powers endeavored to enhance their fleets of ships and submarines. But the Italian Navy's assault craft had not been totally forgotten.

In the spring and summer of 1937, the Operation Plans Office of the Regia Marina prepared two interesting memoranda that took into account, again, the potential of special assault craft. They stressed that they could overcome every enemy port defense and suggested that the navy take advantage of the experience it had gained with them thus far.

The plans foresaw the training of nine crews for the human torpedoes and six crews for four midget submarines. These four submarines needed to be designed to penetrate enemy harbors (although no such attempts would be made in the course of the war). Six SLCs were proposed. These plans remained dormant for several months, at least in part until the fear of a possible war began to emerge with the ongoing

European confrontations. The conservative and hidebound Italian naval leadership represented by Cavagnari refused to allocate men or even a pittance of money for the project.

The Munich crisis of September 1938 showed how much tensions were growing in Europe: Mussolini was still pushing for peace among the Great Powers and seemed capable of helping to bridge the gulf between the democracies and the Nazi state. In March, Hitler had marched into Austria and annexed it; a few weeks later, he encouraged the German inhabitants of Sudetenland in Czechoslovakia to ask to join the Reich. When the crisis became more acute, the French mobilized and Britain mobilized the Royal Navy. At the end of the month, Chamberlain and Hitler signed the famous pact that opted for "peace in our time" in Europe, but it was clear that steps were being taken by all the Great Powers to prepare for war.

Toward the end of 1938 the international situation had changed enough to suggest to the Italian Navy that it should resume the study of assault craft. The day after the Royal Navy mobilized, the Operation Plans Office proposed to the chief of staff to build a Special Weapons Section of the 1st Flotilla MAS at La Spezia under the command of Commander Paolo Aloisi. The flotilla, besides supplying fast attack motorboats, would serve as a cover organization for the training of assault craft personnel. Workshops at La Spezia would be used by the Commissione Permanente, or Permanent Commission, to develop the SLCs, and officers would be trained for the assault craft and would also prepare plans of operation for them. Cavagnari, having seen a secret documentary film on the project, now realized its potential, and he approved the proposal on the same day that he received it. The paperwork still needed to be done, but the decision itself came quickly in the face of the new naval threats.[2]

Later, the Decima Flotilla MAS would be spun off as a special section of the 1st [Primo] Flotilla MAS, but not until March 15, 1941. Meanwhile, the men would operate as if they were training for subma-

rine rescue operations. At the beginning, there were twenty-one officers to operate eleven SLCs and seven MTs. In addition, an improved
model of the MTM (*Motoscafi Turismo Modificati*, that is, modified
touring motorboat) was now under construction. Some of the men
were appointed to study assault operations against possible enemy
harbors. The targets for the SLCs would be Alexandria, Haifa, Oran,
and Algiers. At the same time, plans were prepared for midget submarine attacks against Malta, Toulon, Gibraltar, and Aden.

It was later decided to move these operations from La Spezia to the
Salviati estate at Bocca di Serchio because it was isolated enough to ensure the required security. One side of the estate was closed off by a
gunnery proving ground at Viareggio and another by the royal estate
of San Rossore, where the police watched the area regularly. The assault unit did not need any special surveillance that would have raised
suspicions. Moreover, the mouth of the Serchio River was useful for
tests and training because the seafloor in the area was very regular. Of
course, much of the training took place at night, both for security reasons and for the planned nocturnal war actions.

Life at the estate was hard and sometimes boring. The men were
isolated for long periods of time, and secrecy was not easy to maintain
without the strictest security measures. But the intensive training at
Bocca di Serchio produced several frogmen who would later become
famous, including officers Elios Toschi and Teseo Tesei as well as Gino
Birindelli and Luigi Durand de la Penne.[3]

The year-long training involved four phases. First, frogmen operating
the submarine that would transport the SLCs had to learn how to simulate the approach to the enemy harbor by maneuvering the sub slowly
while hugging the seafloor. Second, the divers had to learn how to exit
the submarine, both by night and by day, with the "40/bis" breathing apparatus. Third, they had to learn how to overcome numerous obstacles
and practice cutting or raising the nets and penetrating the harbor. Finally, the SLC men trained to pilot the "pigs," as they were nicknamed, in
various conditions, and became proficient in detaching the warhead and

attaching it to a target ship. In addition, they received advanced instruction in underwater diving and navigation. One of the operators wrote this excellent description of the final approach to the target:

> You approach, at "observation level," to within about 30 metres of the target. . . . You take a compass bearing, then you flood the diving-tank and the water closes over your head.
>
> Everything is cold, dark and silent. Now you are deep enough; you close the flooding valve, put the motor into low gear and slide onwards. It gets suddenly darker; you know that you are underneath the ship. You shut off the motor and open the valve for pushing the water out of the diving-tanks. As you rise, you lift a hand above your head. You wonder whether it will touch smooth plates or knife-edged barnacles which will play the devil with your fingers, or, worse still, tear your rubber overall and let the sea seep through.
>
> Now you have found the hull. You push the torpedo back, so that your assistant can catch hold of the bilge keel, a couple of hands' breadths wide. . . . You feel a thump on the shoulder: your assistant has found the bilge and is fixing a clamp on it. Two thumps on the shoulder: the clamp is in position. Now you go ahead to get at the bilge keel at the other side. Your second is playing out a line from one side to the other. He fixes the second clamp. And now back again, pulling oneself along by the line stretched under the hull, as far as the centre of the ship. While you clutch the rope with your hands, holding the torpedo between your legs, your second leaves his seat and passes you till he reaches the warhead in front. In the darkness you know that he is fastening the warhead to the rope stretched under the ship between the bilge keels. Now he has detached the head; the firing clock which will cause the 330 kg of the charge to explode in two and a half hours begins to measure off the seconds. . . . Now you may think of escape.[4]

The nickname "pig" was first used by Tesei, who, during training, used the phrase "Tie the pig" to refer to tying the machine to the net.

Under the water, the frogmen could easily speak to one another, thanks to a thin metal sheet that vibrated inside the breathing mask.[5]

A typical two-person exercise at Bocca di Serchio involved raising an iron net like the ones used to protect the harbors. To do this, one of the men would climb the net vertically for some yards and tie it off with a rope, then he and his partner would pull the rope to raise the net. Later, the British made the nets heavier by increasing their length and they became much more difficult, if not impossible, to raise. There were other difficulties, too. To prevent the SLC from being carried away by the river current, the men needed to fix it to the net during the maneuver. The Italian crews also developed a system of cutting the nets instead of raising them and sometimes employed a net "raiser" device utilizing compressed air.

However, the SLC was still in its infancy when it was committed to operations in August 1940. At the time of Italy's entrance into the war there were probably eleven SLC torpedoes available, though this number cannot be confirmed. These models were plagued by several problems. Ongoing modifications were introduced with the active collaboration of CABI, the company developing the second-generation SLCs. These changes improved the SLCs' speed and stability. The length of the new machines reached 7.2 meters (22 feet), instead of the original 6.8, and the engine power was raised to 1.6 hp, with an underwater speed of 2 to 3 knots. Such improvements led to the 100 series, eight machines ordered in July 1940, after Italy had already lost many opportunities at sea. The devices employed in the first operations attempted in 1940 were drawn from the first eleven, and not very satisfying, SLCs. The 100 series was sent into action later, and the follow-on replacement model, the 200 series, only began arriving in late 1941. Three of the latter were presented at Alexandria on December 19, 1941, and more than twenty were built after minor technical problems had been solved.

The first eleven SLCs were built with parts drawn from standard Italian 21-inch torpedoes. The head, 1.8 meters in length, held an explosive charge weighing about 230 kg (260 kg in the third prototype). This feature was modified in the second torpedo produced because of problems with pressure changes after detachment of the head. The solution was a ring that fixed the torpedo to the ship's keel. In the first series, it was fixed with bags inflated with compressed air, which pushed the explosive head toward the surface. In the 200 series, there were two charges, each weighing 125 kg, contained in parallel cylinders that could be fastened together. The charge was activated by a timing device produced by the famous Borletti watch company. The result was a charge powerful enough to cause critical damage to a warship.

The central part of the SLC, where the two-man crew was positioned, contained the mechanisms the pilot needed for driving the machine. It was possible to crash-dive in about 6–7 seconds at speeds of up to 3 knots under water. Surface speeds were a little higher, and surface movement was employed whenever possible to conserve oxygen. The SLC was powered by an electrical motor that moved a single screw, a design that replaced the standard double-screw design because it made for a quieter machine. There were four different speeds plus reverse. Near the screw was the vertical rudder for steering and hydroplanes to control depth.

The pilot and his *Numero Due* (Number Two), sat astride the machine. The pilot had a screen to deflect water resistance (like a windshield) and a control panel supplying depth, battery-charge level, time, and compass direction, all illuminated, in later models by means of phosphorescence. Thirty 60V cells formed the battery, which was inside the torpedo between the two seats.

Later, the Delta assault craft, was introduced. Called the "SSB" because it was produced at the San Bartolomeo works, it was a total redesign where the operators sat inside instead of astride the machine. The design was by naval engineer Major Maio Masciulli and Captain G. N. Travaglini; engineer Guido Cattaneo, who worked for the CABI company, was also involved. Trials were carried out at the beginning of 1943 and were satisfactory. The SSB was not longer than the SLC but

Explosive

FIGURE 3.1 Series 100 SLC

was much heavier (2,200 kg) and could carry a 300 or 400 kg warhead. Its diameter was 78 cm, and it was powered by a 7.5 hp engine and could develop about 4 knots. At the time of the armistice on September 8, 1943, Italy had only three machines available, all prototypes, and by the end of the war another eight were built, this time by the Caproni company, an aircraft producer. Four SSBs survive today and are on display in museums—one is at the Newport News Maritime Museum.[6]

Meanwhile, training for another important group continued. Named the "gamma men" after the "G" in *guastatori* (assault engineers), this group came out of the 1935 trials seeking to build on Paolucci's experience and ideas from World War I. The first training sessions resulted in interesting information for the submarine crews, but less for the divers, who, "walking" on the seafloor carrying a heavy explosive charge, could only manage a speed of 500 meters per hour. Given the short time span that the Davis breathing apparatus provided in 1935–1936, and the fact that the sea bottom was generally muddy, the tests were not satisfactory. Nevertheless, the gamma men would later be used from neutral Spain to attack nearby Gibraltar.

In 1940, somewhat too late, the Naval Academy formed a divers school commanded by Lieutenant Eugenio Wolk. He further developed both the divers and the frogmen with the help of Commander Angelo Belloni. There is an interesting story about Belloni. In 1914, before Italy had entered World War I, he stole a submarine that was to be given to Russia and attempted to carry out a mission on his own against Austria-Hungary. He was put on trial and finally found not guilty. When he was recalled to the colors in 1940, he helped instruct a course for frogmen and armed them with underwater rifles to make the sessions more interesting.

Frogmen were chosen through a strict selection process. Once enlisted as volunteers, they began a short training period that covered the use of the breathing apparatus and basic underwater work. Those who successfully executed this course were sometimes asked to become assault swimmers *(nuotatori d'assalto)*. This additional training lasted ten months and was quite demanding, which explains why only some fifty men were employed in this capacity during the war.

With technological advances in their equipment, the gamma men became a dangerous weapon. They no longer walked on the sea bottom with heavy shoes; instead, after exiting the submarine, they swam with fins to the target ship armed with limpet mines. Much lighter than the SLCs, these explosives were named *bauletti* (little trunks), or *cimici* (bugs). They had to be light so that the frogmen could swim longer distances with them. Weighing about 4.5 kg, the "bugs" worked on a timer that could be set for between one and six hours by simply turning a spring, and a frogman could carry five of them at once on his belt. They resembled eggs and could be attached to the ship's hull directly or in an inflated bag filled with air. A magnetic clamp was eventually developed, but too late to be effectively employed before the armistice.

The bauletti were cylinders containing a more powerful explosive, a charge of some 12 kg of Nipolit.[7] The cylinders could be tied to a ship's bilge keels and were activated when the ship left harbor and reached a speed of 5 knots. At that point, a screw was freed and began to turn, causing, after a certain number of rounds, the trigger to hit the charge. Because the explosion occurred in the open ocean, it was difficult for investigators to determine the cause—which could have been a torpedo or even a mine. Moreover, the increased depth of the water at the site of the explosion usually assured the definitive loss of the ship. Later, when the British began to react by inspecting the hulls of their ships, the charges were fitted with booby traps to prevent their removal.

It is interesting to note that training also extended to the members of the N battalion (N for *nuotatori,* or swimmers) of the *San Marco* marine regiment, who were also trained as saboteurs and commandos for action behind enemy lines. These N marines were later joined by the P (for paratroops) regiment to form the famous NP battalion. All were prepared to damage enemy ships, but they could operate only for a short time and for short distances, and approaching the target continued to present challenges. Despite all the training, the preparation was not enough. When Italy entered into the war, there were few SLCs or explosive fast boats, too few to play an important role against the French and British navies.

The political situation did influence the plans for men and equipment at the 1st MAS. In February 1939, Aloisi was summoned to Rome for a special commission to study and organize the assault craft. The minutes of the meeting show that the participating officers were pushing ahead as they were worried about the lack of progress. By that time, only two out of eight MTs were ready for action, although the other six were expected to become available in March. Eleven SLCs were ready, however, at San Bartolomeo. Aloisi was instructed to immediately train the personnel for the boats and SLCs and to recruit officers and noncommissioned officers (NCOs) coming from submarines with some experience in diving. Moreover, he was told to try transporting the "pigs" to the enemy bases by submarine, despite an earlier decision not to use subs in this manner.

The idea of transporting the boats by air had been dropped, perhaps because the navy did not have its own air force, but more probably because of technical problems that had not been solved. For example, how were the SLC personnel to stay on the torpedo during the flight? And how would the SLCs be launched once on the sea? Moreover, the airplane that was supposed to be used for the task was the slow Cant Z.506, and of course an attack of several SLCs would have to be carried out by a number of such planes without escort because the targets were so distant. These vulnerable, lumbering aircraft, if not intercepted, would certainly have alerted the enemy of an approaching attack.

In July 1939, Admiral Cavagnari ordered the establishment of a Special Arms Section attached to the Navy General Staff under the command of Captain Vittorio De Pace. The Supermarina—that is, the mobilized high command of the navy—also issued an order that read: "The command of the First Light Flotilla is entrusted with the duties of training a nucleus of personnel for employment with given special weapons, and of carrying out . . . experiments and tests concerned with the perfecting of the said weapons."

The navy also began working on plans to attack Alexandria and Gibraltar at the first opportunity when war broke out. If these plans had been completed by the time Italy declared war on Britain and France in June 1940, along with plans for a surprise attack on Malta, the Italian Navy might have achieved a substantial success. Instead, the secret weapons were hastily deployed only after the surface fleet and air force displayed inadequate preparation and effectiveness during early encounters with the British Mediterranean Fleet.

This new form of warfare was not introduced without resistance. As always, in a navy there are different points of view about innovation, especially when the confrontation is between stealth vessels and battleships. One could recall the clash of tactical and strategic theories between the so-called *jeune école* and the battleship schools in the nineteenth century. So, also, in the Royal Italian Navy the assault craft were discounted by a faction entrenched in establishment naval interests and committed to defending them.[8] They argued that the new methods did not have a track record proving their effectiveness in a real war. And of course, there were many problems that would have to be solved before the new weapon would really work. Training and equipment for the fast attack boats were not difficult, and the personnel were highly motivated and had the required esprit de corps. But the divers, gamma men, and "pig" crews had to stay in the water for hours and would have to possess excellent physical conditioning and skills. The selection process was grueling from both the physical and moral point of view.

For the frogmen, even once trained in the skills needed to carry out the missions there were other challenges. Special preventive techniques had to be used to avoid hypothermia from several hours under cold water. The long exposure to the water could inhibit action, lower men's spirits, and lead to a mission failure by forcing the gamma men to the surface. These problems had no simple solutions. For the hypothermia, the Italians had a woolen undergarment for the divers and the Belloni waterproof diving suit over it. This system was still theoretical, as several times water had penetrated through the stitching after several hours under water, and the pressure on the skin caused light injuries that disturbed the frogmen's work. The diving suits clearly would have to be improved.

A long-range breathing apparatus was also needed. The Davis had been standard equipment since the 1920s and was in use in all navies, but Italian submarine personnel had lost confidence in it following some accidents. Several modifications led to a number of new models that were being tested, and in fact, the Davis was being used to rescue personnel from submarines, not for working under water. A Belloni model tried in 1930 included a mask that enabled the diver to breathe without holding an oxygen tube in his mouth, and other models were developed later, especially during the 1935 Mediterranean crisis. A special commission had even been established to study the problem.

The commission, formed by Commander Catalano Gonzaga di Cirella, Commander Giuseppe Moschini, and a surgeon, Major Ferdinando Dorello, was looking for a reliable breathing apparatus that would also be fit for SLC personnel. They were especially interested in safety and favored a continuous flow of oxygen. Rejecting the Belloni model, they wanted a mask-type apparatus that did well in tests both in swimming pools and at sea. They looked at some thirty different models, including "49/bis," produced by AIC, a company of the Pirelli Group. The 49/bis model was finally chosen, but it was not ready to be implemented until the conclusion of the Mediterranean confrontation with Britain, in the summer of 1936. Thus, the 1st light flotilla carried out tests and training with earlier models.

During the war, improved models entered service. The G.50, also produced by Pirelli, supplied oxygen in a closed circuit from two cylinders for long-range employment or from one for short actions. Such high-pressure cylinders could have provided almost pure oxygen so there would be no danger of air bubbles coming to the surface of the water, which could have revealed the presence of the frogmen. But pure oxygen would have caused considerable problems for the men, and therefore the gas coming from the cylinders was a mix. The flow of air was channeled through a valve that reduced the pressure and then to the mouthpiece, and the exhaled air was recycled through a lime soda container.

The frogmen also needed waterproof compasses and watches. These were not available at the time of the Ethiopian campaign or at the ensuing Mediterranean crisis. At the 1st light flotilla's request, the Hydrographic Institute and the Commissione Permanente began to research the problem. The equipment would have to resist salt water, be easily readable under water, and easy to wear with the diving suit. It took some time to find devices that met these standards, but in March 1936, watches were given to the men of the 1st light flotilla. The Lazzarini compass was also adopted in 1936, along with a modified version for the human torpedoes. Although several tests had been necessary to solve the problem, the time spent from September 1935, when the requests were issued, until 1936, when the equipment became available, was not wasted. During the last months before the war, it became more urgent to have the assault craft ready, and these two components, at least, were settled.

Lieutenant Borghese had meanwhile taken command of the submarine *Ametista* of the 600 class, which had been selected as a delivery transport for the "pigs." By the beginning of 1940, training had reached a point where combined exercises could be attempted. Three

SLCs were fixed directly onto the deck of the *Ametista,* which had been fitted with supports for them.[9]

The *Ametista* had already conducted exercises with the frogmen to train them in exiting from the submarine at Bocca di Serchio. The "pigs" were released by night in front of La Spezia base near the isle of Tino, and one of them succeeded in reaching the target after several hours, practically at daybreak, while the second and third ran into technical problems and failed. The target was the old cruiser *Quarto.* Certainly if this had been war, the target ship would have been lost even though two of the torpedoes did not reach the objective. Two frogmen had attached the false explosive charge to the ship's keel.[10]

This was the first experiment in the presence of Vice Admiral Ildebrando Goiran. The results, according to official documents, were "very encouraging." Nevertheless, there were still problems. The position of the SLCs on the deck made possible only short-distance operations; it would be difficult to reach distant enemy harbors. With such a load, the submarine had to navigate at a maximum depth of just 30 meters, and this, in the sometimes shallow and often clear waters of the Mediterranean, would probably be fatal.[11] Moreover, a signal that would allow the assault teams to return to the submarine that was tested in the La Spezia exercise did not work and was abandoned.

In his memoirs, Borghese stressed that these operations were seen from the outset as one-way, that is, everyone knew there was little chance for the recovery of the frogmen after the operation was carried out. As Borghese stated, "No plans should be made for return to the submarine." The pilots preferred to think that "no energy was to be held in reserve for eventual escape," and that every effort had to be made to inflict "the greatest possible damage to the enemy."[12]

CHAPTER 4

Assault Boats and Human Torpedoes

The exploits of the Decima MAS are an example of what courage and bravery can achieve in the face of seemingly overwhelming odds. In a war in which technology occupied a position of growing importance, their exploits were a reminder of an age when character and bravery counted for everything.

Peter Kemp[1]

IN ADDITION TO TOP-SECRET MANNED TORPEDOES and frogman tactics, the Italians continued to create experimental light assault craft. Altogether, these new underwater and assault weapons fell basically into five types, some with more promise than others.[2]

The construction of surface craft, after the first trials of the MA explosive boat and its air-transported cousin in 1936, resumed with the navy's order of September 29, 1938. The Baglietto and CABI companies were asked to build six new assault motorboats to be ready for tests in December. The MTs were not ready until February 1939, when they were given to the navy for final assembly, and were only tested in the late spring of 1939. The tests were a big disappointment. The outer shell of the motorboats, made of canvas, simply did not work, and the order for twelve boats was revised to eliminate the previous weight limits. The limits had been set to accommodate the concept of transporting the craft by seaplane, but delivery by air was now abandoned and the assault boats could be built with more durable materials. The position of the engine was also changed, and the new boats were some 4 inches greater in height than the prototypes.

The next twelve MTs were built only after the first six had been successfully modified with the use of wood for the hull. Also, a life raft was added for the pilot. The raft would serve as his backrest until the moment he was ready to abandon the craft, when he would release it by pulling a special lever. He would then swim to the raft and crawl on top of it, hopefully before the explosive charge went off so that he could escape the shock wave from the explosion. Tests were successfully completed in the spring of 1940, and then production of the next twelve MTs got under way. Only by the end of 1940 were the first assault motorboats available for use, and a complete trial occurred on November 13, 1940, when an MT armed with a reduced explosive charge was launched against the old cruiser *Quarto.*

The MT craft, however, still were not completely satisfactory. The builders continued to improve the materials, and the navy commissioned the MTM, the modified design, which itself underwent several changes. The pilot's station was improved, the hull strengthened for seagoing capabilities, and a reverse gear added to facilitate the maneuvers involved in approaching a target. The MTM was successfully

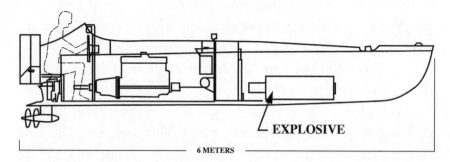

FIGURE 4.1   MTM Explosive Boat

tested on March 1, 1941. In the test, it developed 33 knots at a full weight of 1,100 kg. Nevertheless, the twelve boats ordered following the test were not ready until the autumn of 1941, and the first assault boat actions were carried out with the old craft.

At this point, the new weapons were satisfactory, but it had taken a full ten months after Italy's entrance into the war for them to reach this point. From the planning point of view, assault motorboat tactics counted on surprise. The time lost between 1936 and 1938 was disastrous. It was too late to win a decisive victory. Later the boats were further improved, and a smaller boat was studied at the navy's request. This version was to be contained within the tight cylinders coming into use on submarines for carrying the SLCs to their targets. By then, actual deployment of explosive boats had shown that transporting the craft with surface ships was too dangerous and that the submarine would be a safer option.

In any case, the MTMs became the standard assault boats of the Decima MAS, and they continued to be used after the armistice. They were also well appreciated by the German Navy, which ordered 170 of an improved version, 40 of which were given to the X MAS in 1944 for planned actions against Allied shipping in Italian ports.

Beyond the assault craft, there were two models of fast motorboats armed with torpedoes. They were based on the MAS that allowed Lieutenant Commander Luigi Rizzo in World War I to sink the *Szent Istvan,* but much smaller than the regular motor torpedo boats. Indeed, the MTS (*Motoscafo Turismo Silurante,* or touring motor torpedo boat) was not much bigger than the MTM, measuring 6.5 meters in length, 2.2 meters wide, and 1.75 meters high. Since the engine was the same as in the MTM, the speed was lower, 28 knots, and the range was but three hours. The boats were originally to have two operators, but the seat turned out to be large enough for only one man. Manufactured by the Baglietto Company, the MTS was armed with two modified (smaller) 450 mm torpedoes that were shortened to 3.2 meters and weighed 300 kg, half of which was explosive. They were launched toward the stern of the boat and entered the water at a low speed, stopped, and then began to move forward pushed by their screw. Of course, the MTS had to turn immediately after the launch to avoid tragic accidents.

The MTS design was completed by January 1940 but the first five boats were ordered only in the spring. They were not tested until the summer, when the first, unsuccessful phase of the war had already passed for Italy. In this case, too, the original model was modified; tests on the redesign lasted until the beginning of 1941. Although three MTS boats were employed, the navy was unsatisfied with them because they were too slow and had poor seagoing capabilities. The orders for the last two boats were canceled, and a modified version was placed under study.

The MTSM, featuring two engines and only one torpedo, was the new model. The final "M" in the acronym was originally for *Marino* (Marine) to emphasize the improved seagoing capabilities of the new boat. Apart from several changes in the design, the main difference between the MTSM and the old MTS was a reduction of the explosive, which went from two torpedoes to one and was placed at the center of the boat behind the operators, who now numbered two. Moreover, the MTSM carried two 50 kg charges on its deck sides that could be released against ships. Another interesting improvement was the addition of a radio, and the pilots' cabin was now enclosed. These changes resulted in more than one meter of increased length.

Both the SLC and the MT needed support craft to reach distant enemy targets, but midget submarines could travel independently until reaching the enemy base and then penetrate the harbor to sink ships. The Italians traced their tradition of midget submarines back to World War I, when they built fourteen midget submarines of the models called Alfa, A and B. They had little success, being relegated to harbor defense owing to their poor seagoing characteristics, but the experience was nevertheless useful.

By 1938, two midget submarines, called *CA1* and *CA2*, were delivered to the Italian Navy. They were not registered in the shipping logs as they had to remain secret. "CA" meant coastal type A submarine. They were built by Caproni Taliedo, an airplane factory, displaced 13 tons, were armed with two 17.7-inch torpedoes, and had a crew of two. Trials carried out at La Spezia and Venice, however, proved the submarine was unable to perform its duty in torpedo attacks. A third seaman was added so the midget submarine could be used to deliver assault teams of frogmen. Experiences and tests carried out during the years before the war showed several maneuvering problems, including depth instability (especially after the release of a torpedo), and led to the production of the marginally more successful model, CB.

Thus the CAs were modified and adapted to carry gamma men to distant targets. Their armament consisted of eight 100 kg explosive devices and twenty 2 kg explosive devices. Two additional CAs built in 1943 were also devoted to this kind of mission but had the ability to dive to more than the 47 meters reached by the *CA2* in the winter of 1941/1942 at Iseo Lake in Italy. Also, the 1941 modified version was unsatisfactory because it was difficult to maneuver and very noisy. For this reason, it could not be employed in combat. The midget submarines remained experimental. In actual combat situations, the gamma men would be released by regular submarines, as in the case of the *Ambra* of Commander Mario Arillo.

The last version was developed at the Bordeaux submarine base, Betasom, which the Italians operated with the Germans in the Atlantic, in 1943. The *CA2* was sent to the Atlantic, as in the summer of 1942. The Allied Mediterranean bases were too well protected for the midget submarines because they were not fully developed. Several tests were carried out in the Atlantic in which the submarine *Da Vinci* transported the *CA2* out to sea and released it. At first, the procedure resulted in damage to both craft. After several tests, the *Da Vinci* succeeded in releasing the CA and recapturing it. These final exercises were considered satisfactory.

Finally, the *CA3* and *CA4* were ready in the spring of 1943 and supplied to the navy, but it was too late. The CAs that fell into German hands at the time of the armistice were never employed. The two CAs, however, figured in plans to penetrate two Allied harbors in the Atlantic—New York and Freetown—an audacious plot of which we will speak later.

The improved type CB coastal submarine was more successful and built in greater numbers. Twenty-four of this model were ordered, and of these, twelve were given to the Italian Navy beginning in January 1941. After the armistice of September 1943, several were still in the yards, partially completed by Germany. Six had been sent to the Black Sea theater, where one was lost and the others captured. After that, only one *(CB3)* was fit for action. The Germans gave five of them to the Rumanian Navy, which later had to give them to the navy of the Repubblica Sociale Italiana (RSI, or Italian Social Republic), but the submarines remained ashore and were never employed. Advancing Soviet forces captured four of them in September 1944. The fifth probably disappeared as parts were cannibalized to outfit the other four vessels. According to René Greger's research with Soviet documents, the KGB (not the Soviet Navy) employed at least two CBs until the 1950s.[3] Six remaining CBs were divided between the north and south of Italy after the armistice. The five CBs in the south remained with the Royal Italian Navy, while the Germans at Pola captured the other one.

Nevertheless, the *CB2* also had its problems, and in the spring of 1943—again, too late—another type of midget submarine was designed by two yards that were ordered to supply three prototypes each. The Caproni company (Milan) and Cantieri Riuniti dell'Adriatico (Manfalcone, a port near Trieste) both built their first models, which were named CC and CM, respectively. The navy then ordered eight CCs and sixteen CMs, perhaps because the Caproni company was slower than Monfalcone in building the prototypes. Only one CM was ready before the end of the war. Christened *CM1*, it was launched three days before the armistice. It was later commissioned as *U.It.17* in the RSI Navy. Two more CMs were also in the process of construction but were never completed. The uncompleted *CM2*, which the Germans named *U.It.18*, is still on display at Trieste.[4]

Ten CBs were delivered to the RSI Navy, and of these, three were sunk at Pola *(CB13, CB14,* and *CB15)* by aerial bombing, and *CB18* was scuttled by its crew at the end of the war. Also at Pola, the Yugoslavian partisans succeeded in capturing *CB20. CB17* was sunk near Ancona, and a German boat rammed *CB21.* Finally, the Allies captured *CB16.*[5]

The CB model was much heavier than the CA midget submarine, ranging from 36 to 45 tons. Its speed was about 7 knots, like the CA in the assault submarine version. The CB, at the beginning, was armed with two external torpedo launchers that were detachable. It had a four-man crew and a range double that of the CA, that is, 1,400 miles.

Once the CC and the CM were completed, they were also dubbed CU, for *Costiero Unificato* (unified coastal submarine). They were much larger than the CAs and CBs, displacing between 92 and 116 tons. Each was armed with three torpedo tubes and a twin .50 MG and had a crew of eight. The CM was able to dive to 70 meters, whereas the CA and CB could reach depths of around 40 meters.

The building programs for 1943–1944 foresaw seventy-two midget submarines and only thirty-six standard submarines.[6] The *CM1* would be developed after the war at Leghorn, which would also produce the Cosmos midget submarines, of which we will speak later.[7]

The midget submarines were intriguing vessels that showed great promise. But they were developed too late, and their production was slowed down by poor Italian industrial capacity. Aside from sinking one Soviet submarine in the Black Sea (*CB4*, on August 26, 1943), they accomplished little. (The Italians have long claimed that they sank two other Soviet submarines, in June 1942, but the Soviets never confirmed these losses.)[8]

Italy was not operating in a vacuum, however. It led the way in active operations with underwater and surface assault vessels and frogmen. Other countries had planned similar operations. The British, the Germans, and the Japanese developed similar designs and built several assault means, though not always successfully. The Germans had three types of midget submarines, but only the two-man, diesel-powered

Seehund of 14 tons proved successful. The Japanese built the Type-A class of 46 tons, manned by two and transported by submarine to the place of operation, in 1934. Several were built, along with modified versions, and employed several times in the Pacific campaign, including at Pearl Harbor, with various results.

As earlier stated, for the operations to come for the SLCs and the frogmen, the form of delivery was to be the submarine. There were three submarines adapted for this duty, besides the *Ametista*: the *Iride,* the *Gondar,* and the *Scirè*. The *Iride* was equipped with four supports, like the *Ametista,* for the transport on deck of four SLCs. After the loss of the *Iride* on August 21, 1940, the *Gondar* was equipped with three watertight cylinders that allowed the submarine to reach a depth of 90 meters. The *Gondar* was lost on September 29, 1940. The *Scirè* was modified in the same manner as the *Gondar* in August and September 1940.

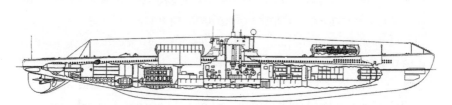

FIGURE 4.2   Scirè 1941

In secret assault operations, the transport submarine had to come near the objective and then release the SLCs. This could be done in one of two ways: The submarine could stay on the bottom of the sea at a depth of between 8 and 15 meters, or it could be at the surface with the conning tower, or sail, alone out of the water. Italian submarines had what they called a "trapdoor" on the roof of the conning tower, which was unusually high compared to most foreign submarine designs. In the first case, the frogmen exited the submarine equipped with their breathing apparatus and opened the watertight cylinders, pulled out the SLCs, and reclosed the cylinders. These were filled with water before the release operations and emptied again after the SLC extraction, because during regular navigation of the submarine they had to stay empty in order not to change the vessel's stability. The *Iride,* incidentally, lacked the watertight modification and could not dive below 30 meters. With the submarine on the surface, the frogmen went out of the conning tower, opened the cylinders, and launched the SLCs. The reserve team, which was generally on board to replace one of the operation teams in case of need, helped to release the SLCs but then returned inside the submarine.

As already mentioned, security and intelligence played an important role in assault craft employment, particularly in the Italian service. Borghese was well suited to secret operations, as we will demonstrate in chapters on the 1943–1945 period. "Secrecy . . . the most absolute secrecy" was the first thing the volunteers of the assault craft had to understand—and not only secrecy about the weapons, as Borghese pointed out, but also about the names of superiors and colleagues, their relatives, and so on. And this was a particularly difficult thing to ask of many Italians. Borghese wrote that it was easier "to get an Italian to lay down his life than to make the sacrifice of holding his tongue."[9] This opinion was echoed by Admiral Franco Maugeri, chief of the Servizio Informazioni Segrete (SIS, the navy secret service), who wrote that successes were achieved "in spite of the fact that Italians generally talk too much and therefore make poor spies."[10]

All training and movement had to be kept hidden from possible enemy agents, informers, and aerial reconnaissance. Every operation had to be carefully prepared with the help of the secret services to ensure the best chances of success. Knowledge of enemy harbor conditions, maps, defense capabilities, and ships had to be precise. The SIS, therefore, had to protect the frogmen and their craft from enemy intelligence activity—and from their own allies, it should be noted, since the Italian intelligence organizations not only worked *with* the German Abwehr and Gestapo but also *against* them.[11]

The structure of Italian intelligence at the time was such that several agencies worked together, and sometimes against each other, with great confusion and a waste of resources (much like the United States in the twenty-first century). Where the navy was concerned, Ambrogio Viviani, author of an important history of the Italian secret services and chief of military counterintelligence in the 1970s, wrote: "The SIS, while the other [services] were unaware, had their own intelligence centers at Alexandria, Tangiers, Algeciras, [and] Ceuta, and had activated and equipped for intelligence duties some motorized fishing boats called *Corrispondenti Beta*."[12]

It was the policy of the chief of Section D of the SIS, Max Ponzo, to plant spy centers in neutral states, as he reasoned that placing infiltrating agents into belligerent enemy states during wartime would be almost impossible. A particularly significant liaison was the vice-consul at Algeciras in Spain west of Gibraltar. Between October 1938 and January 1940, the commander of the SIS was Rear Admiral Alberto Lais, accused by some writers of having sold out his country in favor of a girlfriend named Cynthia.[13] In February 1940, Lais was sent to Washington as naval attaché, and his post was assumed by Rear Admiral Giuseppe Lombardi, who remained in charge until July 1941, when finally Rear Admiral Franco Maugeri was appointed as the head of the SIS.[14]

The SIS was not the only agency that planted people at Algeciras. The Italian Air Force also had some agents there, as revealed by a former agent of the Servizio Informazioni Aeronautica (SIA, or Air Force Intelligence Service), Captain Venanzi. The SIA had its headquarters near Gibraltar in a three-room flat. From there, it was possible to see the Rock, the airport, and the harbor. The SIS was on the opposite side of town at Villa Carmela and had a good observation point but not for the airport.

Although Spain remained neutral during the war, it showed some degree of gratitude toward the Axis for its support to Franco, and Italian and German personnel had a limited ability to transit and recover operatives in Spanish territory. For the operations against Gibraltar, the SIS had a "center" available at Algeciras that monitored the presence of Allied shipping in Gibraltar and convoys that passed the Straits. Moreover, the center recovered personnel after missions against the British.

The SIA transmitted daily reports of ship and aircraft movements to a Balearic station manned by the Servizio Informazioni Militari (SIM, or Military Intelligence Service at the Comando Supremo level), which in turn passed the information on to Italy. The SIS may have eventually worked in the same manner, but certainly at the beginning the navy was running its station alone. The intelligence activity also involved Spanish personnel, as at the SIA base they were present to observe Italian activity. It is interesting to note that the Italians were equipped with radios but only later had a camera available to take pictures of the Gibraltar airport and harbor. The Italian agents operated almost openly, but sometimes agents disappeared, probably neutralized by British counterintelligence.

Admiral Franco Maugeri wrote a couple of pages on the support given by SIS to the *maiali* operations but only in regard to the Alexandria success, leaving us without broader information on the part played by his service. Interestingly enough, he admitted that the reason that Antonio Marceglia and Spartaco Schergat had been captured after the attack on Alexandria was that they had been supplied with British instead of Egyptian currency so were compelled to turn to a bank, where they were noticed while exchanging money.[15]

At the time of the war, Algeciras had a population of 60,000. It has an interesting geographical position, as it is some 10 km from Gibraltar on the road between Malaga and Cadiz, where in August 1974 Prince Junio Valerio Borghese would die. The town's position, as recalled by Captain Venanzi, was unique. "Algeciras was a window open on Gibraltar" and was "literally invaded by Italian, German, British and of course Spanish agents. Italians and Germans were controlled by the Intelligence Service and all of them in turn were kept under the eyes of the complaisant Spanish secret police."[16]

Italy's efforts to create a special naval assault capability were innovative and energetic, but not quite in time for the war that Germany initiated on September 1, 1939. On May 10, 1940, the German Army launched its great offensive against France, and exactly a month later, on June 10, Mussolini brought Italy into the war in support of his Axis ally. Given the spectacle of the British debacle at Dunkirk and the imminent collapse of France, the Duce assumed that he would simply be arriving for the spoils. It would soon be seen, however, that the British were not close to being finished, and their Royal Navy had no intention of ceding the Mediterranean to Italian designs.

CHAPTER 5

The Early Hasty Attacks

Men are by nature prone to fix responsibility in certain directions,
though events are often merely dependent upon the caprices of destiny.

Prince Junio Valerio Borghese[1]

I N JUNE 1940, ITALY OPENED THE WAR WITH VERY
little in the way of naval success. The navy lost ten submarines in the first fifteen days of war, and a valuable cipher book
from one. The French armistice relieved Italy of naval pressure from
that quarter, but it still had to transport supplies to North Africa without the use of the nearby Tunisian ports. This would later entail heavy
losses for Italian transports and escorts.

The first major naval surface engagement, off Punto Stilo on July 9,
1940 (the British refer to it as the "Action off Calabria"), witnessed the
retreat of the Italian fleet and the indiscriminate bombing of both the
Italian and British fleets by the Italian land-based air force, and with
very little to show for it. Further sorties by the Italian fleet were unable
to engage the British, and the transfer of two light cruisers to Leros in
the Dodecanese Islands witnessed the loss of one, the *Bartolomeo
Colleoni,* on July 19. The Italian Navy's losses embarrassed this proud
service, and it became apparent that the service needed to apply all its
resources.

It was now that the Supermarina of the Italian Navy ordered the 1st Flotilla MAS into action. The surface and submarine services of the fleet had been unable to achieve any substantial results against the Royal Navy, and it was the assault craft that now bore the burden of the moment.

Rear Admiral Raffaele de Courten, who commanded the submarines, was also in command of the assault craft when this decision was made. He went to Bocca di Serchio base in late July 1940 to speak to the men there. His words were clear. He explained to the officers that the poor results of the Italian air and naval arms in the first month of war now forced the navy to employ the assault craft against the British Mediterranean Fleet. The seeds of the disaster at Bomba Gulf thus began.

Commander Mario Giorgini, who replaced Aloisi as commander of the 1st Flotilla MAS in spring 1940, was summoned to the Navy Staff and ordered to carry out a mission, against his better judgment, for "strategic necessity," since other weapons had proven ineffective against the Royal Navy. "So, with de Courten as the main driver," according to one history of the frogmen, "the premature date was fixed."[2]

Following de Courten's speech at Bocca di Serchio, on August 10 Cavagnari issued the order of operation for mission GA-1, which had the objective of sinking British naval assets at Alexandria with the following order of priority: first battleships, followed by aircraft carriers, floating docks (used for repair), and cruisers. It is interesting to note that after two months of war the Italian Navy had finally woken up to the fact that the carriers posed a major threat.[3]

The doubts of the commander of the 1st Flotilla MAS did not concern the men who were ready for action, but the craft, which were far from fit for such an important action. Giorgini was well aware that the only "pigs" available were the prototypes used for training and that the new models were still under construction. One of the worst problems still to solve was the fact that these first SLCs were unable to go deeper than 30 meters. Only after the Bomba Gulf disaster were the waterproof cases introduced that could contain the "pigs" and allow them to go a depth of 90 meters.

The men were ready. They had trained for long months before the war, and from 1939 onward they had resumed activities at Bocca di Serchio. As Lieutenant Gino Birindelli later recalled, the eleven officers there slept in a peasant's house, three and four to a room, and ate in a single lunchroom. The heating was supplied by boilers, and the men took baths in an old oil drum!

The mission was one-way only, as the four crews were to attach explosive charges to each of the targets and then try to destroy their two-man SLCs. At this point, the battleship *Lorraine* was the flagship of the French squadron that had partially demobilized at Alexandria after France dropped out of the war. The French contingent also included four cruisers and several smaller ships. The Italians were to close with the French ships and surrender to them. The SLC crews were provided with badges of rank and personal documents in order to be treated as POWs and not shot as spies.

The crews were: SLC 1—Lieutenant Gino Birindelli and second diver chief Damos Paccagnini; SLC 2—Lieutenant Alberto Franzini and diver Sergeant Giovanni Lazzaroni; SLC 3—Engineer Commander Teseo Tesei and diver Sergeant Alcide Pedretti; SLC 4—Engineer Commander Elios Toschi and second diver chief Enrico Lazzari. Luigi Durand de la Penne and electrician Pietro Birandelli were in reserve.

On the night of August 16, the torpedo boat *Calipso*, able to touch 28-29 knots, went as close as possible to the beach of Bocca di Serchio to load the four "pigs" and five crews along with the commander, Giorgini, who was responsible for the operation. The *Calipso* was to transport the crews to the site where they would begin the operation so they would arrive "fresh" for action.[4]

In two days, the *Calipso* reached Tripoli following a route between Sardinia and Sicily, stopping at Trapani, western Sicily. Sailing again from Tripoli, the ship followed the coast until it reached the Gulf of Bomba, where the torpedo boat was to find the submarine *Iride*, which in turn was to carry the human torpedoes to Alexandria. Along the way, the *Calipso* spotted a British submarine, but at first it was thought to be the *Iride*. Arriving at the rendezvous, the frogmen discovered that the submarine was an enemy vessel and that British reconnaissance from No. 202 Group, Royal Air Force (RAF), had already visited the gulf. Unknown to the Italians, the RAF unit had communicated its findings to a Swordfish group temporarily stationed in the western desert from the aircraft carrier *Eagle.*

The commander of the *Iride,* now Lieutenant Commander Francesco Brunetti, felt that the situation was dangerous, particularly because the support ship *Monte Gargano,* which was also there, was an exposed and vulnerable target in the empty Gulf of Bomba, which lay west of Tobruk near Derna (the British referred to the area as El Gazala). In the meantime, Cavagnari informed Marshal Pietro Badoglio on the 20th that the navy was preparing a submarine operation against Alexandria, and an air reconnaissance was requested over the port. This was carried out that morning and it was reported that the Mediterranean Fleet was at anchor. It would probably have been better if Cavagnari had also asked for some fighter and antiaircraft protection for the exposed Gulf of Bomba.[5]

On the night of August 21, the SLCs were loaded onto the *Iride.* The SLCs were held on deck on supports like those used in the first exercise at La Spezia, and the following morning the *Iride* would attempt to navigate with them on board. In the meantime, the commander of the support ship *Monte Gargano,* Rear Admiral Bruno Brivonesi, had offered a toast to the sailors of the 1st Flotilla MAS. But it was just at that moment, when the *Iride* was starting to exit the gulf, that three British aircraft appeared in the sky. They were Swordfish of the fleet air arm operating from Maaten Baggush with the RAF in the western desert, and although the enemy torpedo bombers were old and heavy, their targets were at that moment in the worst position. The *Iride* had just sailed and could not dive in the shallow waters, so the commander ordered increased speed. The support ship *Gargano* was anchored in place and armed only with two .50-caliber AA machine guns.

So it was about noon on the 22nd that the three Swordfish approached the shallow gulf waters from the sea at a height of about 30 feet in a "V" formation. Commanding the center one, slightly back from the two forward planes, was Captain Oliver "Ollie" Patch of the Royal Marines. It was Patch who dropped his torpedo bow-on about 150 meters distant from the *Iride*. It could not be avoided and "crashed straight into the bows of the submarine and exploded." The *Iride* had reacted with machine-gun fire, but the attack by one Swordfish had killed two on the sail, and the submarine was caught by the torpedo and sank immediately. Another Swordfish launched at about 1,000 yards and the torpedo struck the *Gargano*, which was hit under the waterline and began to sink.[6]

As Toschi said, referring to the *Iride*, "We saw a great yellow cloud and nothing more." The *Calipso* was also there and opened fire. The crew later claimed they had hit two Swordfish, but the latter suffered no losses. The third torpedo sank by itself, and it was suspected that it was hit by antiaircraft fire. (See map on page xii.)

Lieutenant J. W. G. Wellham of the Royal Navy later described the attack:

> The first ship to come within range was a submarine which appeared to be charging her batteries on the surface, about 4 miles from the shore. I observed Captain Patch preparing to attack this ship, so broke away from the formation. . . . A few seconds later the submarine blew up, leaving only a small fraction of the stern above the surface. . . .
>
> The destroyer [torpedo-boat *Calipso*] opened fire with pom-poms, multi-machine guns and 0.5-ins. The fire was accurate and at 3,000 yards range my aircraft was struck by an 0.5-in bullet. . . . At a range of about 500 yards I dropped my torpedo. . . . Three seconds later my torpedo exploded on the depot ship just forward of amidships. The ship was left blazing furiously.
>
> Four minutes later there was a further large explosion which caused smoke to rise to a height of 300 feet.[7]

The *Iride* sank in about 15 meters of water, broken in two pieces near the sail. The aft part could apparently still contain living seamen, so Toschi and the others began to organize a rescue. The rescue operations progressed quickly and calls went to Tobruk for special diving equipment. However, it took two hours after the sinking to establish a contact with the submarine because the officer of the assault craft dove without equipment. He noted that from the bow of the submarine the air was flowing out in great quantity (as the bow section filled with water), a very bad sign for those trapped inside. In the aft side of the *Iride,* air was escaping slowly, indicating slow flooding.

Only at 1800 did the rescue operations with breathing apparatus begin, and they lasted through the night as the damaged door refused to be opened. In the end, out of the nine remaining in the submarine, seven were saved and two perished because they did not follow the instructions given by the rescue crew. Of the seven rescued, two more died later. Patch, who survived the war, later met two of the survivors from the *Iride.* The four SLCs were recovered the following day, slightly damaged, and brought back to La Spezia with the *Calipso.* The first assault operation had ended in disaster.

There is some doubt about the intelligence available to the RAF in planning and executing this timely air attack. Air reconnaissance could have been used only to cover the real source of signal intelligence, but as historian F. H. Hinsley has shown, it was entirely the air photographic reconnaissance that allowed the RAF to carry out such successful attacks by aircraft carrier planes on August 22 at Bomba.[8]

Borghese claimed that Admiral de Courten, who was in command of the underwater assault weapons, ordered this operation. But this criticism is not entirely justified, as the orders ultimately originated from Admiral Cavagnari. De Courten could have pushed too hard to initiate this first operation, but it remains a fact hard to confirm.[9]

While the men of the assault craft were being roughly handled in their baptism of fire, the Prince was to receive an important advancement in his career. He had begun the war, in June 1940, on board the submarine *Vettor Pisani.* This 880-ton 1920s design was not very stable as a ship and had to be modified in service. By this time, it had "many wheezy whims, and [was] leaking all over the place," as well as having an immense sail. Like many Italian submarines, it had an overly large conning tower, a feature that would be modified in the course of the war downward as it was easy for the enemy to see and, as technology progressed, even easier to pick up on a radar scope.

Borghese conducted three missions, including being deployed at the early July battle of Punta Stilo (Calabria). In that action, most of the Italian fleet, including its only two fully operational battleships, was covering a convoy bound for North Africa, and Admiral Andrew B. Cunningham was at sea with the Mediterranean Fleet. A brief surface daylight action was fought on July 9. In that action, the *Pisani* was assigned with four other submarines to sortie from nearby Augusta, Sicily, on July 8 to form a submarine ambush line. Cunningham had learned from British intelligence of this submarine line as the action was opening on July 9, and it was one of the reasons for his not pursuing the Italian fleet while it was retiring from action. Borghese then got this old goat of a sub retired to training duties, as it was categorized as "unfit for active war service." He had not seen any action yet.[10]

He was now sent, in August 1940, to Memel on the Baltic Sea, along with two other submarine commanders, in order to attend a course on Atlantic Ocean submarine warfare held by the Germans. It is interesting to note his comments about this course, in which commanders and seamen learned from practical exercises how to react to various situations in action. Italian training was generally less pragmatic and realistic than this. Borghese dove on a U-boat at this time. His claims that Grossadmiral Karl Doenitz held him in great estimation can be doubted, since he had yet to achieve any major successes. Still, it is quite possible that Borghese's spirit and drive could have caught Doenitz's attention even at this point in his career.

Coming back from Germany, Borghese expected to be sent to the Atlantic Italian submarine base at Bordeaux that was being established to operate with the Germans. But Admiral de Courten summoned him and instead assigned him to the command of the submarine *Scirè*, which was operating along with the *Gondar* in the Special Weapons Section of the 1st Flotilla MAS. In doing this, de Courten was probably relying on Borghese's previous training with the lost *Iride* at La Spezia. In any case, Borghese was quite satisfied by the appointment, which changed his life and the lives of many others.

After the Bomba Gulf disaster, it was decided to mount another operation as quickly as possible. The submarine *Gondar* was one of the recently commissioned vessels of the 600, or *Adua,* class, and was chosen to be modified as an SLC carrier. Work in the yard began at the end of August 1940, and in September the *Gondar* set sail for its first and last secret mission. It was fitted with three tight cylinders, built by the OTO yards, that were attached to the deck—two at the stern and one toward the bow. The sub's original gun and ammunition, two torpedoes, and other less vital equipment had been removed. As already explained, the cylinders had to stay tight to withstand pressure at 90 meters depth. They weighed 2.8 tons each and could contain 21.75 tons of water.

On September 19, 1940, the Supermarina of the Royal Italian Navy issued the order for operation GA-2, another assault attempt on the Alexandria base. On September 21, the *Gondar* sailed from La Spezia under Lieutenant Commander Brunetti, who had survived the loss of the *Iride.* On board were also Commander Mario Giorgini and four crews: SLC 1—Lieutenant Commander Alberto Franzini and midshipman Alberto Cacioppo; SLC 2—Engineer Commander RCNC Elios Toschi and diver Sergeant Umberto Ragnati; SLC 3—Engineer Commander RCNC Gustavo Stefanini and diver Sergeant Alessandro Scappino. The reserve team consisted of diver Sergeant Giovanni Lazzaroni and electrical chief Cipriano Cipriani. The human torpedoes were each fitted with a warhead of 225 kg that was to be fixed to the target with an adhesive bag. The timers were to be set at two hours.[11]

The *Gondar* was to stay in touch with the Supermarina using the Special Code G. It sailed directly to Messina, where it arrived at 2100 on the 23rd. There, the *Gondar* refueled by night and landed the secret papers of the ship. It started again on the 24th at 0730. The submarine had steamed three days before it sighted a British warship, which was thought to be a corvette (a small escort). The *Gondar* dove, and after a couple of hours it surfaced again as there were no longer enemy ships in the area.

On the night of the 29th, the *Gondar* spotted several ships steaming at a distance of 500 to 2,000 meters. It was the Mediterranean Fleet, which was engaging in Operation MB-5, with the objective of supplying Malta. The *Gondar* then navigated the rest of the day, surfacing in the evening to take on air and charge batteries. At that point, the Supermarina, having discovered through air reconnaissance that the British fleet was absent from Alexandria, ordered *Gondar* to abort the mission and head for Tobruk. But before the *Gondar* could replenish its batteries and air it spotted the fast-approaching Australian destroyer HMAS *Stuart*. The *Stuart* had accompanied Vice Admiral Cunningham's fleet to sea but had experienced engine problems (a burst steam pipe). Cunningham had signaled the fleet, "*Stuart* is dying on us. I am sending him back to Alex." Now fortune would smile on the Royal Navy. *Stuart* had conducted a series of sonar sweeps while en route back to base.

The sonar picked up a contact on the early evening of the 29th. At 2220 the ship launched its first depth charge attack, and it would operate throughout the night against the *Gondar*. The *Gondar*, which was 60 miles northwest of the Great Pass, dove to 80 meters and remained stationary. The Italians thought they were under attack by three British warships during the night, but it was only the *Stuart* conducting tight attacks and never losing sonar contact. According to the report of the *Gondar*'s commander, the attacks were repeated every hour, with four to six depth charges each time, which caused some damage.

The crew had the opportunity to note clearly how the sonar was detecting the submarine, leaving it few chances to escape. Brunetti tried to escape after six hours of stillness, but the sub was closely followed. At some point, the submarine began to rise, probably due to damage, and rose to 40 meters, receiving hard punishment. A Sunderland seaplane had meanwhile arrived on the scene to help in the hunt. At about 0700 on the 30th, the armed trawler *Sindonis* joined the chase.[12]

Around 0830, the submarine began to take on water, and Commander Giorgini, after conferring with his officers, ordered it to the surface. The men quickly scuttled the submarine at about 0900. Surfacing at about 0920, after eleven hours under attack, the *Gondar* was fired on by the *Stuart* while the *Sindonis* approached, and the Sunderland launched one bomb about 3,000 yards from the *Stuart* near the submarine. The crew abandoned the ship while it was scuttled by several explosive charges. The water was estimated to be 2,000 meters in depth at that point. Forty-seven seamen were recovered by the British, and only one man was lost. At 0925, the *Gondar* sank.[13]

Among the personnel captured were Elios Toschi and other experienced divers. Photographs taken by the Sunderland clearly show the cases on the *Gondar*'s deck, and the British had an idea what they were for. Yet Commander Giorgini was thought to be a "destroyer captain who was taking passage in the submarine," so his cover was a success.[14] As a POW, Toschi was restless and always trying to escape. He finally succeeded and reached Portugal and then was repatriated.

The *Stuart* returned to a hero's welcome that afternoon at Alexandria. Cunningham signaled the fleet, "An outstanding example of a result achieved by patience and skill in operation of asdic gear."[15] After learning about the success, the HMAS *Vampire* sent a more colorful signal to its fellow Australian vessel, the *Stuart*: "Whacko! You did not waste much time."[16]

The loss of the *Gondar* following so closely on the heels of the loss of the *Iride* was a major blow to Italian hopes for a quick success with their secret underwater weapons. The 1st Flotilla MAS was now short of a means of delivery for the SLCs and had to work hard to replace four complete teams of trained personnel. Moreover, Commander Giorgini was now a prisoner and had to be replaced.

It was now time for Prince Junio Valerio Borghese, commander of the submarine *Scirè*, to attempt to salvage Italy's hopes for its novel means of naval assault.

CHAPTER 6

First Blood

For some minutes the bay re-echoed with explosions of all kinds, while the numerous batteries opened intense anti-aircraft fire. Then, as day broke, calm returned; in amazement and wonder, the British realized that they had been taken by surprise and assaulted by Italian seamen with a new, unexpected and unknown weapon.

Prince Junio Valerio Borghese[1]

PRIOR TO THE LOSS OF THE *GONDAR*, ADMIRAL de Courten had ordered another operation to take place at the same time as the assault on Alexandria. On September 24, 1940, when the *Gondar* was still at sea nearing Alexandria and its own doom, the submarine *Scirè*, commanded by Prince Borghese, set sail from La Spezia to carry out Operation BG-1, an assault on the British base at Gibraltar.

The submarine had embarked teams for three SLCs that were encased in the newly built cylinders fixed on its deck. The *Scirè*'s sail had been reduced, and the entire hull was painted pale green, with one part painted a darker color to simulate a trawler with the bow toward what was really the stern of the submarine. Borghese was instrumental in redesigning his conning tower to a smaller size so it would be less visible at sea. He had probably been made aware of this necessity during his training with the German Navy.

Borghese was instructed on September 21 in how to carry out the mission, with every detail, such as route and times, as usual, fixed by his superiors. The attack would happen on the night of September 29/30. The SLC teams included Lieutenant Gino Birindelli, naval engineer Lieutenant Commander Teseo Tesei, Luigi Durand de la Penne, Damos Paccagnini, Alcide Pedretti, and Emilio Bianchi, with Gastone Bertozzi and Enrico Lazzari in reserve.

The submarine was only about 50 miles from Gibraltar on the 29th when it was recalled because Force H had gone to sea, and therefore the mission was aborted. Borghese was ordered to La Maddalena naval base on the northern end of Sardinia, where he arrived on October 3. From there, he returned to La Spezia, where the frogmen waited their next opportunity for action.

The operations of the *Gondar* and the *Scirè* were both canceled at the same time because British forces had sailed from both the target bases. Borghese reflected in his 1954 book that this might have been the result of British espionage, but this was not so.[2] The British were in fact carrying out Operation MB-5, an all-out effort to get a resupply convoy through to Malta. Birindelli commented that the secret of Bocca di Serchio was never penetrated, while in contrast, "Partly for the unquestioned ability of the enemy intelligence services, partly due to the unfortunate national silliness, other secrets, also most important, were not equally well held."[3]

On October 21, Borghese and the *Scirè* were ordered to sail again toward Gibraltar. The plan was practically the same as that of the aborted BG-1 operation. On the deck, he had loaded the three SLCs in their tight cylinders, and the teams were confirmed. Sailing at 0515 on the 21st, the *Scirè* surfaced on October 26 at 2240 but had to wait until the 28th to try to pass the Straits of Gibraltar, as British destroyers heavily patrolled the area. (See map on page xiv.)

The *Scirè* tried to approach the objective on the surface protected by a squall, but then it sighted a destroyer and was compelled to dive. The submarine was detected and had to suffer a hunt by British sonar, followed by depth charge attacks. Fortunately, they were ineffective.

Later, the *Scirè* began to advance slowly and then found a point to remain on the bottom at 72 meters. Here it waited quietly until 1700, when the current began to transport the submarine down the inclined bottom. Borghese then brought the vessel to a point where it was able to remain still on the bottom at 57 meters. It should be noted that the current comes into the Mediterranean from the Atlantic, sometimes at a speed of 6 knots, and moves counterclockwise through the sea.[4]

At 2015, the crew once again faced a strong current, and twenty minutes later the *Scirè* surfaced about 500 meters from the coast. Seeing Gibraltar on his port side, Borghese dove again and forced the Straits successfully, but he had to constantly battle the Mediterranean's strong and irregular currents, which made it difficult for the submarine to hold a constant depth, especially as it was encumbered with the SLC casings.

Borghese's goal was now to find a place quiet enough in Algeciras Bay "for the launching of the operators." Gibraltar proper is a small spit of land ending in Europa Point that thrusts out from the Spanish coast into the Mediterranean. It has a small harbor located on the east side of the spit. Algeciras Bay is named for the main Spanish town that is directly across from Gibraltar, and several smaller towns dot its coast.

Finally, at 0121 on the 30th, the *Scirè* settled on the bottom at a depth of 10 meters, very near the Spanish coast. Then the cylinders were flooded and the submarine surfaced to allow the crews to exit and pull out the SLCs. The *Scirè* dove again to 9 meters at an inclination of 4 degrees in order to help ease the operation. By 0230, the SLCs had left the mother vessel. Borghese took back on the reserve crew, which had helped the others to launch the SLCs, and the *Scirè* immediately crept out of the area.

It was not a simple decision to finally launch the mission. First, after so many failures, the 1st Flotilla MAS was trying an operation for possibly the last time before giving up on the special assault craft. Also, at one point, according to Borghese's estimate of the situation, it might have been better to abort the mission. This was because the submarine's battery was nearing exhaustion, the sub's exact position was unknown, and every maneuver to assess the situation or follow the plan could end in failure and with Borghese being forced to scuttle the vessel.

It was at that point that Birindelli, a former submarine commander, asked permission to speak, which Borghese granted. Birindelli would not normally have been entitled to give his opinion, because the assault teams technically had no official duties before their release. But Birindelli had observed a movement of seaweed from the periscope and had concluded that there was a current of about 3 knots toward Gibraltar Bay. Thus, the operation could be successful, as the current and their engines would propel the "pigs" along.

Birindelli described Borghese's reaction:

> There came out the great soldier and the great commander that Borghese was: he looked straight at me with his eyes like a knife's blade and said: "Are you sure?"
>
> "Yes," I replied."
>
> "We go," he ordered.[5]

According to the available intelligence, the battleship *Barham* was in harbor while a cruiser thought to be the *Kent* and the battleship *Renown* were out on a mission with some destroyers. According to Italian intelligence, there was another unnamed battleship at anchor.

After the release of the SLCs, Borghese avoided the British patrols, sailing the *Scirè* under water for 40 hours before surfacing. At one point he was forced to surface briefly because the crew began to experience problems due to stale air. It was 1900, and the *Scirè* was now 35 miles from Europa Point. The first thing Borghese did was to wire the Supermarina to report that the operation was in progress and that the frogmen would require support. The operation had begun four days after the X-day, and the support foreseen for the crews' rescue in Spanish territory was no longer active—the assault crews were now in the middle of the operation and nobody outside of Borghese's submarine was aware of it. The remainder of the trip proved quiet, and after four days, on November 3, Borghese returned to his home base at La Spezia.

Back at Gibraltar, after their release from the *Scirè,* the SLC teams had stealthily attempted to close on their assigned targets. Borghese, acting on the information available to him, had instructed Birindelli to attack the first battleship, Tesei to attack the other, more distant, one, and de la Penne to look for another big ship, such as an aircraft carrier or cruiser. There were also reserve objectives in case there were no capital ships. In that case, the targets would be destroyers and large merchantmen or at least important harbor facilities such as docks.

As the operators prepared to leave, there had been one small ceremony left to complete. Each of the six men ready for the operation bent over and received a kick in the butt by Borghese! This was for good luck.[6]

The three SLCs were 3 miles from Gibraltar when they were released at 0230. Of vital importance was that—no matter what happened— the operators were not to leave behind any sign of their special equipment for the British to find. The Birindelli-Paccagnini team went on to the Gibraltar port. Besides the Birindelli article already quoted, the experiences of both are described in a report written by Birindelli in 1944 after his return from the British POW camp.[7]

The three teams agreed to meet on the surface near the port entrance after being released from the submarine, but Birindelli's SLC was already damaged before entering action. It proved difficult to pull it out of the host cylinder, and it was slow and unable to hold a certain depth, constantly wanting to sink. Rising to the surface was laboriously slow. It was later determined that the SLC's batteries had partly flooded. Birindelli and Paccagnini decided to continue the action, but a check of the latter's breathing apparatus showed that it was leaking. Nevertheless, they wanted to go on with the action, without realizing that the other two SLCs were facing similar problems. Because of the condition that the SLC was in, they had to navigate close to the surface with only their heads above water, but with the SLC down by the stern.

However, they passed over the obstructions without being detected by the British patrols.

Birindelli now saw the *Barham* before him at 250 meters and headed toward the big battleship. He dove the SLC 45 meters down toward the bottom of the bay, waiting for the terrible feeling caused by sinking in the mud. However, there was no mud, but a rocky bottom with outcrops. His compass and other instruments were visible. The battery was weak, but the compass and the depth indicator worked better. The troubled SLC continued to go on toward its target.

Birindelli wanted to place the explosive charge close to the bottom of the bay. Between the hull and the sea bottom were 4 meters, a good space for enhancing the explosion toward the central part of the hull. Normally, Birindelli would stay on the SLC while the second operator attached the ropes to the keel of the *Barham,* and then both would prepare the explosive charge. But Birindelli was not lucky that night. Paccagnini's breathing apparatus, replaced by a smaller reserve one, was dying. Then, at the same time the SLC stopped, the connection between the engine and the screw broke. Paccagnini had to abandon the attack and headed to the surface to hide from patrols, as it was now almost dawn and the cloak of darkness was slipping away.

Birindelli estimated that he was still some 60 to 70 meters from the battleship. He tried in vain to tow the SLC toward the ship, but the "pig" would not move. After much effort, Birindelli began to feel that his breathing apparatus was working badly, so he activated the time trigger of the explosive charge and came to the surface before passing out.

The fresh air of dawn awakened Birindelli, who began to try to escape, destroying and abandoning pieces of his equipment. He was supposed to swim until he reached the Spanish coast. The rescue plan foresaw that he would be picked up by an Italian agent and returned via air to Italy. If all went well, he would be at La Spezia in twelve hours, where he could show himself in the city, throwing off any informers or spies about his activities.

But he was unable to reach the border and was compelled to exit from the water. Walking on the docks at dawn with a small crowd of workmen arriving that morning proved to be impossible. At first he tried to give money to a Spaniard, but the animated discussion between the two drew the unwelcome attention of a British sailor. So he was captured.

While waiting to be interrogated by an officer, he could hear the big explosion of the charge he had abandoned a few dozen meters from the *Barham*. It caused no damage.

At that point he was questioned, "Who are you?" to which he replied, "Italian officer." Another British officer, a commander, entered and told him: "If you are who I suppose, you are three days late. Your friends were awaiting you," and mentioned a Spanish hotel. This was because an agent had been observed from Gibraltar near the Spanish crossing point three days earlier. This short talk seems to prove that British counterintelligence was efficient and aware of some of the plan, or at least of the fact that an operation would be tried. Birindelli would later report this to Italian authorities.

A British officer saw one of the two SLCs on the Spanish shore and sketched it, but more important, parts of Birindelli's SLC, minus the explosive charge, were recovered. This evidence was combined with information gained through interrogation, especially from Paccagnini. Paccagnini first told a story about being transported by a surface warship, but later he named the *Scirè* and said he was part of a party of eight assigned to the operation. Also recovered were two undamaged diving suits as well as two damaged ones. The British *Chariot* design would be based on the type 100 series SLC.[8]

Birindelli desired to fight against the British as a gentleman, but his class got him into trouble. Before exiting the submarine he had shaved. Later, when he was captured, he was put before a court martial, whose president said that he was not a survivor from a shipwreck as he had claimed, because he was well shaved, and proceeded to ask where he had been the night of the explosion. Birindelli was interrogated in a way that led him to suspect he would be treated not as a POW, but as an irregular combatant and spy, which meant he would be shot. The court martial official's last touch was to ask him if he wanted a chaplain.[9]

Birindelli was not only placed under psychological pressure. In fact, his experience as a POW was somewhat bitter and he was sure the British put him in stressful conditions in the hope that he might die. This was confirmed to him after his release, and he published the account in 1988.[10]

But the British began to become better informed of what was transpiring. The SLC of de la Penne and Bianchi was also going badly. Their torpedo would not sink unless at full speed, and the compass was jammed. They then evaded a patrol boat and four searchlights by diving. It was shortly after this that a small detonation, possibly two, in the motor of the SLC marked the end of the team's attempt.

The SLC sank to a depth of 130 feet, and de la Penne was unable to detach the warhead. He tried to bring it up and could not; he later expressed the opinion that the water pressure stove in one of the ballast tanks. He felt he was about to lose all oxygen when he swam to the surface, where he found Bianchi. Both began to swim toward the Spanish coast, and after two hours, when they were almost exhausted, they arrived safely at a fisherman's house, then found the meeting place. They met Tesei there and learned that Birindelli had failed and was captured.[11]

Tesei and Pedretti began to move toward Gibraltar with their SLC, although its pump was not working and its control instruments had been made invisible by the infiltration of water. After five minutes, at about 500 meters from the coast, Tesei stopped to wait for the other SLCs, which were not to be found.

Tesei was forced to dive to 15 meters to avoid motorboats patrolling the area and was unable to follow a direct course. Several boats hindered his direct approach toward the port entrance, so he lost about an hour in this maneuver, and the compass could not be relied upon. At some point, Tesei discovered that his breathing apparatus was leaking and the replacement (which every SLC carried) was not working. The "pig" was also moving with its bow high out of the water. Since he could no longer dive with the SLC, the team aborted the mission. Tesei at that point detached the explosive charge, and after having reached the Spanish coast, abandoned the torpedo, sending it off to the south. In a short time, the team found "agent N," their contact in Spain, who repatriated them.[12]

Although Tesei destroyed his breathing apparatus and Birindelli and de la Penne sunk their diving suits, the British found some traces of the intruders. Not only had the British captured Birindelli and Bianchi, but when the charge exploded near the *Barham,* they had little doubt of what was happening, although the exact details remained obscure.

Also, Tesei's SLC had traveled around in the bay until it landed on the Spanish coast. The Spanish seized the machine, but it was observed by the British from a distance and pictures were taken. Local Spanish newspaper articles on it also appeared and were picked up by British intelligence. A message reached the Supermarina from the Italian naval attaché in Spain at the end of October, explaining what had happened to the wrecked SLC.

So the cat was out of the bag, and at Gibraltar thereafter, "explosives were regularly detonated in the bay to deter further underwater attacks."[13] Sonar and radar were both also utilized, but the small size of the SLCs protected them from detection. Still, the rescued teams had learned a lot from the problems they had encountered with their equipment and would make good use of their experience to improve the two-man torpedoes (especially the compass and other instruments) and the breathing apparatus for the next time. It also came as a relief that an attack had finally been seamlessly delivered; Prince Borghese and the *Scirè* had returned safely to base in addition to two of the three SLC crews.

But the quasi-success of Borghese's penetration of Gibraltar would soon pale before great setbacks to Italian arms elsewhere. On November 11, 1940, a week after the *Scirè* had arrived safely back at La Spezia,

British torpedo bombers surprised the main fleet while in harbor at Taranto in Italy's far south. The carrier *Illustrious* had crept within 90 miles of the coast and unleashed twenty-one Swordfish torpedo bombers. At the cost of two aircraft, the British crippled three battleships and damaged one cruiser and three destroyers. Taranto, sometimes called "the Pearl Harbor of the Mediterranean," left half the Italian battleship force in temporary shambles. Three days later, the Greeks launched a counteroffensive against the Italian Army, which had invaded that country on October 28. The Italians were knocked back into Albania. The biggest catastrophe subsequently began in December in North Africa, as Archibald Wavell's 30,000-man British Army, spearheaded by the 7th Armoured "Desert Rats," caved in the entire Italian position in Egypt and Libya, advancing 400 miles and taking 194,000 prisoners in a two-month campaign. This first stellar land triumph of British arms in World War II would follow the rule of unintended consequences, however, because the Germans now decided to lend serious support to their Mediterranean ally. On February 12, 1941, General Erwin Rommel arrived in the desert with the first elements of his Afrikakorps.

While the winter passed with various disasters besetting Italian strategy in the Mediterranean, the human torpedo attacks were suspended, at least until the following spring. Strangely enough, the Greek campaign was not supported by any special craft operations, despite the many merchant ships plying the Aegean and entering relatively unprotected harbors with troops and supplies for the Allied cause. But after the several failures, the assault craft needed some reorganization and new equipment.

Nevertheless, a detachment of MT explosive boats was based in the Dodecanese, where it trained under the command of Vittorio Moccagatta on the island of Leros with the objective of attacking Suda Bay on Crete and the British traffic to Greece. But Moccagatta was recalled to Italy on January 23, 1941, and headquartered at La Spezia as commander of the 1st Flotilla MAS.

On March 15, 1941, the special weapons units were split off from the flotilla to form the Decima Flottiglia MAS, or X MAS. Just as the British Special Air Service (SAS) had been given an innocuous name to disguise the fact that it was a commando unit, at Moccagatta's suggestion the Italian naval commandos assumed a name that translated innocently enough into English as the "10th Light Flotilla." It included an HQ unit and two assault craft units, one of surface and one of underwater means. The underwater unit was placed under the command of Lieutenant Commander Junio Valerio Borghese and included the SLC school at Bocca di Serchio, the divers school at Leghorn, the gamma men, and the delivering submarines. Lieutenant Commander Giorgio Giobbe was the commander of the surface unit, which included the explosive MTs and other motorboats. Moccagatta remained in overall command of the special assault units.

Training with the MTs at Leros had shown that it was possible to approach a target using destroyers instead of aircraft, as had been supposed in the early stages of the weapon's development. The two 1920s' converted destroyers employed were *Crispi* and *Sella,* and both reached a high level of training. They were equipped for the transport of six MTs each and were provided with electrically powered cranes for placement of the MTs on the water. Such an operation was carried out in an average time of about 7 minutes, although a time of 35 seconds was also reported. The additional training involved overcoming net obstructions, simulated attacks under searchlights, and maneuvers in formation.

At the beginning of 1941, the MT unit was ready for an attack. The plan for the attack was to hit the British ships employed in the supply of Greece after Italy had invaded that country. In the spring of 1941, the Germans and Bulgarians would enter the war in the Balkans, but the attack against Greece was more urgent for Italy. Along with a surface squadron action (which resulted in the Matapan disaster), there was to be an attack on Suda,[14] a bay in the northwestern part of Crete with a mouth facing the east. It was 4.5 miles long, and its entrance was 10 to 12 meters deep, while in the middle it was between 70 and 120 meters deep.[15]

Twice in January and February the planned action was canceled, and only in conjunction with the famous Gaudo operation, which ended in the battle of Matapan, was the attack at last launched. And it finally became the first successful operation of the special Italian assault craft.

On March 25, 1941, the destroyers *Sella* and *Crispi,* which had embarked six MTs for the action at Suda, sailed from Stampalia. The destroyers had to launch the explosive boats 10 miles from Suda's entrance. On the 24th, fresh aerial reconnaissance pictures arrived of Suda Bay with a clear and updated situation of the British ships at anchor. There were a cruiser, two destroyers, and twelve merchant ships. Later information indicated that only a cruiser and eight transports were in the bay, but by the time the operation was launched there were more targets: the heavy cruiser *York,* the large light cruiser *Gloucester,* the small AA cruiser *Calcutta,* the destroyer *Hasty,* the support ships *Cherryleat* and *Doumana,* and finally three tankers, *Desmoulea, Marie Maersk,* and *Pericles.* The *York* had arrived there at 1400 on the 25th with the *Gloucester* after operation MC-9. (See map on page xii.)

At 2330 hours on March 25, the Italian destroyers arrived at the spot where they had to release the boats, and they launched them into the sea in just a few minutes. The destroyers then safely returned to base. The boats started toward the objective, reached it safely, and quickly began to overcome the outer obstructions. Only one of the MTs was blocked by the outer defense, but it succeeded later and joined with the MT formation near a little isle near the bay's entrance.

The commander, Luigi Faggioni, regrouped the boats, and the advance was resumed at 0245 on March 26 toward the third obstruction, which was some 3 miles away. During the advance, two searchlights began to sweep the darkness. They were really assisting the entering AA cruiser *Coventry,* but the attackers suspected that the searchlights were for them.

At 0430, Faggioni sighted an upcoming obstruction, which was bypassed by the rocky coast, then the MTs steamed along the net toward the middle of the bay. To regroup there silently, the MTs used oars.

The flotilla had to wait because it was too early and dark for the attack. So Faggioni instructed the pilots, distributing the targets: Two were assigned to the *York,* which was some 500 meters distant. Two other boats, including Faggioni's, were in reserve to attack the *York* in case the first two should fail; the last two were to attack the merchant ships present in the harbor.

The attack began just after 0500, just as dawn broke. The first two MTs approached the *York* and stayed some 300 meters distant for about 15 minutes, waiting for the sky to lighten, then started at full speed toward the ship. The pilots abandoned their boats at about 80 meters from the *York.* On board the cruiser, the service officer heard at 0511 the noise of an engine at full speed, which was thought to be an aircraft, but before the alarm could be launched, the ship was hit.

Another two MTs attacked the tanker *Pericles,* which was hit, while Faggioni tried to aim at the *Coventry,* which had entered the bay during the night, refueled near the *Pericles,* and was just getting under way. But Faggioni did not hit the cruiser and his boat exploded on the coast, as did another of the MTs. Finally, one remained intact and was captured by the British. The attackers survived and were all captured.[16]

The *York* had begun to go down, listing to the side after being hit near the stern. Both engine rooms and boilers were flooded. The *York* "had no power for pumping, lighting or for working turrets." The destroyer *Hasty* towed the cruiser toward the shore and ran it aground to save it from sinking. In the months to follow, however, it became a favorite target of air attacks until it was finally abandoned. In this way, the Mediterranean Fleet lost its only cruiser with 8-inch guns.[17] The *Pericles* initially survived the attack but lost 500 tons of fuel from the opened wounds in its hull. On April 14, while being towed to Alexandria, the tanker sank in a heavy storm.[18]

The *York*'s destruction was the first truly successful action of the assault craft. The pilots were captured, of course, but the boats proved to be a well-developed and dangerous new weapon. One MT was captured intact, but a trigger charge went off while the MT was being examined, injuring a British officer and damaging the craft.[19]

The POWs were well treated at first. Faggioni remembered a British sailor's fair comment: "Good work, isn't it?" to which followed several interrogations in which some psychological attempts were made to force Faggioni and his men to speak. They were gathered before what appeared to be a firing squad while an officer held a black strip in his hand. Then they were returned to prison and the same officer asked them if they needed a chaplain.[20]

There was one other small operation at this time. An offensive reconnaissance of the assault craft took place in the Corfu area in April 1941. It was carried out by two MAS (535 and 539) and two MTS (2 and 4), with the MAS towing the MTS until they were near the objective.[21] The MAS and assault craft sailed on April 2 under the command of Moccagatta and arrived at the point of release of the MTS toward midnight on the 4th. The MTS began their mission steaming toward Port Edda but were soon discovered, illuminated by searchlights, and shot at by heavy machine guns. Therefore, the crew was compelled to abort the mission, as the element of surprise had been lost. The following day, the MTS boats were back at the Saseno base.

Another operation against Gibraltar was planned for the next month using the same units from the earlier failed operation. Therefore, in May 1941, Lieutenant Commander Junio Valerio Borghese and the submarine *Scirè* loaded three SLCs and sailed toward Gibraltar. Among the new details approved for the operation was shipping the SLC teams by airplane to avoid the fatigue of the long trip inside the submarine and have them in the best possible physical condition at the outset of the mission. The previous attempt had shown that the physical effort required of the crew was so great that it may have reduced their effectiveness.

The frogmen arrived in Spain at Cadiz harbor. The *Scirè*, after passing the Straits of Gibraltar, would be resupplied from the merchant ship *Fulgor*, take on the frogmen, and then return to Gibraltar. The *Fulgor*—also called *Base C*—was a tanker that had remained in Spain after the outbreak of the war. It had been equipped as a secret submarine support ship. Of course, the SLC personnel were traveling under cover names with false documents in order to fool both Spanish and British intelligence.

Borghese's voyage to Gibraltar began on April 15 when the *Scirè* sailed from La Spezia; the other frogmen had arrived the day before at Base C. Steaming to Spain, Borghese found heavy seas near the Spanish coast that caused some delay. However, at dawn on May 24 his submarine began to dive some miles from Europa Point to begin the difficult operation to pass the Straits, an increasingly difficult task because the British fleet was more likely not to be caught by surprise after so many failed attacks. The *Scirè* had to stay under water at 40 meters for some time, fighting the currents, but by 2300 it had surfaced and easily entered Cadiz around midnight. It was a rare pleasure for a submarine crew to take a bath in the support ship.

On May 25, the *Scirè* was again en route to Algeciras Bay. But in the approach it had to escape being hunted by a British destroyer and come to terms with the strong currents, which made it difficult to enter the bay. At this point, Borghese had to wait through the daylight before making the final approach to the release point for the SLC.

But the twenty-four hours that Borghese decided to wait were enough because Force H left Gibraltar on a mission, leaving the Italian assault craft with no major targets available. Borghese had already brought the *Scirè* to the mouth of the Rio Guadarranque and was resting on the bottom at a depth of 10 meters, with the SLC teams ready to exit the submarine, when the Supermarina sent a message informing him that the major British warships had left the base. It was 2330, and at that point Borghese decided to order the attack on the transport ships in the outer Bay of Algeciras. Then, at 2358, he brought the *Scirè* near the surface and released the SLCs. The frogmen received some drugs (Simpamine or Dextropur—a form of "speed") to aid them in their extreme physical effort. Drugs were commonly used during these operations, just as they are today by some special assault forces, to counter fatigue. After the frogmen had exited the sub, one of them, Amelio Franchi, got sick and was replaced by Antonio Marceglia, who would later be one of the attackers at Alexandria.

Borghese, with the two remaining frogmen, now sailed for La Spezia, while the six men on the SLCs began to move inside the bay. They were Lieutenant Decio Catalano, with NCO diver Giuseppe Giannoni; Lieutenant Amedeo Vesco, with Lieutenant of Naval Construction Antonio Marceglia; and Sublieutenant Licio Visintini, with NCO diver Giovanni Magro.

As always, things went partially wrong: The Marceglia and Vesco SLC did not start up properly, and this forced the other two SLCs to take on board a frogman each while the warhead of the jammed "pig" was transferred to Visintini's SLC. Catalano's SLC was much slower than Visintini's, and Catalano, fearing that his machine could stop at any time, detached the other frogmen and instructed them to attack the targets, which were now visible. Catalano chose a transport ship, but this time, while the team was working the "pig" under the hull, a problem suddenly rose. Marceglia suddenly could not receive air from his breathing apparatus; shortly thereafter he did not respond, as he was fainting, so Catalano had to help him. To wake him up, his comrades slapped him vigorously in the face, and this caused Marceglia to cry out, which drew the attention of the sentries. While the crew was doing this, the SLC sank to the bottom of the harbor in an area too deep to be retrieved. This compelled the team to leave the place after destroying their breathing apparatus in an attempt to reach the coast at the meeting point.

At the same time, Visintini, Magro, and Schergat, sitting on the other SLC, were examining the possible targets. Two were hospital ships and they could not attack them, and one possible target was a tiny 600-ton out-of-service transport. Finally they found another ship that appeared to be a tanker, but it was only a small oil storage ship. Touching the hull, Magro began the operation of attaching the rope to the ship's rudder, but at some point he disappeared. He had started to pass out. While saving Magro, Visintini lost control of the SLC, and it, too, sank to the bottom. Visintini had to give up at 0240, and after destroying their breathing apparatus, the men swam with a strong current, arriving on shore at 0415.[22]

The SLCs of all three teams were lost, and the only trace of a silver lining in the operation was that it had failed so completely that the British didn't realize they had been attacked, and so did not increase their defenses. But Borghese's conduct on the *Scirè* had been outstanding, and all six pilots were awarded the Silver Medal. The Straits of Gibraltar became an ever more dangerous deathtrap for Axis submarines throughout the war (as vividly portrayed in the movie *Das Boot*), yet Borghese, twice in succession, had surmounted the difficulties. All that remained next time was for the "sea devils" he delivered not to be betrayed by their experimental equipment.

CHAPTER 7

The Glorious Failure

When you will receive this letter I will have had the finest honor; that is to give my life to the King and to the flag.

Teseo Tesei[1]

MUCH OF THE WAR IN THE MEDITERRANEAN swirled around the island of Malta, one of the prizes that Britain had presciently held on to after the Napoleonic Wars. A vital piece of real estate since at least Roman times, Malta had for centuries been occupied by the Knights of St. John, who had fought off an epic Turkish siege in 1565. (Today they are commonly known as the Knights of Malta.) Napoleon seized the island from the aging remnants of the Knights while en route to Egypt in 1798, but then British Rear Admiral Horatio Nelson's pursuing fleet grabbed it for England in 1800. And like Gibraltar, Suez, the Falklands, and Hong Kong, it remained one of those small but strategically vital knots that tied Britain's global empire together. A glance at the map describes its importance in World War II. Lying just 90 miles due south of Sicily, between Sicily and Libya, the island is also nearly equidistant between Gibraltar and Alexandria. Its sheltered port of La Valletta features a natural harbor with a narrow entrance shadowed by limestone heights crowned with forts.

Naturally, the island was bombed by the Regia Aeronautica and then the Luftwaffe from the beginning of the war, but the British had their own fighters and bombers in place on the island, as well as ships that would sally out from the harbor. Most dangerously, at the turn of 1940/1941, the U-class of British submarines took residence in Valletta and proceeded to wreak havoc on Axis shipping, using the port as a base of operations.

The U-class, incidentally, is not to be confused with German U-boats, a general term based on *Untersee*. These British subs were smaller than most oceanic boats, thus more suitable for the Mediterranean, and their names simply all began with "U"—for example, *Upholder, Urge, Unbroken, Utmost,* and *Uproar*. Whereas British submarine efforts in 1940 had been dismal, sinking sixteen ships in the Mediterranean at the cost of nine lost subs, the arrival of the U-class at Malta spelled doom for tens of thousands of tons of Axis shipping.

Leery of the British fleets at both ends of the Mediterranean waiting to pounce on any major Italian surface action against Malta, the Supermarina called on its special operations craft to more stealthily attack the British harbor. Unfortunately, this would result, in June 1941, in a combined attack of motorboats and SLCs that failed in the face of a prepared garrison. To attack Malta was not a simple task, as the base was very well defended and the harbor entrance narrow, and the Italians had little chance to gather intelligence on the harbor defenses. The main source of intelligence was aerial photographs, and from this source every detail had to be carefully planned, especially after the harbor defense forces had begun to take countermeasures against possible motorboat attacks.

It should be said that before the attack at Suda Bay, the first plan had been to attack Malta, and for this reason the explosive MT boats were transferred to the Augusta naval base in Sicily to prepare the operation. But after the *Gondar* disaster and the capture of Commander Giorgini, things changed, and so Moccagatta tried to build the MTs into an effective weapon and did not want to launch them in a rushed and dangerous mission.

After Suda Bay, de Courten wanted more successes and ordered Moccagatta to resume the planning for an attack on Italy's main Mediterranean problem, that is, Malta. (See map on page xiii.) The operation against the island's harbor was planned after scrutiny of all possible assault craft: Moccagatta examined every possibility and finally opted for the MTs as his main weapon. This was because the SLC could not be brought there easily, and not with a submarine, owing to the unknown local minefields. A means of surface transport would be required, but it was not available at the moment. It was also impossible to release gamma men from a CB midget submarine, since there were unfavorable conditions off the Maltese coast.

Moccagatta thus concluded:

MT: with these means a surprise action must be excluded, the Valletta harbor entrance is 300 to 500 meters wide and the port guard in the middle, so the MT would be spotted in the most dangerous moment, i.e. while almost immobile passing the obstructions.

An action by force should therefore be studied and it is what we are planning, with the sacrifice of three or four MTs to destroy the obstructions and the possible defense (machine guns, searchlights) on the docks.

Of course it must be necessary to operate with at least eight MTs to achieve some results.

Moccagatta also drew attention to the fact that moonlight did not provide sufficient illumination and that the assault had to take place at dawn in order for the crewmen to be able to see the port entrance. The entrance was "very tight," the limestone rock of Malta was close to the surface, and there were outcrops near the harbor entrance.

Some reconnaissance operations by MAS boats were also carried out, though these were of limited effectiveness because of the need to avoid alerting the British defenses. One of these was carried out on May 25, and another on the night of May 27/28 by Moccagatta himself. The MAS boats used their auxiliary engines for a quiet approach to the island and were able to observe the sea and wind conditions near la Valletta's entrance. Apparently there was no Italian naval seaplane surveillance. But bad weather intervened and the operation was delayed. Reconnaissance resumed in the middle of June, with direct observation of Malta's entrance.

At sunset on June 28, the assault craft sailed from Augusta under the direct command of the commander of the flotilla, Moccagatta. They consisted of eight MTs and one MTS, towed by MAS. The MAS boats were numbered 451, 452, 509, 556, and 562. The force was unlucky, encountering bad weather; one MT sank and others were taking on water, so Moccagatta was forced to postpone the mission.

The same thing happened two days later, when, on the 30th, the same force encountered a strong wind approaching Malta from the southeast, and again around 1500 an MT was in danger of sinking and was sent back to Augusta. Moccagatta waited until 0800, when the wind finally ceased, and then verified the state of his craft before unleashing them against the island. But at that moment, an MT lost its towing rope and was unable to make its engine function. After more than an hour, the MT was left behind, but in a short time a MAS suffered a breakdown and all attempts to repair it failed. Moccagatta still wanted to continue the attack, but the commander of the surface craft, Giobbe, was reasonably contrary. In the end, the naval force had to return to Augusta.

Moccagatta remained determined to carry out the operation, but this time with some planning changes. The new attempt, now with the added employment of SLCs, would be known as Operazione MALTA-2. Destroying the obstacles at the port entrance was the duty of an SLC; another human torpedo had to penetrate the submarine mooring at Marsa Muscetto on the west side of Valletta. The SLC would be transported by a *Motoscafo Turismo Lento* (MTL, slow motorboat) in convoy with the 32-knot sloop *Diana*. This sloop was the support ship for the expedition and carried nine MTs until Point C, 20 sea miles from Malta, in order to avoid the technical problems caused in the past attempts after the long travel from Augusta to Maltese waters. One would be damaged during the launch and later lost while being towed.[2]

MAS 451 and *MAS 452* were escorting and towing vessels, especially *MAS 451,* which had the duty of towing the MTL transporting the SLCs from Point C to Point B, which was only 1,000 meters from the harbor entrance. Point A was where the base had to be penetrated, and the MTL had to bring the SLC there, while the MTSM had to bring the MTs to Point B and then join *MAS 452.*

The MTs would then race past the outer boom, after the net was destroyed, and pass into the harbor. The inner boom had a 2-meter-wide gap for the passage of small craft, including Maltese fishing craft, and the MTs would pass through there in single file to spread out and attack shipping. A convoy, ships from British Operation Substance, had just arrived and would be prime targets.

The air force was also asked to cooperate by conducting three bombing waves through the night to draw the attention of the searchlights and defenses on the sky while the real threat came from the sea. Fighters would cover the retreat of the ships from the Malta area against pursuit by British aircraft. The projected date of July 26 was confirmed because the recently arrived convoy was a very good target for Moccagatta's explosive boats. Unfortunately, the Italian air effort would be minor, in part because it was employed earlier against the approaching convoy. The operation was quite complicated, especially considering the degree of cooperation (or more properly, the lack of cooperation) to which the Italian armed forces were accustomed.

Teseo Tesei, who had not taken part in the recent Gibraltar operation because he was not in the best of physical condition, was to lead the SLC that had the duty of destroying the obstruction called "breakwater viaduct," by the British, St. Elmo Bridge to the Italians. An unusual man, Tesei had once said, "The success of the mission is not very important, nor even the outcome of the war. What really counts is that there are men ready to die in the attempt and really dying in it: for our sacrifice will inspire and fortify future generations to conquer."[3]

On the night of July 23, the MAS carried out a final reconnaissance, and after the aerial photos were studied, the operation began. The travel to Malta was comfortable, with good weather, no wind, and without the disappointing breakdowns that marked the previous attempts.

During the entire time, the defenders of Malta were aware that something was planned. First, a Special Liaison Unit on the island conducting ULTRA interception and decoding alerted the garrison to a possible attack. Second, the radar unit on the island picked up the *Diana* at 2055 on July 25 as it closed the island to release the attackers. Finally, the noise of the engines of the boats was heard from 2220 on.[4]

At 2300, the party regrouped just in time at Point C. All started out well, but then the towing rope of the *MAS 451* became slightly entangled with the screw, which caused the vessel to hit the MTL and damage it. The MAS had to leave the formation. As the party neared the breakwater viaduct, two searchlights opened up, but the MTL continued to approach the obstruction. The two SLCs were launched, but Lieutenant Commander Franco Costa's refused to work. Tesei therefore had to act alone, and a lot of time was lost trying to get the second SLC working.

By that time, Malta's radar had already detected (at 2230) the naval formation and the defenses were on alert, though some patrolling Swordfish failed to sight any of the Italian vessels. Also, a weak Italian air attack at 0425, meant to distract the defenders, instead had the effect of further alerting the garrison artillery.[5]

Tesei was seen starting with his second man for St. Elmo Bridge, determined to blow the obstruction by 0430. Tesei was well known at

Bocca di Serchio for his austere attitude and long talks, but he was devoted to his mission. According to Costa's after-action report, Tesei had said, "At 0430 the net must blow and it will blow. If it is late, I will regulate the fuse to the very minute."[6] Since the operation depended on removing the obstruction, Tesei meant to blow himself up with the bridge if that was the only way to maintain the schedule. What subsequently happened under St. Elmo Bridge is difficult to understand. All that is known for certain is that at 0445 the obstruction net blew up together with the bridge just in time for the charge of the eight explosive boats toward the harbor entrance.

According to British sources, Tesei was spotted while some 300 yards from the bridge by a sentry, a Maltese corporal named Zammit of the Upton battery, who opened fire with an automatic 6-pounder gun. It is possible that Tesei and Pedretti were killed before reaching the obstruction. As Joseph Caruana argued in a 1994 article, the SLC retrieved by frogmen at Malta in 1966 was Tesei's, and therefore this would prove the effects of Zammit's fire.[7]

It is also quite possible that Tesei sacrificed himself, considering that he was described by all his friends as devoted first and foremost to duty and the fact that he was beginning to suffer heart problems, in part brought on by his intensive training. If his SLC was lost, he might have detached the explosive charge and either personally set it off at the bridge or, as some thought, placed it where by chance it was detonated by defensive fire or by one of the following MT boats.

The MTs were numbered from 1 to 9 (Number 5 was the damaged one) and assigned specific duties. Number 1 had to lead the charge but wait for 2 or 3 to blow the obstruction in case Tesei failed in his attack. On balance, it is most likely that it was one of these two MTs that destroyed St. Elmo Bridge and brought it tumbling into the waters below, further blocking the entrance.

The following MTs had to penetrate into the harbor and attack the ships inside as planned. Number 9 was assigned to attack possible fixed defenses, such as gun emplacements or machine-gun nests. When Number 2 attacked, its pilot, Lieutenant Roberto Frassetto, jumped away, but the operator of Number 3 blew up with his boat, according to Frassetto, in the attempt to open the way for the others. But instead of opening a passage, the explosions caused the bridge to collapse in such a manner that it totally blocked the way that the explosive boats needed to use to get past the outer boom. The remaining MTs now charged toward the sound of the explosion, which was slightly starboard instead of dead ahead because the current had carried them somewhat to the east.

British defensive fire was heavy from the start. It included airplanes from the nearby airfield and every kind of gun and machine gun shooting at the motorboats. The coastal defense guns were manned almost exclusively by Maltese, who fought well. According to one report, "For a few minutes the illuminated area of the harbor mouth was criss-crossed by devastating fire of tracer bullets. The whole party had been caught in the beams of the searchlights and one boat after another was sunk or blew up. The attack was utterly broken." Only NCO Fiorenzo Capriotti's boat was not hit, and he waited until dawn, thinking he would try later, but when he approached he was fired upon and jumped into the sea. He was able to help one wounded man reach a boat, and they waited there.[8]

Costa's SLC was still trying to approach the harbor, but it was steering badly, and after five hours, and many airplane attacks, Costa activated the self-destruct. He reached the coast and was captured there with his number two man.

And further disaster was still to come. During the return trip to Augusta, the RAF attacked the MAS and other vessels. The Regia Aeronautica, from the navy's point of view, had performed little of their planned operations. The first bombing of Malta did not seem to take place at all, and just a few BR.20 bombers were used to carry out the second and third raids. And most important of all, the ten fighters sent to escort the returning ships were not enough to counter the thirty RAF planes that raced out from Malta in pursuit. Raked repeatedly by swooping aircraft, the little convoy was destroyed. The X Flotilla MAS commander, Moccagatta, the commander of the surface boats, Giobbe, and the medical officer of the assault craft, Captain Bruno Falcomatà, were all killed. With a total balance of 16 killed, 18 taken prisoner, and only 11 men escaping, the operation was a complete disaster. Owing to the bravery of the attempt, however, it would be known by the Italians as the "Glorious Failure."

Cunningham would write in his war diary that "Grand Harbour was heavily attacked by about 20 E-boats and one-man torpedo boats at dawn 26 July. The attack was repulsed most successfully. The E-boats scored hits on the viaduct of St Elmo breakwater but the harbour defence guns prevented any E-boat or torpedo craft from following through, and in about three minutes the attack was entirely frustrated."[9]

The vice admiral at Malta later sent a message on July 27 and a fuller report on August 13 detailing the attack. The August document included the translation of the Italian orders for the attack, which had been captured on the MAS boat. Also captured intact was an MT. These allowed the British to fully understand the method of attack. The MT was taken to Gibraltar and later to Britain, where ten "Boom Patrol Boats" based on the MT design were built with the idea of launching them from a Lancaster bomber, but the idea was later abandoned.[10] After this, Cunningham warned all Mediterranean bases, including Gibraltar, of the possibility of midget submarine attacks.

At Gibraltar, these warnings were heeded foremost by Lieutenant Bill Bailey, the "Render Mines Safe Officer," who was soon joined by the famous Lieutenant Lionel K. P. Crabb. Volunteers were called for underwater training in order to routinely check the hulls of the ships in harbor to detect and neutralize explosive charges that might be clamped onto them.[11] Crabb and Bailey formed the core of what would become one of the busiest units at Gibraltar, the Underwater Working Party, or UWWP.[12]

On the Italian side, the X Flotilla MAS found itself without two of its three commanders. The only one remaining was Lieutenant Commander Junio Valerio Borghese, the leader of the underwater craft.

The heavy losses at Suda Bay and the Glorious Failure before Malta—both in casualties and in trained men taken prisoner—put the X MAS in a crisis. Borghese, who retained command of the underwater teams, temporarily took command of the flotilla.

The unit had also suffered severe losses in equipment. New SLCs had to be built, hopefully improved models, as the series employed in the actions to that point had always shown a number of disappointing breakdowns and problems. Rear Admiral Carlo Giartosio replaced Admiral de Courten, but this was not necessarily on account of the failures. It is more likely that de Courten's efforts were appreciated and thence rewarded with a sea command. He would become minister of the Royal Italian Navy after the September 1943 armistice.[13]

Giartosio assigned the submarine *Ambra* to the X MAS as a means of transport for the SLCs. The *Ambra* was of the 600 class and under the command of Lieutenant Mario Arillo, who proved to be a daring and capable leader.

The experience gained during the fruitless attacks on Gibraltar to date had shown that several of the target ships always at anchor were transport ships, for which the SLC warhead was simply too big. It was for this reason that Lieutenant Eugenio Wolk would begin to train the gamma men, who were included in this period in the X MAS underwater unit now under Borghese's command, for the sabotage of merchant ships in enemy and neutral harbors. The frogmen were armed with much lighter explosive charges than those carried by the SLCs, though they were still enough to sink commercial tankers and transports.

Besides improving the SLCs and transforming the *Ambra* into an SLC carrier, there was much that needed to be done with the surface unit, which had suffered terribly. Lieutenant Commander Salvatore Todaro was appointed commander, and he had before him a difficult task in rebuilding the MTs, and especially in training the men.

The following months were therefore used to improve both boats and men. A new transport system was also developed. It consisted of two fishing boats, the *Cefalo* and the *Sogliola,* and the sailing ship *Costanza* (which had limited engine power). A new boat, the MTSM (MTS, modified) was also developed at this time, though it would not be ready for operations until 1943.

It was following this reorganization that another operation against Gibraltar, Operation BG-4, was planned. The operation's blueprint was the same as for the BG-3 action: Borghese's submarine *Scirè* would carry the three SLCs to Algeciras Bay, where it would release the two-man torpedoes. The teams were also the same. However, this time the machines were well worked over, taking into account the mechanical glitches that had occurred in the previous actions.

To take advantage of longer nights, Borghese had to wait until September before beginning his fourth attempt to force Gibraltar's port, which was now always illuminated. The operation was to be carried out between September 18 and 22, when there would be complete darkness favorable for the release of the SLCs, and a low tide.

On September 10, 1941, the *Scirè*, with Borghese in command and SLCs 140, 210, and 220 in their casings on deck, sailed from La Spezia toward Spain. It arrived on the 16th at the Straits of Gibraltar, which was successfully forced while submerged. The next day, Borghese lay on the sea bottom near Cadiz and waited for night to enter the harbor so he could take the frogmen on board. Then he resumed the move toward Algeciras. On the following night, he met a convoy coming in the opposite direction escorted by destroyers, but he was not spotted by the enemy.

On the next night, the 19th, the *Scirè* entered Algeciras Bay and moved up to the mouth of the Guadarranque River. It was 0120 on the 20th when the SLCs were launched into the sea to begin their adventure. Borghese now turned his vessel and headed back to La Spezia.

The SLCs began to steam slowly toward the harbor of Gibraltar, having as targets a battleship of the *Nelson* class, an aircraft carrier, and a merchant ship. The Amedeo Vesco and Antonio Zozzoli team was to penetrate the harbor and mine the battleship, but they ran into a patrolling motorboat, and at some point, at about 0330, Vesco heard underwater explosions and suspected his team had been spotted by hydrophones. Therefore, he changed his target to one of the ships in the bay. Having chosen a transport, he applied the charge and headed toward the Spanish coast. He suffered problems with his breathing apparatus, drank water poisoned by the absorbing salt of the apparatus, and was compelled to use the replacement. At the same time, his number two man had become faint from similar problems. But the SLC worked well, and they accomplished their mission. They landed and hid their breathing apparatus and then were arrested by Spanish sentries. The two men claimed they were shipwrecked sailors, however, and were shortly rescued by an Italian captain named Piero Pierleoni who then busied himself destroying the breathing apparatus.

The SLC of Decio Catalano and Giuseppe Giannoni began to move regularly at around 0130, but this team also detected a patrolling boat before the entrance of the harbor. The boat appeared perfectly silent and was not heard at a distance of 50 meters. To escape from the boat, which seemed to be following their "pig," Catalano dove and remained under water for a quarter of an hour. Then he came to the surface but estimated that he was too far away and too late to try to enter the harbor, and so decided to attack one of the ships in the outer bay.

At first, he and his partner mined a ship that they then discovered to be Italian, the *Pollenzo* from Genoa, so they detached the charge and mined another merchant ship. At 0516, Catalano set the timers and swam away, sinking the SLC (activating the auto-destruction device) and destroying the breathing apparatus. At 0715, the team finally touched the coast, and Catalano observed that the SLC was destroyed from a large white patch on the surface. He remained to observe. At 0916, he saw a 30-meter-high pillar of water on the stern of the ship, marking the successful explosion.

Meanwhile, the other team, consisting of Lisio Visintini and Giovanni Magro, was also encountering difficulties on the way to the harbor. Their target was the aircraft carrier *Ark Royal*, but although Visintini's team was the only one to succeed in entering the harbor, it proved difficult to approach a warship. Visintini found the patrolling boats before the entrance, but he was not detected; at some point he was compelled to dive, however, and a boat passed over his SLC.

At 0345, Visintini and Magro steamed at 11 meters depth toward the net. They overcame that obstruction and entered the harbor, where they passed what appeared to be a cruiser of 7,000 tons. There was not enough time to reach the carrier *Ark Royal*, so they had to choose another target. Visintini reflected that the cruiser was too near the entrance, where there were continuous explosions of depth charges, and so chose a loaded tanker.

Their mining operation went well, without any of the technical problems that had previously plagued the frogmen's operations. The team escaped the harbor and successfully reached the Spanish coast.

On the morning of September 20, 1941, three ships in the Gibraltar harbor exploded. The tanker *Fiona Shell* (mined by Vesco) of 2,444 tons broke in two pieces and sank, and then blasts ruptured the armed merchantman *Durham* of 10,893 tons (owing to the work of Catalano and Giannoni) and the tanker *Denbydale* of 8,145 tons (by Visintini with Magro). This last blow did not cause fires to break out on other ships, as Visintini had hoped, because the Royal Navy used an oil of high density that did not easily ignite. The *Durham* was heavily damaged, and the *Denbydale* sank, spilling a great deal of oil into the harbor. It was later raised and repaired.

Vice Admiral Somerville wrote of the aftermath of the attack: "Ships in harbour were ordered to close all watertight doors and to raise steam. Motor launches were sent out . . . to sweep the head of the Bay. . . . Motor boats, armed with depth charges, were sent to patrol inside booms at both entrances. A breathing apparatus, picked up in the Commercial anchorage, where an oil hulk, the *Fiona Shell* had been sunk, and SS *Durham* damaged, indicated that the probable cause was attack by two-men submarines."[14]

After this first important success of the two-man torpedoes, all the men were awarded the Silver Medal for gallantry in war. Borghese was promoted to commander and received an audience with King Victor Emmanuel III. It was only then that the king learned that training for the Decima MAS took place next to his estate. He later visited the training center and would witness a submarine exercise with the SLCs.

Borghese's citation read, in part: "In every one of these operations he succeeded in bringing back his submarine and its crew to the base, despite the difficulties due to determined pursuit by the enemy and to navigation underwater driven to the limit of human endurance, thus providing a splendid example of organizing capacity and leadership."[15]

According to the German naval attaché, Admiral Werner Löwisch, in his report of October 2, the Germans were well informed of the details of the operation. But Admiral Giartosio did not reveal the fact that the frogmen had arrived in Spain by air, perhaps to avoid explaining too much of the secret Italian support net in Spain.[16] In fact, the degree of protection the Italians maintained around their secret assault craft resulted in another report from Admiral Löwisch in which he claimed that the Italian Navy did not show him details of these secret weapons.[17]

The British, too, remained vague about exactly what kinds of devices had hit them, but after Borghese's next mission, all doubts about their destructive potential would be erased.

CHAPTER 8

Triumph at Alexandria

Please report what is being done to emulate the exploits of the Italians in Alexandria Harbour. . . . Is there any reason why we should be incapable of the same kind of scientific aggressive action that the Italians have shown? One would have thought we should have been in the lead.

Winston Churchill to General Lionel Hastings Ismay for
the Chiefs of Staff Committee, January 18, 1942[1]

D URING THE FALL OF 1941, THE AXIS AND THE British Commonwealth exchanged moves and countermoves as the war in the Mediterranean escalated. The Royal Navy, having established supremacy over the Italian surface fleet, had been shaken, if not stirred, by the Decima MAS's penetration of its anchorage at Gibraltar; but its control of that vital strait continued to constitute a stranglehold on the mouth of the Middle Sea. An aggressive cruiser squadron, Force K, had meanwhile taken up residence in Malta, within easy grasp of Axis convoys to North Africa; and the powerful Mediterranean Fleet—now strewn with battle laurels—was still inviolably based at Alexandria. The upshot of the British buildup in the theater came in December when Rommel, starved of supplies, was unable to withstand Operation Crusader, a British offensive that relieved Tobruk and pushed the Axis armies back across Cyrenaica (modern Libya), gaining new land-based airfields within easy reach of the Italo-German supply route.

But the last few weeks of the year would see a striking series of events that would tilt the seesaw war once more in an Axis direction. On December 2, Hitler ordered the II Fliegerkorps transferred from Russia to the Mediterranean. This was not because the Germans couldn't have used more air support during their concurrent crisis before Moscow, but because the onset of the worst Russian winter in half a century had made most air operations there, as well as airfields, untenable. (One can imagine the delight of Luftwaffe personnel at being transferred south, and they immediately vented their renewed spirits on Malta.)

The introduction of German U-boats into the Mediterranean, beginning in September, also had a dramatic impact. On November 13, the *U-81* sank the British aircraft carrier *Ark Royal* off Gibraltar with a single torpedo, and twelve days later the *U-331* caught the battleship *Barham* with a deadly spread. In this remarkable action, the U-boat's commander, Hans-Dietrich von Tiesenhausen, dove beneath the British destroyer screen and closed in on a line of three battleships. After destroying the *Barham,* which sank in three minutes with the loss of 861 sailors, the *U-331* accidentally broached the surface and was almost run over by the next battleship in line, the *Valiant* (the third being the *Queen Elizabeth*). A crash-dive barely avoided a collision, and the *Valiant*'s furiously firing dual-purpose (DP) guns could not depress low enough to hit the submarine beneath its nose. Tiesenhausen, now submerged, was somehow able to creep from the midst of the British fleet to return to his base unscathed. By way of adding further injury to insult, the British cruiser *Galatea* was finished off by the *U-557* on the night of December 14.

Thus, even as Rommel fell back across Libya, German naval and air forces were simultaneously decimating British naval power to his north, reopening his line of supply. And now Italy was poised to make its greatest contribution to the Mediterranean naval war. Ironically, it would not be delivered by the capital ships of the Regia Marina, but by a few brave men of the Decima MAS. Prince Borghese would command the operation, and his instrument of destruction would be the SLCs.

British intelligence had picked up word of the coming attack. There had been some forewarning from decrypts that the Italians were planning a covert mission against the fleet anchorage at Alexandria. Admiral Cunningham, having learned of a possible attack, "warned the fleet by signal that attacks on Alexandria harbour by air, boat or human torpedo might be expected in calm weather" at 1025 on December 18. One of the problems noted by Cunningham was that he was unsure which weapon Italy would use—explosive surface torpedo boats such as those used in the destruction of the heavy cruiser *York* at Suda Bay, or the rumored submergible "explosive motor-boat . . . fitted with apparatus for lifting nets." Neither Cunningham nor any of the other sailors serving that day at Alexandria had a clear idea of how they were about to be attacked or how to counter it. It must also be remembered that most British sailors thought that Alexandria—because of its relatively remote location, the harbor's own defenses, and the strength of their fleet—was perfectly safe from enemy attack. Still, "steps to increase vigilance had been taken by ordering out the greatest number of patrol craft. . . . The defences were inspected and lookouts increased." In addition, a second net was to be added, along with newer sonar and radar. They arrived after the attack.[2]

Prince Borghese had trained the SLC crews with a great deal of night practice in a harbor containing the kind of obstacles that might be encountered at Alexandria. The training also included mock attacks at La Spezia naval base against their own ships. In one exercise, Borghese's crew "sank" the Italian battleship *Giulio Cesare* and the elderly armored cruiser *San Marco,* now employed as a wireless-controlled target ship. In the process, the men became extremely fit. All three manned torpedoes were of the new 200 series and were loaded after dark on December 3 at La Spezia. For security, they were loaded after the *Scirè* was under way, partially down the channel on its way out of port. The three captains of the SLCs then carefully checked their submersibles for any possible defects. The attack was dubbed Operation GA-3.

Borghese was helped by captured maps of the minefields around Alexandria, recovered from the wreck of the British destroyer *Mohawk*. The *Mohawk* had been lost in a convoy action in shallow waters off the Tunisian coast on April 16, 1941, and Italian divers had afterward found a trove of Royal Navy documents. Air reconnaissance meantime kept track of the British vessels at Alexandria, including where the big ships were moored. On the eve of his departure, Borghese obtained additional information on the harbor obstructions from Rear Admiral Franco Maugeri, the head of SIS naval intelligence.[3]

The SLC operators now left the *Scirè* and went to Brindisi, where they boarded a plane for Port Lago on the island of Leros in the Dodecanese Islands, there to rejoin the *Scirè* when it steamed to that island. This was done in part to keep the crews fresh for the coming operation. Mussolini had personally shaken the hands of all the men ordered on this mission, wishing them luck and informing them that, if successful, they would receive Italy's highest award for bravery, the *Medaglia d'Oro*, or Gold Medal.[4]

The *Scirè* experienced only one unusual event while sailing to Leros. Off the coast of Sicily, Borghese sighted a surfaced British submarine and for a tense period the two craft actually traveled parallel to each other under a moonlit sky. But neither Borghese nor the British commander chose to attack. The deck gun of the *Scirè* had been removed for the SLC casings, so the sub was armed only with torpedoes, while the British boat had two deck guns. After about an hour, much to Borghese's relief, the British craft veered away just as silently as it had appeared. After daylight, however, the *Scirè* found itself sailing among the depressing wreckage of a convoy, a vast field of debris and life jackets floating on the sea—perhaps the handiwork of that same British sub.

After arriving at Leros, the *Scirè* reembarked the ten SLC crewmen and also removed the camouflage that had shielded the cylinders on deck from air reconnaissance or Greek spies. An awkward situation occurred when the local base commander wanted to see a demonstration of the SLCs, which was a command Borghese had the authority to refuse, and he did. He didn't want to risk accidents and also wanted his SLC crews to be fully rested.[5]

The crews for the human torpedoes were Lieutenant Commander Luigi Durand de la Penne (a veteran of the Gibraltar mission) with petty officer Emilio Bianchi as his number two; Antonio Marceglia with seaman Spartaco Schergat; and Vincenzo Martellotta with seaman Mario Marino.

The reassembled crews then departed on board the *Scirè* for the approach across the eastern Mediterranean to Alexandria. (See map on page ix.) The plan was to attack on a moonless night, with Commander Ernesto Forza at Athens coordinating any additional reconnaissance and intelligence information that might arise. Forza had been appointed commander of the Decima MAS and would retain that position until May 1, 1943, so Borghese was no longer in temporary overall command. Moon, weather, tides, and the naval situation at Alexandria were all favorable for the attempt.

It was known that the *Queen Elizabeth* and the *Valiant* were in port—they were the last two British battleships in the eastern Mediterranean, except for an older, unreconstructed one based at Gibraltar (the Italians had five in service). These two battleships were to be the main targets unless an aircraft carrier was present.

The secondary objective was to ignite fuel oil. This task would fall to the third SLC crew that was to attack one of the ten reported tankers in the military harbor—if they could not locate an aircraft carrier. Two of the three "pig" teams were also equipped with timed incendiary floats in case they were lucky enough to split open a loaded tanker in the harbor. They were timed to go off after oil had spread on the surface, but not so early as to precede the main charges. Only de la Penne's crew would not employ this weapon.[6]

As Borghese brought the *Scirè* creeping toward Alexandria, the weather was bad and he delayed the attempt for one day. On the next night, December 18, he ordered the attack, as word had arrived from Athens confirming that both battleships were still in port. The *Scirè* approached within 1.3 miles of the harbor's mole submerged at a depth of 15 meters. It stopped just short of a line of shore-controlled sea mines and settled into the mud of the seafloor. Borghese had come to within a few meters of his objective point after an excellent feat of underwater navigation.

He then surfaced just enough for the conning tower to be out of the water so he could pop out of the "trapdoor" and look around. Preparations for launching the three SLCs began. Marceglia's team would attack Cunningham's flagship, the *Queen Elizabeth*, while de la Penne's team would go after the *Valiant*. The overall command of the SLCs was de la Penne's. Left on board the *Scirè* were two reserve teams, including a medical sublieutenant, Giorgio Spaccarelli, who had daily checked on the medical condition of the men during the voyage. Interestingly, the three volunteer commanders of the SLCs represented all three divisions of the Italian Navy: gunnery, engineering, and deck officer. De la Penne would later write that he and the crews had "complete faith in our 'chariots,' and in the submarine *Scirè*. We also had confidence in Commander Borghese and, of course, in ourselves."[7]

Borghese gave the SLC crews their ceremonial kick in the rump just before their departure.

In the process of releasing the SLCs, the submarine remained partially submerged while all ten of the X MAS men, equipped with diving suits, worked at getting the SLCs released. During this procedure, one of the doors for the casings was found to be damaged; it was hard to open and would not close. This would adversely affect the navigation dynamics of the *Scirè* on its way home. The submarine was now free to leave for Leros between 2000 and 2100.

Another mishap occurred when Spaccarelli damaged his diving equipment while working on the launch of the SLCs and nearly drowned. Very fortunately, he settled on the deck of the submarine instead of slipping overboard, and after the SLC crews signaled by pounding on the hull, the *Scirè* surfaced and Spaccarelli's almost lifeless body was recovered. What is even more remarkable about this is that Borghese had removed all the railings on deck so that there would be fewer obstructions on the *Scirè* that might snag a mine cable. After much CPR and injection of drugs, Spaccarelli recovered, though finally only after hospitalization at Leros.

After the "pigs" had been released, between 2000 and 2100, the *Scirè* was free to leave for Leros. Italian agents on shore and an additional sub had been arranged to try to retrieve the crewmen after the attack. Now the frogmen were on their own. They slowly approached Alexandria astride their torpedoes, only their heads above the water. (See map on page x.) While approaching the main harbor entrance, the three crews rendezvoused. A small meal was consumed by some of the men, along with stimulant drugs.

They were a bit ahead of schedule and discussing how best to enter the outer harbor when providence smiled upon them. Three destroyers of Rear Admiral Philip Vian's squadron, retiring from the First Battle of the Sirte that had just been fought, were approaching from the open sea. The harbor's lights, including the main lighthouse just 500 yards from the Italian frogmen, came on to help guide Vian's approaching ships. The three SLCs were now almost at the boom and could see a motorboat on patrol that was periodically dropping small depth charges. According to de la Penne, "We heard—and felt—sharp underwater explosions which painfully constricted our legs."[8]

Suddenly the entrance signal lights went on. The SLC crews knew this meant that ships were about to enter port and that the boom would open. The three destroyers, showing no lights and steaming at about 10 knots, approached as the boom slowly opened at 0242. And the SLCs scampered in with them. Martellotta's team and Marceglia's team went in with the first destroyer, and both were almost rammed by the second destroyer. De la Penne's SLC would literally be under the second destroyer, and the surge of its bow wave forced his "pig" down into the mud. The third destroyer's bow wave pushed him up again, against the inner boom buoy, but no damage resulted. The boom closed again at 0315, but now the manned torpedoes were inside.

Getting into the harbor unobserved was considered the second most difficult part of an operation. De la Penne now considered the most serious problem: the cold. No matter how much training the men had performed in cold-water conditions, their bulky diving suits could not fully protect them. Also, during the many stages of an operation some damage would usually occur to their suits, allowing the freezing seawater to seep in against their flesh.[9]

Now past the mole, the SLCs began to proceed deeper into the harbor. They were now no longer sailing together but seeking out their individual targets.

First we will trace de la Penne's attack. He passed the third destroyer, which was now anchoring, again with just his head out of the water. Two cruisers loomed up in the night's dark, anchored with their sterns to the quay. Then he came upon the French battleship *Lorraine,* which at that point in the war was a noncombatant. Up ahead was the British *Valiant.* As de la Penne approached, there was one more boom directly surrounding the battleship. He and his number two manhandled the SLC through by literally pushing it between two floats. De la Penne's suit ripped during this procedure and the icy water spread against his skin, but the noise they made, fortunately for them, was not heard by the sentries.

So at 0300, and after six years of training and practice, de la Penne was within 100 feet of his target. As he approached the battleship, his hands were too cold to control the "pig"; it struck the hull and then dove to the bottom, about 45 feet below. De la Penne then surfaced, looked around to determine where he was, and went down to find that his number two, Bianchi, was gone. Bianchi's respirator had failed and he had surfaced, semi-conscious, but recovered; so as to not disclose the operation, he had quietly swum to a nearby buoy to hide.

De la Penne also discovered that a cable had become entangled with his propeller and that he could not fix it. What to do? He was still some distance from his target, which was *uphill* on the muddy seafloor. He literally began "to drag the torpedo along in the mud by main strength until directly beneath the ship. The mud was extremely gooey and cut out all visibility, but I guided my 'pig' by the noise of one of the pumps on board the enemy ship. The frightful effort made me sweat as if I were in a Turkish bath. Seawater seeped into my mask, and I had to drink it to avoid drowning. Although I was submerged in water and was drinking all the time, I had a continuous sensation of terrible thirst."[10]

After about twenty minutes, with longer and longer rests between efforts, de la Penne bumped against the battleship's hull. He then settled the charge under the ship's centerline, about 15 feet below the vessel, and set the timer. There was no need for him to set the "pig" for self-destruct, as it would be destroyed in the explosion because it was so close. De la Penne now surfaced and threw away his respirator. "As I was swimming away, someone on the battleship's deck almost over me saw me and ordered me to stop. I paid no attention and kept on swimming until a hail of machine gun bullets induced me to change my mind."[11]

De la Penne then swam to the buoy, where he discovered Bianchi. Then, not thinking, he started to swim to the side of the battleship, until another burst of machine-gun fire dissuaded him. Both men were then picked up by a patrolling British motor-launch.

At 0325 on December 19, the *Valiant* reported that "two foreigners had been found on her bow buoy." They were de la Penne and Bianchi. By now the British knew what the presence of two Italians in diving suits within one of their harbors implied. The prisoners were questioned and moved about, even told it was too bad their mission had failed, and their itinerary included a short stint on shore where they were given the third degree. The two clammed up—it was name and rank only at this point. Taken back to the *Valiant*, at Admiral Cunningham's suggestion, they were placed in confinement deep in the bowels of the battleship, where they would be the first victims if they had indeed staged an attack. (Incredibly, Bianchi fell asleep!) Warnings had been issued of the presence of "human torpedoes" in the harbor. Various ships tried to pass lines underneath their hulls to locate the weapons, and the *Queen Elizabeth* did snag an obstruction, possibly the SLC's charge, but was unable to do anything about it.[12]

Marceglia's team, unlike the other two, would proceed down the harbor completely submerged as it approached the *Queen Elizabeth*. The men approached the battleship and accidentally noisily hit the hull with their SLC, but no alarm was sounded. They detached the warhead and hung it from a line 4 feet below the hull. At about this point, Marceglia's number two became disoriented and could no longer work under water. Marceglia set the explosive timer, and at 0315 they began to surface by riding the SLC. They broke surface amidst foam and splashing water, this time attracting a searchlight that scanned the area but failed to find them. They then deployed their incendiary flares, set their SLC for self-destruct, and headed for shore. Their attack had been the closest of the three to a textbook operation and would yield the greatest results.

They made it to shore and posed as French sailors, then discovered that the money they had been issued to help them in escaping was British and that they needed Egyptian currency. While exchanging money, they caught the attention of the Egyptian police. They did make it in the course of the day to the Rosetta stone, and the submarine *Zaffiro*, which had come to pick them up, was off the coast about 10 miles when they were caught. The plan was for them to find a boat and head out to meet the submarine. The *Zaffiro* would surface for most of the night two days later, but no one arrived for the rendezvous, as all six operators had been captured.

Martellotta's team had the farthest to go and took roughly the same route as Marceglia's team. As Martellotta and Marino passed by the *Lorraine*, Martellotta saw a French sailor smoking by the rail and used his flashlight to read the ship's name. One sailor from a nearby French cruiser shone "a torch from the gangway." This incident is probably the root of the story that made the rounds of the British lower deck after this action, that a French sailor, upon being asked where the British battleships were, directed the Italian frogmen to their berths![13]

Proceeding down deep into the harbor, Martellotta determined that no aircraft carrier was present and so began looking for a tanker. He and Marino did come upon a "large ship and decided to attack, but when only a few yards away he noticed that it was a cruiser. . . . As he was very near the ship, he decided to navigate alongside, holding himself off with his hands, so as to reach the stern without being seen, and thus get away quietly. During this operation he was nearly discovered while he was under the ship, and he had a hard job keeping his assistant quiet, for Marino could not bear to give up such a wonderful opportunity to attack."[14]

The team next saw a large tanker, the Norwegian oiler *Sagona*, nearby and proceeded to attack it. Moored next to the oiler, bow to the *Sagona*'s stern, was the newly arrived destroyer *Jervis*. Martellotta was hit on the head by an oar of a native boat passing over at this point and began to vomit repeatedly. He could no longer dive, so he had Marino mount the attack. By himself, Marino could not place the explosive charge directly under the centerline of the tanker, but he did place it below the stern and set the timer. The men then set the explosive self-destruct on their SLC, placed their incendiary flares, and made it to shore, where they managed to change clothes. However, they would be captured a short time later while trying to get out of the harbor area.

So the weapons were all in place. Now, would they work?

On board the *Queen Elizabeth*, Frank Wade, a midshipman, was awakened at 0400 "by the alarm rattlers buzzing us to action and stations and a bugler blowing the alarm" over the intercom. Wade's friend, Sublieutenant S. Nowson, was sent over from the *Queen Elizabeth* to the *Valiant*, where de la Penne and Bianchi were being held, as he spoke fluent Italian. Nowson found the two prisoners "unexpectedly calm after their ordeal."[15]

At 0550, de la Penne, deep within the bowels of the ship, finally warned a British officer that an explosion was about to occur. He refused to give other details and was left below, but the ship's captain, Charles Morgan, had the foresight to order all hands on deck. At 0558, the first charge detonated, sinking the tanker *Sagona* and damaging the bow of the nearby *Jervis*. This explosion was fortunate for the British in that it blew up the stern, flooding the engine room, but did not substantially rupture any fuel tanks. Thus, little in the way of fuel was released.

On the *Jervis*, several men thought they had been torpedoed. Signalman George Kean was on watch when the charge went off. It "hurled me across the compass platform on to the deck," he said. "Our bows had jumped up, and as I scrambled to my feet they were dropping down again causing me to think for a second or two that our end had come." The ship suffered hull damage and a small fire, but no casualties. It would go into dock the following day and be under repair for the next month.[16]

This first blast was followed 7 minutes later, at 0605, by an explosion from beneath the *Valiant*, which now had its crew up from below and all watertight doors shut. No one was lost, but the forward main magazine and shell room were flooded along with some additional compartments. Eighty feet of the ship's underside was damaged, and the trunk to its "A" turret of two 15-inch guns was distorted. The *Valiant* suffered less damage than its sister ship because the explosion was further away and the sea bottom slightly deeper, so the energy of the blast was more dissipated. After temporary repairs, the ship would proceed to Durban, South Africa, in April and be under repair until July 7, 1942.[17]

The next and most destructive blast occurred at 0616 on the *Queen Elizabeth*, where most of the now nervous crew had been summoned from below decks. The ship's A, B, and X boiler rooms, and other compartments, were flooded, and the explosion "cut off all power and light." Some engine personnel were below deck, and eight would die. Between the upward heave followed by the downward motion of the ship, Admiral Cunningham and Midshipman Frank Wade, both of whom were standing on the bridge, were thrown a few inches in the air. Wade later wrote: "Again there was the low, rumbling underwater explosion and the quarterdeck was thrown upwards about six inches, maybe more. I bent my legs and threw out my arms to keep my balance as the huge ship lurched beneath me. A blast of thick smoke and flame shot out the funnel. Then the ship seemed to settle rapidly."[18]

Damage to the ship's bottom extended 60 feet by 190 feet. The *Queen Elizabeth* lost all hydraulic power, and the next day two submarines would move alongside and supply power to the crippled flagship. The *Sagona* and the *Queen Elizabeth* settled to the shallow harbor bottom, while the *Valiant* and the *Jervis* listed but did not sink. The *Queen Elizabeth*, after temporary repairs in Alexandria, would proceed to Norfolk, Virginia, and undergo repairs for another year, until June 1, 1943.[19]

When Borghese had left Leros, he had sent a secret message to Ernesto Forza in Athens: "Departing at dawn. Foresee cavities developing in Lion's mouth." Now it was time to prove that the operation had been a success. The operators would later send secret coded messages back to Italy from their prisoner-of-war camp, but Axis air reconnaissance already had solid results. On January 8, 1942, the fact that the *Valiant* was in dock under repairs was clear, and war bulletin N.586 on the following day noted that both battleships had suffered heavy damage. The British, in order to conceal their losses, had corrected the lists on their damaged ships and even blew smoke from the *Queen Elizabeth*'s funnels—while the ship was sitting on the seafloor—in order to fool German reconnaissance planes. But the full details would emerge over time.[20]

After the attack had proved a success, de la Penne freely gave many of the details of the operation to his interrogators. These details included their flight from Rome to Leros, the embarking on a submarine, and a complete story of how the operation unfolded at a tactical level in the harbor. Some have called this treason, though in hindsight it could probably be more accurately termed overexuberance, and today a warship of the Italian Navy sports his name.[21]

When asked about Borghese, the prisoners told their captors, "The Captain of the *Scire* is *Capitano di Fregata* Borghese who had been a member of the party that attacked Gibraltar. He was decorated and specially promoted for his part in the attack. Great admiration was expressed by P.W.s [prisoners] for this officer who showed great calm and courage at all times."[22]

Cunningham later wrote "that as the possibility of attack was expected the defences were on the alert, but that protection must not rely on the comparatively out-of-date methods of lookouts, boats and nets. Warning of approach by modern scientific methods is essential. Some method of neutralising a charge once it has been placed is important, in this instance there was three hours warning."[23]

At the time of the successful attack against the *Valiant* and the *Queen Elizabeth,* the port admiral, Rear Admiral G. H. Cresswell, in charge of the defenses of Alexandria was thought by some to be "not up to his job." It is possible that he was not relieved earlier by Cunningham because he was in his class at Dartmouth—the British equivalent of Annapolis.[24]

But a board was convened and later issued "Report of Board of Inquiry: Attack on Alexandria Harbour, Dec 1941." It concluded that there had been "a failure of the look-out system, a lack of supervising officers, the absence of radar, the inability of submarine (detection methods including sonar) to range far enough to locate the parent submarine, a shortage of patrol vessels, lack of illumination, the failure of the dusk air patrol to detect the submarine, the inability of antisubmarine nets to prevent the attackers reaching their targets, and the lack of safeguard when the boom was opened." Radar and sonar that had been ordered in late October but had not yet been installed was quickly deployed now. Interestingly, Cunningham's biographer, Michael Simpson, feels that the admiral deserves some of the blame because he was less than interested in "shore administration"; but he concludes, quite rightly, that "full credit must be given to Italian skill and courage."[25]

The last two British battleships in the eastern Mediterranean had been "Tarantoed."

After delivering the SLCs to within a mile of the harbor, the *Scirè* had crept back out, and after thirty-nine hours of being under the surface, set a course to Leros and arrived safely. The *Scirè* flag was awarded the Gold Medal, and its commander, Borghese, the Military Order of Savoy.

As 1941 drew to a close, it appeared as if the steady, hard-fought projection of British power in the Mediterranean had suddenly come unraveled in a matter of weeks. The newly arrived U-boats had made their presence felt in devastating fashion, and the arrival of II Fliegerkorp carried ominous consequences for Malta as well as for British fleet or convoy actions. With Japan's entry into the war on December 7, the Royal Navy had assumed a vast new obligation to protect Britain's eastern possessions. This effort got off to a disastrous start when the battleship *Prince of Wales* and the battle cruiser *Repulse* were sunk by Japanese aircraft off Malaya, putting to death, too, the theory that capital ships could not be trumped by aircraft in the open sea. Another consequence of the Japanese onslaught was that all Australian vessels immediately vacated the Mediterranean in order to protect their own homeland.

In still another setback, the Malta-based cruiser squadron, Force K, which had wreaked havoc on Axis supply convoys to North Africa, stumbled into a catastrophe. Sallying out to intercept another convoy on December 18, Force K steamed into an unexpected Axis minefield. The cruiser *Neptune* was disabled and, while drifting helplessly, ran into two or three other mines until it sank with all hands (one man survived to become a POW). A destroyer trying to help the *Neptune* also hit a mine and sank, and two more cruisers were forced to limp back to Malta with partially blown hulls. Force K had been crippled and was soon withdrawn, as was Britain's flotilla of U-class submarines, which now found their base at Valletta untenable.

But the most galling loss to the British was the loss of their last two battleships in the Mediterranean at the hands of the Decima MAS in Alexandria Harbor. It was at dawn on December 19 that explosions began ripping apart the most valuable ships in the fleet's anchorage, the *Queen Elizabeth* and *Valiant*, afterward described by Churchill as "useless burdens." Of perhaps equal significance was a sudden change in the British attitude toward their Italian opponents. As Midshipman Wade, who had been aboard the *Queen Elizabeth* at the moment of its devastation, wrote, "All of us thought that the Italian navy was hopeless, inefficient, and even cowardly. . . . However, we soon revised our opinions about their heroism and ingenuity."[26]

Admiral Ernesto Forza, who had commanded the X MAS between October 1941 and May 1943, later concluded that by the start of 1942 the British were aware of the Italian methods and knew that a new generation of weapons would be needed. In addition, the Italians knew that from that point on they would need defenses against the same type of attack by the British.[27]

The balance of power in the Mediterranean Sea had shifted.

CHAPTER 9

The Siege of Gibraltar

Among professionals there are no secrets—or at least, only a few.

Admiral Franco Maugeri[1]

AFTER THE SPECTACULAR SUCCESS AT ALEXANDRIA, Borghese had to relinquish his command of the *Scirè* because he could no longer fulfill his duties as commander of the underwater units of the Decima MAS while also commanding a submarine.

The British naval setbacks at the end of 1941 had allowed significant Axis reinforcements to reach North Africa, and in January Rommel knocked the British back to a position known as the Gazala Line. The focal point of Axis strategy in 1942 was a projected offensive against Suez, which had to be coordinated with the continued neutralization of Malta in order to maintain the supply route of Axis troops in Africa. Malta was thus heavily bombed by the Luftwaffe and Regia Aeronautica during April and May 1942, and the Decima MAS was called upon once again to support the siege of the island from the sea.

For this reason, the surface assault craft were partly based at the naval facility at Augusta, Sicily. There, an MTSM squadron under the command of Sublieutenant Ongarillo Ungarelli was ordered to ambush Malta harbor's entrance to try to intercept the merchant ships that escaped the air and naval attacks of the Axis.

Ungarelli worked closely with Lieutenant Giuseppe Cosulich, and both collaborated with the Special Naval Force established under the command of Vice Admiral Vittorio Tur for the conquest of Malta that had first been contemplated in 1940. The planned invasion had been code-named Operation C3 by the Italians and Herkules by the Germans, but it never took place because Hitler refused to commit to the attack.[2] In early 1942, Hitler's quandary was whether to expend airborne and amphibious assets on an island that had already been effectively neutralized, or to continue the flow of all available resources to Rommel's conventional armies in North Africa. Hitler had been unnerved by the loss of paratroopers in the invasion of Crete the previous year and no longer had a stomach for pitting them against the 28,000-man, more concentrated garrison of Malta. So while Axis attention remained focused on the tiny island, the object was only to suppress it while feeding supplies to Africa, where greater results seemed within grasp.

MTSMs *214* and *218* landed two agents on Malta to gather information, one of them with a radio. The torpedo boat *Abba*, under Commander Max Ponzo of the SIS with *MAS 574* and *MAS 576*, sailed from Augusta on the evening of May 17, 1942, to carry out the missions, called "110" and "111." However, once landed, the two agents were captured, and one of them, Carmelo Borg Pisani, a Maltese by descent, was hanged as a traitor on November 28, 1942. Nevertheless, the missions around the island were helpful in gathering fresh information on the sea currents and coastal conditions, and also served the gainful purpose of keeping the weary British garrison on edge.[3]

One further operation was attempted against Alexandria with the submarine *Ambra* under the code name of Operation GA-4. Borghese and the Supermarina had it mounted because Axis aerial reconnaissance had shown that the *Queen Elizabeth* was very likely under repair in the floating dock at Alexandria (the Axis was unaware of the full extent of damage inflicted on the Mediterranean Fleet at this time). Reconnaissance operations had also spotted the support ship *Medway* (displacing 14,650 tons), which was thought to play an important role in the submarine threat to the Axis supply lanes to Africa. This assessment was accurate, as the ship indeed housed important supplies, including torpedoes, for the British submarines operating in the Mediterranean.

The large floating dock was a vital objective in itself as it was an important support factor for battleships coming from other theaters of operation. The nearest dock of this size was at Durban, South Africa. Therefore, of the three human torpedoes the *Ambra* could transport, two were assigned to the dock, and the third to the *Medway*. Operation GA-4 would be difficult, for after the devastating December 1941 operation more security measures had been taken. The *Ambra*'s commander, Mario Arillo, had to release the operators just at the last light of sunset to allow as much darkness as possible for the SLC teams.

The teams consisted of Supply Captain Egil Chersi and Petty Officer Rodolfo Beuck; Engineer Luigi Feltrinelli and Petty Officer Luciano Favale; and Midshipman Giorgio Spaccarelli and Petty Officer Armando Memoli. Chersi would become ill; the substitute team that replaced him and his number two was made up of Midshipman Giovanni Magello and Petty Officer Giuseppe Morbelli. Also on board was an X MAS doctor and one additional diver.

The *Ambra* sailed from La Spezia on April 29 and reached the Aegean island base of Leros, the starting point for the mission. Sailing from Leros on the evening of May 12, the *Ambra* reached the point of release on the evening of the 14th. But Arillo failed to note the speed of the current off Alexandria, which displaced the vessel some 1,000 yards westward, and the SLCs were released too far from the objective.

The submarine surfaced at 2020, and by 2100 the release of the two-man torpedoes was completed. The *Ambra* dove just afterward because the coastal searchlights were sweeping the dark and Arillo did not want to be spotted. So close to the shore was the *Ambra* that the shallow sandbanks caused some difficulty.

But soon more pressing problems arose: The Feltrinelli SLC refused to work and was therefore sunk, and the crewmen destroyed the equipment and went to Alexandria, where they made contact with

Italian agents. On May 29, however, they were located and captured. The other two crews spent the hours of darkness trying to locate the entrance to the harbor and in the end had to sink their SLCs and swim for the coast, where they were captured. The operation had failed, and specialized equipment and trained personnel had been lost. The British had been in a high state of readiness for this operation, as it turned out. ULTRA had intercepted an Italian radio transmission on May 5 that had alerted them to the upcoming attack.

Meanwhile, Borghese's attentions were occupied to the west with the changing situation at Gibraltar. His intelligence network had kept him informed of the growing volume of shipping in the area, much of it stopping off there before proceeding either north or south in the Atlantic. Borghese was always one for tactical enhancement, and he pushed for new methods to take advantage of the situation. The volume of the merchant shipping was such that much of it was in the outer, more exposed Algeciras Bay, with many British merchant ships closer to Algeciras than to Gibraltar. Borghese also recognized that British defenses, especially against submarines, were improving, thereby limiting the potential for attacks. Also, delivering attacks by submarines demanded the long nights of fall and winter, whereas a nearby base might allow for year-round attacks. Finally, sending a submarine from Italy required several steps and days, while a high-value target at Gibraltar might have already steamed off. With a sympathetic Spain nearby, Borghese, with his talented staff, developed a strategy for a veritable siege of Gibraltar.[4]

Borghese, of course, did not expect to capture Gibraltar, but he did expect and did succeed in diverting British men and materials to defending the port, which would now start to suffer a series of attacks. The Decima MAS operated from several bases at home and abroad during the war, but its most famous base became the *Olterra*, a secret installation that the X MAS created and maintained in the very shadow of the Rock.

The *Olterra* was a merchant ship built in 1913, displacing 4,995 tons, which happened to be in Algeciras Bay when Italy entered the war. Rather than let it fall into the hands of the British, the ship was scuttled by its crew, under the command of Captain Amoretti di Imperia, in Gibraltar Roads. A month later, the ship was raised and towed to the Spanish port for sale, but the British refused to let the vessel leave from Gibraltar. From the ship it was possible to see British installations at Gibraltar, about 6 miles east.

It was only in 1941 that Decima MAS agent Antonio Ramognino reported the opportunity to use the ship as a base for the SLCs so that they would no longer need to be transported there for each mission by submarines. Ramognino was a boat racer and on his own had designed an assault craft similar to the MTM. On May 2, 1941, he was received by Admiral de Courten, but the bureaucracy was too slow for Ramognino. He had a talk with Commander Moccagatta before the latter's death, and finally, on August 24, 1941, a discussion with Borghese at the X MAS base at La Spezia. At that point, he already had a wooden prototype. The Prince listened to him with great interest and approved the assault boat, which was named "R." Construction began shortly afterward, and the first two boats were ready in January 1942. The enthusiastic Ramognino tested one himself between January and March.[5]

Ramognino also had another virtue: His wife was Conchita Peris del Corral, and they both spoke Spanish. The X MAS sent them to Algeciras to organize the base. They went to Spain on June 22 and rented a house, later called "Villa Carmela." This house would later become the main base of the gamma frogmen. Located in the vicinity of Maiorga Point, several dozen meters from the sea near the mouth of the Guadarranque River, the house was just on the other side of Algeciras Bay. It was not too difficult for Ramognino to rent it, as he explained that his Spanish wife was recovering from an illness and needed to live in a hot and comfortable place with sea air.

From here, the gamma men would be able to scrutinize every naval movement into Gibraltar with the use of a powerful set of binoculars, which, incidentally, were stolen from the British consulate at Algeciras.[6] The British and the Spaniards were not easy to deceive. Ramognino later recalled that, beginning on the day of his arrival, a

British car sat for several nights near the house. He and his wife also received many Spanish visitors, all of whom were very interested in what they were doing and what was in the house.[7]

Observation of the bay took place from a post prepared by Ramognino that was hidden in an aviary he had built for a green parakeet. From inside the aviary, it was possible to covertly observe the British base, as the villa was just a couple of miles north of Gibraltar and very near the Spanish *La Linea* (literally, "the line," or border). Spanish and British counterintelligence alike continued to keep a watch on the villa, however. The Ramogninos had to keep their windows closed when the gamma men were preparing their equipment and used every caution when buying food and other daily supplies to avoid rousing the curiosity of British surveillance.

It should be noted that while many ships could find cover and defense under the Rock, many others had to stay in the large bay, as many convoys sailing on the Atlantic stopped there, and the space available in the inner harbor was not enough for all. Therefore, there were often some thirty cargoes in the bay that were potentially easy victims for an underwater attack.

At the same time, Italian Air Force Intelligence, the SIA, had established an observation post on the other side of Gibraltar Bay and gradually obtained wireless apparatus and camera equipment (the latter only in June 1941). On that side, just in front of the Vittoria Hotel, which housed the British consulate, was the *Olterra*.

The *Olterra* base has been called "the masterpiece of Licio Visintini"[8] because it was this distinguished lieutenant who organized the transformation of the old ship into an SLC base. Explaining to anyone who was interested that the hull had to be cleaned, men started work on the ship in September 1942. The men of the X MAS had arrived from Italy a few at a time, simulating the arrival of workers coming to Spain to repair and improve the ship.

Covered by the noise made by the scraping of the bow of the ship, they cut an exit door on the starboard side of the *Olterra*'s hull that was 1.2 by 2 meters in size. They then built a window that would show no irregularities when shut. The window was 6 feet under the waterline when the *Olterra* was in its ordinary position, serving as the exit to the sea for a room that was both a base and a workshop for the Decima MAS. Reaching the secret room from inside the ship was made quite difficult, with false doors, true but closed and locked doors, and so on, in order to fool unauthorized visitors.

Equipment arriving from Italy was ostensibly intended for repairs, but inside the containers were components of the SLCs to be assembled in the hidden workshop. The torpedoes arrived as tubes and were shipped without warheads and tails, while the breathing apparatuses were sent in fuel oil drums. The warheads also arrived in drums, the subterfuge maintained because the containers presented for the inspection of Spanish guards had a surface section filled with real fuel oil.

The *Olterra*, as a tanker, would have been a good ship to sell, and therefore these extraordinary maintenance measures appeared natural. The underwater "window" allowed the SLCs to exit the ship and sail toward their objectives. It was cleverly designed. An aperture would open for the SLCs to exit, and then the welded doors would shut again.[9]

The work of transforming the *Olterra* took the entire summer of 1942. It took place under the watch of a patrol of Spanish Carabineros who were charged with making certain all activity was strictly in accordance with international rules regarding interned shipping in wartime. Visintini took care to supply them with good food and wines in order to draw their attention as far as possible from the working party that was converting the ship into a base for saboteurs.[10]

The *Olterra*'s original crew was gradually replaced by seamen who appeared to come from the merchant trade but were in fact warriors. The degree of cover-up work the project required shows the high level of cooperation with the SIS that was part of X MAS work. Borghese would become involved later, after Italy's armistice and during the postwar era, in other secret activities.

As Maugeri later surmised, the Spaniards could have looked the other way when work was under way on the *Olterra,* but it was more difficult for the Italians to bring their supplies and equipment in. The list of items sent to the *Olterra* included 30 explosive charges, 120 revolvers and 65 rifles, 25 breathing apparatuses and diving suits, 70 underwater lamps, and 17 heavy underwater motors. Still more difficult was keeping the movements of about 100 men secret, especially from British intelligence. The Italians had an organized net in Spain and were helped by the fact that the two regimes were political friends. An Italian volunteer, Bepo Martini, who had remained in Spain after the end of the Spanish Civil War, organized the covert movement of the Italian personnel. He gave them various identities and cover stories— they posed as hikers crossing the Pyrenees, tourists arriving from elsewhere in Europe, or sailors leaving interned merchant ships.[11]

At the General Staff level, there were few references to the work of the Decima MAS, and only a few lines even when operations were successful. This cover-up strategy seems to have worked. The British GC&CS closely scrutinized German reports from the Gibraltar area to the Abwehr in Berlin and was well informed about German activities, but there is little evidence that it had any such knowledge of Italian activity in the area, despite the fact that there was so much of it occurring.

In more than one case, the British considered destroying the German observation post, especially when it became evident that the Germans were using "high-tech" methods to watch British shipping by night. But such a solution would have involved action that could have hurt the Spanish-Allied relationship, and the Allies needed the Gibraltar base. Only specific complaints were addressed to Franco's government, which did bring about some limited results.[12]

By the time of the Allied invasion of French North Africa in November 1942, called Operation Torch, German activity had become much less effective. Italian effectiveness did not suffer in this way. For example, Licio Visintini was able to enter Algeciras acting as a merchant seaman, and many other X MAS men were also able to sustain a cover before being sent into action. For the most part, the British never solved this ruse. Visintini, incidentally, went on to be part of the gamma unit of the Decima MAS from 1943 to 1945, when the X MAS operated in northern Italy under the rule of Mussolini's RSI.

Another interesting point is that even the Italian Foreign Ministry thought the X MAS men in Algeciras were asking for too many forged personal papers. The ministry refused to supply them in the amount requested. But the X MAS, in close contact with the SIS, stole the papers from the ministry's office! Thus, stolen papers were often used to equip the men who went to Spain to work on the *Olterra* (and the *Fulgor*—another *Olterra*-style vessel).

The X MAS operated quite autonomously in many ways. In fact, no other unit in the tightly controlled Italian armed forces enjoyed the same freedom of action. In general, the Italian military, like all institutions under fascism, was a very "top down" organization, allowing only a limited degree of independence. It was one of the cardinal problems with Italian fascism. But key personnel inside the X MAS were of noble stock, and this enabled them to win the support of top-level officers. It also made it possible for them to be in direct contact with the companies that supplied and developed craft, new weapons, and equipment for the flotilla.

The *Olterra* base was a solid and well-developed idea, but it came a bit late to be of real use. The base was ready only toward the end of 1942. It was only after the armistice, and before the Spanish could destroy the evidence of the plot that they, too, had only just discovered, that the British came on board. When Crabb and two torpedo experts, Lieutenant Commander John Anthony Noel Malim and a Mr. Clark, boarded the *Olterra,* they found three SLCs, or parts of them, and in rather good condition, and from them they could assemble two working machines.[13]

It was a new and exciting experience for Crabb to operate the human torpedo, now called *Emily,* with leading seaman Bell. They took it around and outside of the bay and *through* the torpedo net.

Tests continued, but an SLC was lost on January 7, 1944, when the machine suddenly sank.[14]

Before using the *Olterra,* the Italians used the ship *Fulgor,* a tanker of 6,504 tons lying interned at Cadiz, anchored in the Guadalete River, as a base. There, the Italian SIS organized the arrival of food and operators as well as regular supplies and new seamen. Borghese had already used the *Fulgor* when, with the *Scirè,* he had embarked from the *Fulgor* the crews of the human torpedoes for an earlier attack.

Another ship, the *Gaeta,* also acted as a base for the clandestine activities of the SIS and X MAS. A transport displacing 4,457 tons, it was anchored at Huelva, in the Cadiz Gulf near the border with Portugal. Huelva was also a point of major traffic for Allied ships transporting raw materials and weapons, so the *Gaeta* became a base from which the X MAS could attack them.[15]

The first operation under Borghese's overall command carried out by the gamma men was at Gibraltar on July 14, 1942. The *Olterra* base was still under construction but was nevertheless used as a base for the operation, which employed a team of twelve frogmen: Sublieutenants Agostino Straulino and Giorgio Baucer, and Petty Officers Alfredo Schiavoni, Alessandro Bianchini, Giovanni Lucchetti, Vago Giari, Evideo Boscolo, Bruno Di Lorenzo, Rodolfo Lugano, Carlo Bucovaz, Carlo Da Valle, and Giuseppe Feroldi.

They were shipped in two groups. Six were sent to Betasom, the Italian submarine base at Bordeaux, and from there, helped by Italian secret agents, passed the Pyrenees border, partly on foot and partly on trucks with a false bottom, until they reached Madrid. The other six acted as sailors of the merchantman *Mauro Croce* who "defected" at Barcelona. They went on to Madrid after being denounced as deserters by the cargo crewmen, who were not aware of their secret. All twelve were then sent to the *Fulgor* by car. From there, they cautiously made their way to the *Olterra,* as the Spaniards controlled the access to Algeciras Bay and had to at least act as if they were trying to stop the Italian operations, although their secret police helped the Axis.

There they found Visintini and could observe their targets on the enemy base. Finally, on the night of July 12, following various routes to avoid the British watch, the frogmen arrived at Villa Carmela, where they could examine their equipment and study the target ships. The operation, named "GG-1," would involve sinking some of the numerous cargoes that were in the bay.

They gamma men were very lucky. Neither the numerous Spanish Carabineros nor the British counterintelligence agents spotted their movements. At 0030 on July 14, the frogmen exited from the villa and reached the beach following a prepared trail and slipped through the patrols of Spanish guards.

Each of the assault swimmers was equipped with three explosive charges and swam in the bay very slowly to avoid British surveillance. Boats were patrolling the waters of the bay, and intermittent depth charges were continuously launched.

The frogmen did their work, and by 0320 the first two men came ashore at the point where they had entered the water. Three Italian agents were waiting to rescue them. Despite the difficulty of seeing a man in the water at night at a distance of more than 6 or 7 meters, seven of the swimmers were captured by the Carabineros. They were freed later, thanks to the intervention of the Italian vice consul at Algeciras, Commander Germanico Bordigioni. One frogman went ashore near the La Linea bridge and reached the Italian consulate undetected. The others arrived back at the home base.

The results were slightly disappointing, as the charges apparently failed to work properly. Four ships were damaged by the explosions: the *Meta*, displacing 1,575 tons; the *Shuma*, of 1,494 tons; the *Empire Snipe*, of 2,497 tons; and the *Baron Douglas*, of 3,899 tons. But none of the ships were sunk, and they were quickly grounded on the shore to avoid the total loss of their cargoes. Two frogmen were wounded, one by the explosion of a depth charge, and the other by the screw of a British patrol boat. However, all the frogmen eventually returned safely to Italy.

The British had begun to build an underwater working party, later termed the UWWP, and Crabb and Bailey and this new outfit of British divers were able to find some mines before they could explode. Moreover, a British agent at Huelva reported finding an intact limpet mine on the beach. It was one of the standard mines the Italians attached to bilge keels that would explode outside of port to avoid any suspicion of sabotage. This discovery was of great help to the British. Now Crabb and other divers could go under water to inspect every ship arriving at Gibraltar from the Spanish coast.

But a few days later, a cruel loss hit the Decima MAS: the sinking of the *Scirè*. This happened during Operation SL-1, which was mounted employing the submarine *Scirè* under the command of Bruno Zelich with the aim of attacking the naval base at Haifa in British Palestine.

Following the offensive launched by Rommel's Axis army on May 24, 1942 (Operation Venezia), which resulted in the fall of Tobruk on July 21, the Mediterranean Fleet left the threatened base of Alexandria and was displaced partly to the Red Sea and partly to Haifa. The Italian Navy planned to attack the base at Haifa, thinking that the defenses were newer and much less effective than at Alexandria. The gamma men were embarked on the *Scirè* and were to be released near Haifa.

These operations in the eastern Mediterranean were based out of the Dodecanese Islands and, as in the case of Operation GA-4, the submarine *Scirè* had to start from the base at Leros. The action was planned making use of aerial reconnaissance to supply the needed intelligence on the Haifa defenses. Assistance was solicited from the German Luftwaffe because the Italians did not have high-altitude aerial reconnaissance. Radar, antiaircraft artillery, and RAF fighters heavily defended the area.

On August 4, the gamma men arrived via airplane at Rhodes and then went on to Leros. The next day, Lieutenant Commander Max Candiani, who was in charge of coordinating the entire operation, carefully examined the plan with the commander of the *Scirè*, establishing that Operation SL-1 would take place on the 10th. The aim was to sink Allied ships, but a new priority was placed on submarines, which were becoming the main threat to Rommel's supplies. The months of July and August 1942 were the hottest months of the supply war for the North African front: Rommel so much as accused the Italian Navy of treason for not having supplied enough fuel to his troops during the last days of August. This accusation was another result, and an extra one at that, of ULTRA. In the list of priority targets, the submarines were followed by cargo ships, destroyers, cruisers, and finally, support ships and other minor vessels.

On the following morning, August 6, the *Scirè* sailed from Leros, steaming toward its objective and its fate. Interestingly enough, the *Scirè* maintained daily wireless contact with Commander Candiani at Leros, thanks to which Zelich was informed of the situation as seen by German air reconnaissance over Haifa, where it was reported that there were two cruisers and three destroyers, plus eight merchant ships. On the 10th, contact with the *Scirè* was lost. According to the plan of operation, the submarine was to release the gamma men at sunset and then wait for them until 0300 on August 11.

The craft was lost while approaching the port to launch the attack. At about 1030 on the 10th, the *Scirè* was approaching Haifa harbor when it was discovered. It is unclear how it was first spotted—it may have been by aircraft—but it was certainly then hunted by the British armed trawler *Islay*, which damaged the *Scirè* with a set of depth charges. The *Scirè* surfaced but was fired on by coastal guns and sunk with all hands: 48 submariners and 11 frogmen. Four corpses were found in the following days, and there were no survivors.[16] The *Scirè* was found many years later and several sections are now in museums. This was a grievous personal loss for Borghese, who knew all the men.[17]

After the sinking of the *Scirè*, the Decima MAS command preferred to act on the other side of the Mediterranean, where the Spanish coast near Gibraltar had proven to be an excellent support base for their missions. The secret bases of Villa Carmela and *Olterra* were working out well, and four successful missions were executed there before Italy capitulated.

There were many reasons why the operations in Gibraltar were successful. The approach to Gibraltar from Spain was narrow, and every day hundreds of workers came from the little Spanish town of La Linea to work on the docks. Various points on the Spanish coast offered excellent vantage points from which to observe the bay and harbor. This allowed Axis agents to know everything about the ships at Gibraltar, many of which were taking cover from the U-Boat "wolfpacks" then on the loose in the Atlantic.

Gibraltar was completely illuminated, but not because the British felt safe under the Rock. Rather, imposing a blackout would have meant their ships would be well silhouetted and visible against the Spanish coast lights. The British trusted in their radar and fighters to resist Axis bombing missions; their more important task was to stave off insidious naval penetrations.

By May 1942, British counterintelligence, which had enjoyed excellent success against the German Abwehr, had also picked up some traces of the Italian activity in Spain and had noted the fact that Spanish Cara-bineros protected Italian operations.[18] British countermeasures con-sisted of continuous patrolling of the bay with three launches, which played their lights among the ships at anchor and routinely launched ex-plosive charges throughout the night in the water around the ships.

It was a good system of defense, but it was not enough. At least it helped to avoid more losses on the night of September 14, when three frogmen (Lieutenant Agostino Straulino and Petty Officers Bruno Di Lorenzo and Vago Giari) entered the water before Villa Carmela at 2340 and tried to attach mines to the ships in the bay. They were greatly disturbed by British patrols and only Di Lorenzo was able to place his mines. He was assigned the transport ship *Ravens Point,* a ship that displaced 1,787 tons. It sank. The frogmen safely returned to the *Olterra,* and then to Villa Carmela, before returning safely to Italy.

The tireless Visintini, under Borghese's direction, mounted a more complex operation at the end of the year. He wanted to penetrate the inner harbor to attack the valuable British warships there, including the battleship *Nelson* and the aircraft carriers *Formidable* and *Furious.* The operation was called BG-5 and foresaw three SLCs exiting from the *Olterra*'s underwater portal, then penetrating Gibraltar's inner harbor and attaching warheads under the three warships. Several "bugs" would also be carried by the frogmen for possible use against smaller targets.

The three SLCs were manned by Sublieutenant Licio Visintini and NCO diver Giovanni Magro; Midshipman Girolamo Marisco and diver Dino Varini; and Sublieutenant Vittorio Cella and Sergeant Salvatore Leone. They started at 2330 on December 7, 1942, from the *Olterra*, but all were forced to return to the base because of problems with their gear. They all restarted with their SLCs in order, but of the six men, only one, Cella, would succeed in returning to the *Olterra*.

Visintini and Magro were killed, perhaps while trying to overcome an obstruction, as this was opened, or perhaps by an "irregular shot from the modified Northover projector," which launched charges made by Crabb, Bailey, and the harbor defenses.[19]

The Marisco/Varini team was spotted and fired upon with depth charges. They set their torpedo for auto-destruct and were then captured by American ships. During their interrogation, they let the Allies think they had been released at the bay's entrance by the submarine *Ambra*.

As for the remaining manned torpedo, Leone was killed by a depth charge that exploded near his SLC. Cella was able to get back to the *Olterra*.

The depth charges (which were cans filled with TNT, not regular depth charges) were launched too often and formed a barrage that Visintini was not able to pass. He had already been awarded two Silver Valor Medals, and after his death he received the Gold. His family was not lucky—his father-in-law was killed in the so-called *foibe* (deep caves in the ground, from a few yards to hundreds) by Tito's partisans, and his suffering mother had to abandon their home to take refuge at Venice.

The bodies of Visintini and Magro were recovered in the bay in the following days and buried by the British. A special memorial wreath was placed on their graves, and two Italian flags dedicated by Crabb and Bailey, who displayed great chivalry.[20]

Crabb and the Underwater Working Party had a huge task to perform after discovering the attackers. They had to inspect the keels of a large number of ships, beginning with the carriers and the *Nelson*. Then, they had to try to find the SLC of the two prisoners, but every effort, including the use of a very old diving bell, proved fruitless.

The Italian Navy could not strike against the assembled Allied fleet in a conventional action, and did not want to, but continued trying to mount special assault craft operations. The X MAS was almost proposed for an operation against Tobruk that summer, but the fortress fell to the Afrikakorps without the Decima's help.

At end of August 1942, however, when Rommel launched his offensive at El Alamein, which would be checked at Alam Halfa ridge, the so-called Autocolonna Giobbe (a motorized column) and the fishing boats *Sogliola* and *Costanza* operated on the coast near the front to harass Allied shipping. It was entirely a surface (and land) operation, employing MTSM and MTM boats with fifteen operators under the head of the X MAS, Commander Ernesto Forza. Among the objectives of the assembled force were possible attacks against Alexandria, Haifa, or Suez in an attempt to disrupt Commonwealth supply lines.

These objectives were rather difficult to attain in the face of Allied air superiority. However, when British destroyers bombarded the coast near the front, *MTSM 228* succeeded in badly damaging the destroyer HMS *Eridge* near El Daba on August 29 with a single torpedo. (The British thought it had been attacked by a German E-boat.) The *Croome, Hursley, Eridge,* and *Aldenham,* all small *Hunt* type destroyers, had been detailed for coastal bombardment work. The *Aldenham* would tow the *Eridge* back to Alexandria, where the latter would never again operate at sea but did act as a base ship.[21]

After the climactic battle of El Alamein in October 1942, the column succeeded in retreating with the rest of the Axis forces to Tunisia, but before that, the X MAS personnel had carried out successful sabotage actions on the British rail line and the coast beyond the British front in Egypt.

CHAPTER 10

Last Attacks Before the Armistice

While the Italian Navy steadily retreated, their Tenth Flotilla advanced.

Marshall Pugh[1]

IN EARLY NOVEMBER 1942, THE ALLIES LAUNCHED Operation Torch, a powerful series of invasions of Morocco and Algeria that quickly overcame Vichy French Resistance. These seizures of French North Africa marked the beginning of the end of the Axis in Africa. Rommel was now in full retreat from El Alamein in Egypt and being pursued across Libya by the British 8th Army. The Axis sea- and airlifted new forces into Tunisia to prevent the Germans and Italians from being crushed in a vice, and to form a new bastion in the part of Africa closest to Sicily. The Axis forces won this "race for Tunisia," thereby ensuring that the war for North Africa would continue for another six months.

Following the Torch landings, the Decima MAS mounted Operation NA-1 against the harbor of Algiers, to be carried out by both human torpedoes and gamma men. They would be brought there by the submarine *Ambra* under the command of Mario Arillo to attack the ships in the bay, which were reported to lie there in great numbers. The gamma men would attack the transports and light warships such as destroyers, while the heavier warships were to be attacked by the SLCs, which in this case were equipped for the first time with two warheads, each of 150 kg.

The *Ambra* sailed on December 4, 1942, from La Spezia and arrived off Algiers on December 7. Arillo waited three days for better weather, and on the 11th moved in close to the harbor. But the fact that Allied destroyers patrolled the area, and that the *Ambra*'s sounding lead was broken, caused the submarine to navigate blindly, hitting underwater rocks and wrecks. When the *Ambra* stopped at 18 meters depth, Arillo assumed he was in the right place, but after a look through the periscope he realized he was too far off the coast. Approaching closer, he finally brought the *Ambra* to where he could release the frogmen and SLCs.

The time was 2200 and the *Ambra* was now among six cargo ships, about 2,000 meters from the port's entrance. By 2224, ten frogmen had been released, despite delays due to some jammed or broken equipment, and an hour later, at 2320, the three SLCs were launched.

The submarine waited in place until 0300, but by then the harbor was on alert and Arillo's vessel was in danger. None of the frogmen had returned, so the *Ambra* slipped out of port and steamed back to La Spezia.

The ten frogmen were under the command of Lieutenant Agostino Morello, who had been instructed by Borghese to send two men for each merchant ship displacing more than 10,000 tons. The gamma men were NCO Oreste Botti; sergeant of the grenadiers Luigi Rolfini; two Bersaglieri sergeants, Alberto Evangelisti and Gaspare Ghiglione; underchief diver Giuseppe Feroldi; underchief gunner Evideo Boscolo; engine room stoker Rodolfo Lugano; seaman diver Giovanni Lucchetti; and infantry private Luciano Luciani. The composition of this team gives one a sense of how swimmers were by then being drawn from various parts of the armed forces.[2]

The crew for the first SLC consisted of Lieutenant Giorgio Badessi and NCO diver Carlo Pesel, but their SLC broke down almost imme-

Commander Junio Valerio Borghese proudly wears his medals, including the Gold Medal, Military Order of Savoy, and Germany's Iron Cross.

CC Valerio Borghese, 1942. (Achille Rastelli collection)

Submarine *Ambra* with caissons shown in foreground. (Achille Rastelli collection)

This view shows how an SLC was secured inside a caisson that was mounted on the deck of a submarine. (Author collection, from the Venice Arsenal Museum)

SLC is hoisted aboard for placement in on-deck caisson. (Achille Rastelli collection)

Two views showing details of
SLCs. (Achille Rastelli collection)

A later, improved model of the SLC,
the SSB. (Achille Rastelli collection)

An MT, or one-man explosive boat—similar to the boat used to sink the British heavy cruiser, *York*. (Author collection, from the Venice Arsenal Museum)

Lieutenant Licio Visintini prepares for an undercover assignment in Spain, 1941. (Achille Rastelli collection)

CC Valerio Borghese (left) with his commander, CF Ernesto Forza. (Achille Rastelli collection)

Wartime poster depicts an MT attack on the British heavy cruiser, *York*, on March 26, 1941. (Author collection)

The SLC attack on Gibraltar is depicted in this wartime propaganda poster (Author collection)

Award ceremony in April, 1942, for the crew of the submarine *Scirè* (shown in the background) for its part in the successful raid at Gilbraltar. (Achille Rastelli collection)

Inscribed, "On December 19, 1941, the Decimas MAS penetrated the port of Alexandria, Egypt, and sank two British battleships, *Queen Elizabeth* and *Valiant*," this wartime propaganda poster is more stylized than accurate. (Author collection)

Commander Umberto Bardelli, who led the "Barbargio Battalion" was a distinguished submarine commander and helped Borghese rebuild the Decima MAS Flotilla. (Archivo Centrale dello Stato, Rome)

New recruits of the "Barbargio Battalion" entering the front lines. (Archivo Centrale dello Stato, Rome)

An NCO of the Decima MAS wears Italian and German medals. Note that the Savoy Royal Army star has been replaced by the "gladio," a Roman short sword. (Archivo Centrale dello Stato, Rome)

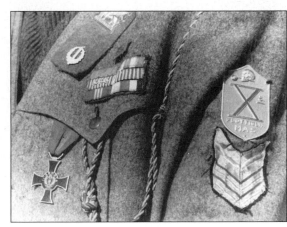

Commander Valerio Borghese contemplates his command.

Commander Borghese and his wife visiting the Imperial War Museum in the early-1960s.

diately and they were unable to attack. After rescuing a frogman, they went ashore and were later captured.

The second SLC, manned by Guido Arena, lieutenant of the naval engineers, and diver Ferdinando Cocchi, began with the handicap that Arena was very seasick; however, they succeeded in placing both charges under a transport ship before trying to regain the *Ambra*. After an hour of fruitless searching, they landed. They also rescued two frogmen (Luciani and Ghiglione), who still had their explosives. These men were also captured.

The third SLC, of Midshipman Giorgio Reggioli and diver Colombo Pamolli, headed to what seemed like a tanker and attacked it. Although unable to find the bilge keels, they attached one of the two charges to the left screw, fixing the timer at 0135. Then they reached another ship and by 0215 had set the timer on the their second charge. This action was the most flawlessly executed of the operation. But this crew also failed to find the *Ambra* and had to land. They, too, were captured. All the SLCs were destroyed before the crews landed.

The leader of the frogmen, Morello, drew the attention of a searchlight at one point, but he only had his head out of the water, masked with seaweed, and this saved him. Of the ten gamma men, six carried out their mission while four encountered difficulty and gave up. Of these, three men (Ghiglione, Luciani, and Lugano) were rescued by the SLCs with their unused charges. Seaman Lucchetti gave up and was taken prisoner by personnel on the transport ship that Morello was attacking, an act that caused the general alert of the port.

According to Morello's report, the results were lower than expected because the gamma personnel were not all at the same high level of training; some men came from the army and suffered seasickness. However, beginning at 0500, explosions began ripping apart ships throughout the port. As a result, the transport *Berto* (1,493 tons) was sunk, while the *Ocean Vanquisher* (7,174 tons), the *Empire Centaur* (7,041 tons), and the *Armattan* (6,587 tons) were badly damaged.[3] A total of 22,000 tons of Allied shipping off Algiers had been put out of action.

The port of Bone on the Algerian coast had also attracted Borghese's attention. A combined action was planned against shipping at this important logistics point. The operations BO, G-1, and Beta foresaw the penetration of the harbor by three MTSMs with the support of MAS boats. Then, while three MTSMs, under the command of Commander Agostino Calosi (whom we will meet again after the armistice), landed 16 "N" (swimmer) operators to destroy as much as possible at the Bone airfield, the explosive boats would bring three gamma men to mine cargoes in the harbor.

The action was to be launched on the heels of the Algiers raid and was somewhat complex. At this time, Borghese was in charge of the underwater department of the X MAS and not of the surface unit. Moreover, cooperation with the air force was, as usual, a failure, as the planned bombing of Bone did not take place.

Starting from Bizerta at 1700 on December 12, 1942, Lieutenant Commander Salvatore Todaro reached La Galite Island. He arrived there with a torpedo motorboat and three gamma men, but the sea was so rough that the operation had to be canceled. The following day, the *Cefalo*, with MTSMs *230, 258, 260,* and *264,* arrived. Since the Italian naval command in Tunisia did not send the required MAS boats for the support of the explosive boats, Todaro decided to attack with three MTSMs. He had one, another was manned by Ungarelli, and the third, manned by a Lieutenant Corrado Dequal, broke down shortly after the start of the mission. Todaro had to give up, as the sea was too rough to continue.

Back at La Galite, the X MAS group was attacked by two Allied airplanes that heavily damaged the *Cefalo*, destroyed or damaged the MTSMs, and killed Todaro, who was sleeping after his tiring bout with the rough seas. The group went back to Bizerta, where they arrived on the 15th and joined the Giobbe column that was now stationed there.

On the morning of February 18, 1943, the Allies received warnings that the Italians were preparing to assault the shipping off Tunisia. These pieces of intelligence were not arriving only through ULTRA,

but also from "SIS agents operating from Rome." This proves that the
X MAS was quite correct to emphasize secrecy in its operations, even
from fellow Italians.[4] In fact, a landing of saboteurs was made on
Tunisian coasts by the submarine *Malachite* on the night of February
7, but the submarine was sunk while returning to Cagliari on Sardinia.
The landing yielded little.

However, in April 1943, the Decima MAS tried again to penetrate
the port of Bone, although by then the African campaign was clearly
nearing its bitter end for the Axis. On the night of April 6, three
MTSMs tried, starting from La Galite, to reach Bone to release some
gamma men, but at the port's entrance the noise of the boats alerted
the Allies and the operation had to be aborted. On May 9, 1943, the X
MAS team sailed to Italy as the Axis forces in Tunisia had already
begun to surrender en masse, a process that would be completed on
May 13.

We now return to Gibraltar, and the further attacks planned for
that port.

After the costly operation of December 1942, when Visintini lost
his life, the X MAS had to wait several months before rebuilding its
Olterra team and attempting another attack against the shipping
near the Rock. It was Commander Ernesto Notari who was placed in
charge. He arrived, along with Lieutenant of the Naval Engineers
Emilio Tadini and the divers Ario Lazzari, Eusebio Montaleoni, and
Salvatore Mattera, to help the only survivor of the previous action,
Cella.

The effective defensive measures adopted by the Royal Navy to protect British ships and the harbor forced the *Olterra* men to choose
ships in Algeciras Bay as their targets. Visintini's death was proof of the
impossibility of entering the inner harbor under the Rock, where the
important warships were usually anchored.

Therefore, Operation BG-6 was planned for the month of May after
accurate observation of the targets could be completed. Notari chose
loaded cargoes in the bay at anchor near the British base. They were far

from Algeciras, but, from a military point of view, they were better ob-jectives than closer ships. Notari also reasoned that the distance would mislead the British about the starting point of the attack. (See map on page ix.) He did not want the defense to suspect the *Olterra* base.

The action was carried out on the evening of May 7, 1943, when, at 2235, three SLCs, manned by Notari and Lazzari, Tadini and Mattera, and Cella and Montaleoni, left the secret underwater door in the *Olterra*'s hull. Each of the SLCs was equipped with two warheads and some "bugs." All the SLCs faced the same main difficulty—the water currents that flowed against them. For Notari, it took two hours to reach the target, and his team was unable to mine more than one mer-chant ship, as the physical effort required to hold the pig under the keel was too much for the two frogmen. They placed both their charges on the same ship, and by 0345 on the 8th, they had returned to the *Olterra*.

Tadini and Mattera were able to mine two ships after passing through the British patrols and searchlights, while every 6 minutes de-fensive charges exploded in the water, their tempo increasing as the night passed. They were able to return to the base at 0415.

The impression of ever-increasing British depth charges was not false, as that same night Crabb had Operation Tadpole under way (a preemptive action against the X MAS). He had summoned six divers to Jumper's Bastion, located in part of the older fortress section of Gibraltar. After "ten minutes' hell," they dove and cleared a convoy that had to sail the next day. The other convoy was not cleared, as there was not enough time.[5]

The third SLC team was the first to reenter the *Olterra* base, at 0215 on the 8th. From Cella's report, it is clear that he faced the same prob-lems as the other two teams. He succeeded in attaching one charge under a ship, then felt he was being chased and depth-charged. It was probably just the routine checking carried out by British patrols that he noticed. Perhaps influenced by his previous experience, Cella dove and swam far from the surface targets. There were no motorboats nearby, but his number two had a leaking diving suit, so they came back.[6]

Since all the crews had returned safely to the *Olterra*, the British had no warning before 0615 on the morning of the 8th when the first charge exploded. By 0640, the other two had blown up, severely damaging a total of three cargo ships, the *Pat Harrison* (7,000 tons), the *Mahsud* (7,500 tons) and the *Camerata* (4,875 tons). All three were hastily towed ashore before they could sink, and therefore it is too much to say that "20,000 tons of enemy merchant ships were taken deep," although this was certainly a successful operation.[7]

On the keel of the "Liberty" ship *Pat Harrison*, Crabb found the second charge that Notari's crew had applied for good measure. Its timer had malfunctioned because it was damaged by the explosion of the first charge. The British UWWP was not convinced by Notari's acts of deception, which had included abandoning pieces of diving equipment on the beach on the north, Gibraltar side of the bay. While pondering how the Italians had once more penetrated his defenses, Crabb cast a suspicious eye on the *Olterra*, although no unusual movement had been noticed on board. His proposal to inspect the innocent-looking tanker under water was rejected.[8]

This was one of the last actions of the Decima MAS in the war. When the Allies landed in Sicily, there were two bases of explosive boats, one at Augusta naval base in Sicily and another at Cagliari in Sardinia. There was little activity from these bases, although in one case an Allied bombardment was snuffed in the bud by a diversionary attack of explosive motorboats.[9]

Interestingly enough, the Sicilian campaign witnessed collaboration between the San Marco marine regiment and the Buttazzoni battalion of the army to carry out sabotage beyond the Allied lines. The technique of combining units from various branches would be developed by Borghese after the September 8, 1943, armistice.

Borghese was placed in command of the entire flotilla from May 1, 1943, replacing Forza. He had developed a good relationship with the men of the surface squadron of the Decima at Augusta, and personally with Admiral Tur, who had been involved in preparing for the invasion of Malta. Borghese had words of praise for some of the officers, especially Cosulich and Ungarelli. The latter would become one of his closest and most loyal officers after the armistice.

An operation against the shipping at Syracuse, now an Allied port, was attempted by the *Ambra,* which carried three *Motoscafi Turismo Ridotto* (MTRs, reduced motorboats). These were a torpedo version of the explosive boats that could be placed inside the SLC containers mounted on the sub, which was under the command of Renato Ferrini. The *Ambra* reached Messina on July 16, 1943, and approached Syracuse but was discovered on the surface by airplanes and bombed. Suffering damage, the *Ambra* had to abort the mission and return to Naples and then La Spezia.

The last important operation of the X MAS took place in August, just a month before the armistice. The target was once again Gibraltar, and it was called Operation BG-7. It involved three SLCs, manned by the same men who had performed the successful attack on May 7 and 8. The operation began during the evening of August 3 as the three "pigs" slipped from the secret, submerged door of the *Olterra.* Notari headed for the *Harrison Gray Otis* of 7,176 tons and mined the ship, but then his SLC sank and Notari lost contact with his number two, Andrea Gianoli. Gianoli was captured, but Notari was able to return to the *Olterra.*

Cella, with Montaleoni, mined the merchant ship *Thorshovdi* of 9,944 tons, and Tadini and Mattera mined the freighter *Stanridge* of 5,975 tons. It is surprising that the operation succeeded, because Crabb and his men had begun to employ still another kind of defense—they had strung barbed razor wire around ships some six feet above the bilge keels. From this, additional wires were strung, hanging down ten feet at ten-foot intervals, and kept in place by weights.

Nevertheless, with the first light of dawn came the first of a succession of massive explosions in the bay. All three Allied ships had to be beached, and only the *Stanridge* was recovered. Crabb's Underwater Working Party had been as vigilant as possible, but that night the

UWWP simply arrived too late: Bell was just jumping into the sea to check the hull of the *Stanridge* when the charge blew up, and he was barely missed by splinters. The same blast killed the sentry who was guarding the captured Gianoli.

After taking full command of the Decima MAS, Borghese did not neglect the other side of the Mediterranean. In May 1943, he dispatched a single gamma raider to neutral Turkey, who would enjoy the greatest success of any individual gamma sailor.

Luigi Ferraro had been one of Wolk's best divers at the Special Operations branch of the Leghorn Academy. He had volunteered for the assault craft after witnessing British warships bombarding Tripoli in 1941, but only in 1942 was he admitted to the divers' school, where he proved to be one of the best, as he was a "natural" in the water. Training included silent swimming under water with fins, use of breathing apparatus, and the ability to find one's bearings while submerged. Fins were introduced by Wolk; without them it would have been very difficult to carry out any operation.

After his training, Ferraro had been ordered to North Africa for a daring operation. It was later aborted because of the fall of the Italian-German front at El Alamein. If it had been carried out, he would have been helped by his wife, who was also a good swimmer; her presence would have been useful for building a cover in case he had to work in neutral countries. After this mission was canceled, he returned to Italy.

On May 1, 1943, Borghese, who had taken command of the flotilla the same day, summoned Ferraro and instructed him to study Lisbon harbor in order to accomplish some acts of sabotage there. But a few days later, Borghese ordered him to go instead to Alexandretta harbor in Turkey, near the Syrian border, to sink Allied transport ships that were embarking chrome while supplying Turkey with arms. The decision not to go to Lisbon was most likely for political reasons. Since Turkey was neutral, the damage to the ships could only be done by covert action.

Incredibly enough, Ferraro was supplied with documents that had to be stolen from the Foreign Ministry. These established that he was a consulate employee traveling in the Balkans and destined for the consulate station at Alexandretta. He was equipped with four heavy diplomatic bags, each holding a couple of explosive charges, plus, of course, his gamma equipment.

X MAS and Borghese were always operating with secret procedures, even toward other Italian services and agencies. Of course, any study of the relationship between the Office of Strategic Services (OSS), created in July 1942 by President Franklin D. Roosevelt, and the U.S. State Department will reveal similar antagonism between an older government bureaucracy and a newer covert organization springing from World War II. In the Decima's case, however, strict secrecy was certainly one of the keys to success, given the mix of Italian loyalties as the war went on.

Ferraro took the Orient Express. On the same train there was a Captain Mario Vespa of the SIS. Ferraro disembarked at Istanbul, where an Alexandretta Italian consulate secretary, one Mr. Giovanni Roccardi, took him to the objective harbor. In reality, Roccardi was his contact there; he was a navy officer of the SIS and covered Ferraro before the consul, who was unaware of the operation.

Establishing great friendships with the consulate personnel, Ferraro studied the harbor and the many unarmed ships lying there. He busied himself the first month in Alexandretta letting people think he had exploited his good connections to avoid actual fighting, and he let it get out that he was unable to swim, although very inclined to every other kind of sport. According to Ferraro, British intelligence had him under watch for three weeks in an attempt to ascertain who he really was. His mission, incidentally, was quite dangerous for its possible diplomatic consequences—the war was going badly for the Axis, and Turkey would not then have needed a large shove to be drawn in on the Allied side.

The problem for Ferraro was how to arrive on the beach, which was under surveillance by both the British consulate and Turkish sentries, with his equipment. He solved the problem by continually going to the beach with a case containing sports equipment. One day, he hid his gamma tools under the sand in his beach cabin, and later he used the sports equipment case to bring explosive charges and diving gear.

On the evening of June 30, Ferraro entered the water at 2330. He returned at about 0300 on the following day. He had attached two 12 kg charges to the bilge keels of the *Orion,* a Greek cargo. The *Orion* sailed on July 7 and blew up and sank a few hours after. A small screw activated by movement in the water triggered the charges.

It was good luck for Ferraro and the X MAS that the ship's crew suspected a submarine ambush, but the second mission revealed the true cause of the explosions. The second mission involved the British freighter *Kaiatuna* of 4,914 tons, which arrived in Mersina harbor soon after the successful first mission had been carried out. Ferraro and an SIS agent reached the harbor by car on the night of July 8–9, and Ferraro accomplished his job in about three hours. However, of the two charges he placed, only one exploded, on the 19th. The *Kaiatuna* was beached, and the unexploded charge was found. The ship would later be repaired.[10]

The next assault took place again in the same port of Mersina, where Ferraro planted a charge under the keel of the *Sicilian Prince,* a transport ship which was about 4.5 km from the coast. Ferraro had to swim for a long time to reach it. But after the *Kaiatuna* discovery, the keel of the *Sicilian Prince* was inspected before it sailed and the charges were removed.

In the meantime, there had been an important change in the situation in Italy: Sicily was invaded on July 10, and on July 25 Mussolini was arrested and the king had summoned Marshal Pietro Badoglio to be head of the government. Negotiations with the Allies for an armistice would shortly begin.

Two days after his attempt against the *Sicilian Prince,* Ferraro attached his last two charges to the Norwegian transport *Fernplant,* which sailed on August 4 from Alexandretta without being examined. But for some reason the ship returned to harbor the same evening, still intact. Evidently the ship's slow speed failed to trigger the charges. But two days later, the ship sailed again, made sufficient speed, and this time was sunk.[11]

Ferraro had no more charges and had to return to Italy, which he did by simulating a sudden illness so he would be immediately repatriated. According to Ferraro's account, his name was known to the Allies after the armistice, when the Italian consul Ignazio di Sanfelice, who by now was aware of the subterfuge, disclosed the fact to his British colleague at Alexandretta.

Ferraro later worked with the X MAS of Borghese in northern Italy, when he became the deputy commander of the gamma group under Wolk and played an important part in the protection of industrial plants in the last days of the war.

Besides these activities, a contingent of MTSMs and midget submarines was dispatched to the Black Sea in June 1942 and operated there until March 1943. It was requested by the Germans to help in the blockade of Sevastopol. Known as the "Moccagatta motorized column," it served with limited results. Italian source material often incorrectly states that the Russian flotilla leader *Tashkent* was sunk by *MTSM 216*.

After Borghese was promoted off the *Scirè*, he devoted himself to the underwater unit of the X MAS. In 1942 he also traveled to Germany and other countries to gather documentation that would be useful in planning actions in the Atlantic against important Allied harbors in North America and South Africa. His long trip brought him to Paris, Berlin, Bordeaux, Lisbon, Madrid, and Algeciras. In Paris, where the German Submarine Command, or BdU, had its headquarters, he met Admiral Doenitz, with whom he had a friendly talk. The reports of the German Navy command in Italy show that the Germans were quite interested in the Italians' development of underwater and surface assault weapons. The Prince, in turn, observed the German approach to assault units, both on sea and, more successfully, on land, and was freely shown reports and given a great deal of information.

Nevertheless, the German liaison officer got the impression that the Italians were reluctant in their collaboration. The impression was not a false one, as Borghese confirmed recalling his visit to Germany. The Italians had orders to show unreserved goodwill toward the Germans but to reveal to the German Navy "something but not everything"—in other words, only what was already known to the British owing to the loss of personnel and equipment.[12] Borghese and the command of the Tenth, however, disagreed with this view. The Prince and his commanders by and large wanted to cooperate with the Germans to a greater degree than the Supermarina allowed.

Borghese then reached Bordeaux and thereafter flew on to Lisbon on board a Ju-52. After Lisbon, he went to Madrid, where he had talks with his Algeciras agents on the situation there. The long trip finished with the same tour, back to Bordeaux and Paris and finally La Spezia. These visits with the Germans were friendly, and after the Italian armistice Borghese was well received by Doenitz.

X MAS operations were always going on. After their costly failure in 1941 against Malta, the Italians tried to operate with frogmen against the British submarine base. Five frogmen would be brought there with MTSMs *240, 246,* and *256* and released near the harbor entrance. But the operation was aborted several times because of unfavorable weather and for the breakdown of one craft. Perhaps, considering the effectiveness of Malta in 1942, it was best for the X MAS that these attacks didn't come off.

When Borghese went to Germany in the summer of 1942, he clearly had ideas about how to duplicate the same attack methods that had proven successful in the Mediterranean in the Atlantic theater. The Germans were most interested in this possibility, as they had already given up on major surface actions in the face of the huge Allied fleets, and looked more to stealth weapons to damage Allied shipping.

Nevertheless, when the Italian naval attaché in Berlin, Rear Admiral Giuseppe Bertoldi, asked the German High Command (OKW) for the use of one submarine as a transport for frogmen, the OKW refused and argued against the attacks planned by the Italians. The Germans had developed their own plans to attack the Atlantic coast, which involved land sabotage teams and blocking the Panama Canal, but all the operations either failed or were canceled. Some spies had been caught and executed.

Because of the lack of interest in the Italian plans, Borghese went to Paris again to see Admiral Doenitz and attempted to convince him that an attack against New York was a good idea. The Italians did not expect to achieve a large tactical success, but they wanted to score a great moral victory, which indeed it might have been. But the Germans at that time preferred war operations against shipping in the Mediterranean.

The Italians decided to deploy one of their own submarines, and so a tiny CA midget sub was shipped to Bordeaux by train in July 1942. The CA was to be employed without the two torpedo launchers, and equipped instead with eight 100 kg explosive charges and twenty "bugs."

The submarine chosen as a carrier was the large *Leonardo Da Vinci*. The sub was based at Betasom, and there, during the month of August, it was transformed to carry the CA on its deck, with Borghese and Sublieutenant Eugenio Massano as advisers. When the *Leonardo Da Vinci* was ready, it performed several trials between September 9 and 23, 1942. The tests were encouraging, but during the procedure both the CA and the *Leonardo* were damaged. The X MAS men were rather satisfied, but the operation would require more planning.

It seems that Wolk and Massano had thought of the possibility of bringing the frogmen near the objective with the CA and CB submarines. But tests using this plan were halted by the X MAS headquarters, which was not convinced. However, the two officers succeeded in organizing a test with a surface craft towing a frogman at 8 knots. For this reason, two CAs were made available and modified, and one of them was sent to Iseo Lake in the middle of the Alps, where in the cold winter of 1941–1942, tests took place. Particularly difficult for the frogmen was exiting from the submarine. The vessel reached 70 meters of depth during these tests.

After these trials, the plan of operation was revised. The employment of the submarine was planned without the trained X MAS frogmen, instead training the three men of the crew to perform the same actions normally carried out by the gamma men. This would mean that when the submarine reached an enemy ship, it would lay underneath it while a frogman exited from the special compartment in the conning tower, attached an explosive charge, and then reentered the submarine. The midget would then move to another point of the harbor to look for another target. But the submarine plan had a lot of problems, and not all were eliminated.

At first the action was planned against Rio de Janeiro for the eventuality of a Brazilian entry into the war, but when Borghese summoned Massano to La Spezia, he was thinking of the raid against New York. Massano was enthusiastic about the plan and was sure that it would be successful, although Rear Admiral Romolo Polacchini, commander of Atlantic submarine operations, was not so sure.

Then the plans were stopped by the fact that the *Leonardo Da Vinci,* which was to be used to transport the frogmen, was sunk in the Atlantic during a regular war mission, and this left the X MAS without the basic equipment for the plan.[13] The X MAS was left to wait for the development and improvement of the new series of CA midget submarines, and this again delayed the action. The assault against New York—which, if successful, would surely have ranked prominently among the Decima's actions—was finally foreseen for the end of 1943, but the armistice finally halted the project.[14]

After the change of government on July 25, 1943, the new minister of the navy was Admiral de Courten, who in the past had been responsible for the assault craft. One of the first things he did was to visit the X MAS at La Spezia in the first days of August, accompanied by Vice Admiral Varoli Piazza, chief of staff of the inspectorate of the assault craft. Among the operational topics discussed was the employ-

ment of the new SSBs against the capital ships in Gibraltar scheduled
for attack in October.[15]

But as we now know, Mussolini's overthrow was only the prelude
to Italy's official resignation from the entire war, though for a few
weeks it was pretended otherwise. Borghese afterward claimed to be
unaware of the political machinations then in progress, thinking only
of how to fight the enemy.[16] But given the Prince's contacts in the SIS
and the Abwehr, as well as his and other Decima officers' connections
to the highest levels of Italian society, this statement can be reasonably questioned. The handwriting on the wall, leading to the
armistice—or de facto capitulation—in conjunction with the invasions by the British 8th Army and the American 5th Army on the Italian mainland, could not have been completely invisible to the naval
commando leaders at La Spezia. In any case, all further counteroffensive operations planned by Borghese and the Decima MAS were
brought to a temporary halt by the announcement of the armistice on
the evening of September 8, 1943.

All in all, the performances of the Decima MAS from the time of
Italy's entrance into World War II to the armistice were far superior to
those of the Italian surface fleet. Big ships built with a great expendi-
ture of funds and resources turned out to be much less effective than a
few highly trained, daring men armed with experimental equipment.

This reality was recognized by other nations. The British immediately began to imitate the Italian SLC with their own version of a
manned torpedo, the "Chariot," two of which were launched against
the German battleship *Tirpitz* in Norway. The Germans, like the
British, sought to draw on as much expertise as they could. And most
enduringly, virtually all the methods that Borghese and the X MAS
had developed would later be adopted by the U.S. Navy SEALs—from
frogmen to underwater delivery vehicles, to their very credo of daring
small-unit operations against large targets.

In his World War II memoir, Borghese listed the ships that the X
MAS sank or damaged from March 1941 up to the 1943 armistice.

Subsequent research by the Italian Navy has revised his totals from 265,000 tons of Allied shipping to about 203,000, but the X MAS and its predecessor, the 1st MAS, carried out 22 attacks by various means, of which 12 were clearly successful. The total of tonnage pales before the extension of British and Allied defensive measures—including manpower, equipment, expenses, and constant vigilance—that was employed to stave off the Decima attacks. Sunken British battleships, transports, and merchantmen aside, the X MAS had achieved the ultimate goal of a special operations force by compelling the enemy to commit disproportionate resources to defend against a relative few.

As for Borghese himself, the royal coup, followed by Italy's armistice with the Allies, shook the floor on which he had stood. Even if he suspected the consequences that would ensue from Mussolini's ouster, higher command prudently kept him out of the loop, correctly assuming he would not agree. Or, as one major historian of the period put it, "His private war had become so very private that the Italian Navy had not troubled to tell him that the big war was over." But his private war would continue until the very end of World War II and would resume again later underground.[17]

CHAPTER 11

The Decima MAS
Hits the Land

The most feared units of the Italian armed forces were semi-autonomous groups over which Mussolini had little or no control. He tried to explain this by arguing that such volunteer corps were part of an Italian tradition dating back to the Middle Ages. The most notorious and ferocious was the Decima Mas under Prince Valerio Borghese.

Dennis Mack Smith[1]

ON THE EVENING OF SEPTEMBER 8, 1943, Marshal Pietro Badoglio went on the air to announce that the Italian government had concluded an armistice with the Allies. He said nothing of Italy's relationship with Germany but instructed the armed forces to react against any aggression.

Most of the officers and men of the Italian armed forces were caught completely by surprise, and many men waited several days for orders that never came. Most Italian units scattered through Europe began to disband, while the Germans committed instead to a determined operation to disarm the Italian armed forces according to the plan "Achse" (Axis). In the following days, they succeeded in disarming with force, tricks, and negotiations some 800,000 men. They also gathered an immense quantity of material, much of which was shipped to

Germany. When it was seen that a number of Italian units were still resisting, Hitler issued orders to shoot all the officers of those units that opposed German action, and to deport the soldiers and NCOs to the Reich to be used as laborers.[2]

The Germans were able to occupy much of Italy thanks to their success in disarming the Italian troops and to the surprisingly effective defense they mounted against the Allied landing at Salerno. On September 11, 1943, Hitler personally issued secret directives that divided Italian territory into operational zones: the front zone of operation and two more special zones of operation called Alpenvorland and Adriatische Küsterland. Moreover, he placed his minister for armament and war production, Albert Speer, in charge of the exploitation of the economic resources of northern Italy.[3]

According to instructions received, most of the Italian fleet took to the sea steaming to Allied bases, the major warships reaching the Allied ports of Malta and Bone. A notable exception was the modern battleship *Roma,* which was chased down by the Luftwaffe and destroyed with a glider bomb. The Spanish in the Balearics interned some vessels, and many other ships were scuttled because they were compelled to do so or chose not to surrender to either the Germans or the Allies.

The Germans had little hope of taking over Italy's fleet as easily as its army, since in early September the navy was still estimated to be a well-trained force with high morale. Further, the fleet could now be assisted by the massive Allied navies and air forces offshore. Therefore the Germans would act as soon as possible against the brain of the Italian Navy: its commanders and headquarters.[4]

The Germans did succeed in sinking, capturing, or damaging 386 Italian ships of war for a total of 292,771 tons. The warships captured in the yards numbered 199, adding another 210,653 tons to the already great war booty. The merchant navy was no exception and suffered heavily in this process, since 1,214 merchant ships, totaling 976,902 tons, remained in German hands.

There were also naval units and sailors who did not want to join the Allies and either disbanded or joined the Germans. Of these, the Decima MAS of Prince Valerio Borghese was the most famous. His unit was based at La Spezia. Borghese reached an agreement with the Germans on the basis of direct cooperation between the flotilla and the Third Reich. In those days there was a vacuum of power in Italian institutions, as the Italian armed forces had vanished, and the king was arriving at Brindisi in Apulia with his ministers and many high-ranking officers. Nor had Mussolini's Social Republic yet been established. Into this vacuum of authority stepped Borghese.

According to Borghese's memoirs, he learned of the Italian armistice from the radio announcement and was just as surprised as anyone else. At first he asked for information from the chief of the MAS HQ, the Prince of Aimone of Savoy, Duke of Aosta, nephew of the king, but he was equally surprised and replied to Borghese that the broadcast could be "enemy propaganda." Borghese could see the main fleet anchored at La Spezia, with the battleships *Vittorio Veneto* and *Littorio* still in the harbor.[5]

With the duke and other officers he tried to contact the Supermarina in Rome, but only after several hours were they able to find Rear Admiral Umberto Rouselle, who replied, "There are no particular orders, wait for directives." But at the same time, the admirals at La Spezia fled and Duke Aimone received an order to embark on the large torpedo-boat *Indomito* to join the king. According to Borghese's diary and later trial declaration, he was unable to receive orders from the navy command and reasoned that an armistice was not peace; it was only a lull in the war, and he had to stay under arms and wait for orders, though these never arrived.

The official position of the Navy Ministry was quite different, as the navy issued orders to "destroy X MAS equipment," and the naval commander of the North Tyrrhenian area reported that this order was about to be carried out. Assuming that such a statement could have been made only after Borghese's report of the situation, some authors have concluded that Borghese was informed of such orders. But the issuing of orders to the Italian armed forces for the September 8 armistice is—along with the World War I disaster at Caporetto—still one of the most controversial episodes in Italian history. It was certainly a very confused and poorly handled process—except by the Germans![6]

Once captured, Borghese told Allied interrogators that he chose his own course because he considered that his primary goal was to save Italian prestige, though considerations of strategic interest also played a part. He thought that Italy had two main enemies: Great Britain, which had lines of communication to the east that could not tolerate Italy's natural expansion into North Africa and a stranglehold upon the Mediterranean that remained a constant menace to Italy's security, and Germany, with its age-old aspirations for an outlet on the Mediterranean and its claims to certain Italian territories (such as Alto Dige in the Alps and Trieste). In the present circumstances, Borghese believed that the balance of power was best served by siding with Germany against England. According to his official interrogation report: "He explained that there were at least three reasons why he had chosen to join the Germans, i.e. that it would be easier to shake off the German rather than the Allied occupation, that peace terms would be harsher if the Allies won, and finally that the anti-German feeling spreading in Italy could have preserved better the 'national spirit while the Anglo-American influences were likely to be disruptive.'[7]

Several attempts were made by the Germans to enter the X MAS barracks, but, according to Borghese, "We repelled them easily, the enormous odds notwithstanding."[8] This statement has seldom been disputed, and the firm attitude of the flotilla is often taken as an example of what could be done with a unit of high morale in those difficult days. But the Germans were mainly interested in the X MAS Flotilla because they did not have, in the Prince's words, "any preparation nor knowledge of the special sea assault means." Therefore, the German Navy was interested in developing good relationships with the

Decima MAS in order to outfit units of the same kind, having so little in naval resources with which to fight the Allied navies.

On his side, Borghese soon had a chance to go to Germany, where the newspaper *Völkischer Beobachter* covered the news of his visit. The trip allowed him to better understand German special land operations, and he likely paid special attention to sabotage and commando actions behind enemy lines. Borghese would later build similar units, and after the war he was considered a "counterinsurgency specialist."[9]

According to an officer's memoir, on the evening of September 9 there was a meeting of the X MAS officers. Here, they discussed possible courses of action—that is, whether to continue to fight alongside the Germans. Borghese said, "The oath we took remains."[10]

Lieutenant Commander Luigi Longanesi Cattani was instructed to place himself in the service of Prince Aimone's family and to act as a liaison with the Germans. When Mussolini's Social Republic was declared, this officer, who was loyal to the royal family, declared he would not collaborate with the X MAS under such conditions. Borghese replied to him that until the end of the war any personal ideas regarding the form of the state would be "closed in briefcases." Afterward, when problems arose with the Fascist authorities, Longanesi Cattani resigned from the X MAS.[11]

On the 11th, Borghese rounded up his men and explained his decisions, telling them that those who did not agree with him could be dismissed. Most of the men left the unit and preferred to go home.

The basis of the agreement reached by Borghese and his 1,300 men with the Third Reich after the armistice was Germany's interest in Italy's special assault capability. And Borghese's unit certainly seemed to be a formidable enough resource. After the armistice, the Italian flag had come down over La Spezia naval base, and up had gone the flag of the Decima MAS. The Germans arrived to speak with Borghese after a message had arrived to them from the X MAS with the following words: "Commander Prince Borghese, Chief of the Italian 10. Flotilla Mas Spezia (assault boats), unreliable personnel dismissed today, and collaboration offered." The message arrived through Naval Intelligence, and the German Naval Command wanted to check the situation to be better informed of the Prince's intentions.[12]

This is easily understandable if we take into account that on the 3rd, when the armistice was signed at Cassibile by General Giuseppe Castellano, Borghese "had talks with an Abwehr representative."[13] When the armistice occurred, the X MAS had been training about fifteen German officers and sailors under Lieutenant Commander von Martiny.

The text of the agreement signed by Borghese and Korvettenkapitän Max Berninghaus, commander of the Ligurian coast, who arrived there on the 12th, is printed in several books on the basis of what witnesses remembered, and more recently from the recollections of Mario Bordogna, Borghese's aide-de-camp:

1. The X MAS Flotilla is a combined unit of the Italian Navy fully independent in logistic, organizational, disciplinary and administrative fields.
2. She is an ally of the German armed forces with the same duties and rights.
3. She may display the Italian flag.
4. It is acknowledged that her members may use any weapon.
5. She is allowed to recover and equip with the Italian flag and crew the Italian vessels found in Italian ports: the operative employment is under control of the German Navy.
6. Commander Borghese is the acknowledged chief with the rights and duties of this appointment.[14]

This agreement took place mainly because Borghese was what in the past was termed a *condottiero,* a captain of fortune, of the kind that led bands of mercenaries in medieval Italy. The Germans agreed because they needed to cooperate with the "secret weapons" of the X MAS, which had achieved better results during the war than the surface battle squadrons.

But how did Borghese explain his choice to side with the Germans? In an interview, he declared, "On 8th September, when I heard Badoglio's communiqué, I shed tears at that time but not after. . . . Because at that time I had suffered all that I could."[15]

The situation at the time of the armistice was all the more confused because Mussolini, after being taken prisoner by the Royalist government in July, was being held incommunicado on a precipitous mountain peak in the Apennines. But on September 12, in one of the most spectacular special operations of the war, German SS Colonel Otto Skorzeny led a force of glider-borne commandos into the midst of 100 Italian guards to rescue the dictator. By the end of September, Mussolini, sponsored by Hitler, had established a new government in the north of Italy, the Repubblica Sociale Italiana (RSI), or Italian Social Republic, best known, after its capital, as the Salò Republic.

At this time, Borghese traveled first to Rome, where he met Captain Ferruccio Ferreri, who became the general secretary of the navy of the Salò Republic, and then, on the 28th, to Germany to report to Grossadmiral Doenitz.

The German Naval Command war diary notes that Admiral Eberhard Weichold reached an agreement with Borghese for the quick employment of his specialized units against the Allies. From the German point of view, the X MAS was an Italian Freikorps, or volunteer corps, with Italian personnel remaining under the command of Borghese, as any attempt to build up such a German unit would require too much time. In fact, after the war SS General Karl Wolff used this very term to describe the X MAS.[16]

German documents also mention the fact that Commander Enzo Grossi of Betasom, the Italian submarine base in the Atlantic, joined the Germans to continue the war.[17] At the Italian submarine base of Betasom at Bordeaux the Italian submarines *Bagnolini* and *Finzi* were still operating. They were at Le Verdon, ready after yard-refitting to sail to Singapore. In the Far East there were also the *Cappellini,* the *Giuliani,* and the *Torrelli,* and in the Indian Ocean the *Cagni.*[18]

Lieutenant Commander Mario Arillo, while training his crews with German submarines at Danzig in the Baltic, was also surprised by the armistice. Arillo had been a daring commander through much of the war and was probably the second most famous Italian submariner. The Italian submarines in German service would be used primarily as transports and were renamed with a preface of an "S" and numbered 1–9.

In the German Navy's view, Grossi was to speak with Marine Gruppe West about the reorganization of the Italian Navy, and then he would come to Berlin with Italian Captain Sesto Sestini and Prince Borghese before reporting to Mussolini.[19]

Commander Grossi went with Borghese on October 5 to visit the Duce. Mussolini, confined in a villa at Salò on Lake Garda, received the two officers, and Borghese was struck by the "very human dimension" to which Mussolini had been reduced. Mussolini was angry about the surrender of the fleet, which "had cost the Italian people many sacrifices."[20]

In the meantime, several groups of disbanded military and volunteers organized by political parties began to put up armed resistance against the German occupation, but especially a deadly struggle against the new Fascist government. Sometimes there were initial forms of spontaneous resistance, such as helping Allied POWs to flee from prisoner-of-war camps.

Italy was now rent by a civil war throughout the north and central sections of the peninsula. Thrown in were the German and Allied armies fighting in the skies above, in the seas on either side, and especially on a vicious front that stretched across the south. Longtime quarrels were being settled, while the "outs"—the old Fascists, faced off against all those who had been repressed for over twenty years. Fascism, with its ideals of a bygone age, was now fighting for its life against modern democratic ideals and the United Nations of the future.

An underground movement was formed on a political level by the Comitato di Liberazione Nazionale (CLN, Committee of National Liberation) composed of members of several political parties, ranging from the Christian-Democrats to the Socialists, the Communist parties, and the Action Party.[21] The committee was formed in Rome, and when that city was liberated by the Allies in early June 1944, the northern part of it remained divided, changing its name to CLNAI—the CLN of Alta Italia (that is, upper or northern Italy)—based in Milan. The CLN took control of the partisan bands already formed, and these in turn depended on the committee for money, weapons, and equipment. Allied assistance was delivered through the CLN; therefore the guerrilla formations could survive only if they joined with some political party inside the umbrella organization. This point is important for understanding the development of the guerrilla/counterinsurgency operations and the relationship between Borghese's Decima MAS and the Resistance.

There were two main types of guerrilla formations: the disbanded military units and the units organized by CLN. Of the latter, the Garibaldini, or Communists, were the largest single group, mobilizing at least 40 percent of the partisans. The Socialists formed the less numerous Matteotti brigades, while other units included those formed by the Catholic Church.[22]

Borghese did not take part in Mussolini's return to power, devoting his energies from the start to the enlargement of his unit. In this process, the *marò*, as the men of the Decima MAS were called, rallied everywhere they could along the coasts to build up the unit. Many volunteered for the new X MAS, as the unit was famous for its accomplishments and especially for its commander.

Why would young people enlist in this unit? Perhaps a typical case is that of Luigi Del Bono, a navy physician who saw the advertisement, "Why do you not enlist?" He later described his reaction: "It was a fraction of a second. The war was lost. The honor of the Italian Navy must be defended. My doubts, my scruples, my spiritual depression vanished. . . . I signed my enlistment papers to the X MAS of the RSI."[23]

In other cases, it was the hope of finding "a place in the mess, a bed to sleep on, a kind of discipline, a salary," that led men to enlist, or the lure of the Italian adventurer. In Ferruccio Parri's opinion, who was at the head of the CLN, and would be the first Italian premier after the war, "A good many were attracted by pay and the good conditions; among them there were also minors. They enlisted and loved to show the weapons and inspire fear; they liked to act the master and to plunder."[24]

The core, according to the X MAS veterans, would be the men of the submarines and the sailors. Certainly it was not mandatory to be a sailor to enlist in the flotilla, and the fact that Borghese wanted only volunteers ensured him the highest morale and spirit in his rank and file.[25]

New service regulations established in the flotilla stipulated that:

1. the mess would be the same for privates and officers,
2. the cloth for the uniforms had to be identical,
3. no promotions would be granted until the end of the war, with the exception of promotions in the field for war actions,
4. there would be volunteer recruitment only, and
5. the death penalty would be in force for every X MAS enlisted man found guilty, by regular trials, of robbery or plundering, defection, or cowardice before the enemy.[26]

Reactions among the armed forces and the population to the X MAS were mixed, ranging from praise for the discipline of the men to claims of arrogance and lack of discipline.[27]

The X MAS volunteers were not required to take the oath of allegiance to the Salò Republic, and this fact caused problems between Mussolini's newly formed RSI armed forces and Borghese. As we will see, this tension would come to a head with Borghese's arrest in January 1944.

By November, the Decima Mas had enough volunteers to cede some 5,000 of its men to be sent to Germany for training as the core of the future San Marco Division, which was intended to be a marine unit. In December, Mussolini instructed the navy undersecretary to detach 1,000 of these volunteers to fight the guerrillas in Piedmont. At the same time, the navy (not Borghese) tried to build up a 9,000-man force as Marines, but the Germans became uneasy about these uncontrolled initiatives.[28]

Admiral Ferruccio Ferrini, undersecretary of the RSI Navy, proposed to send the volunteers to fight at the Anzio beachhead instead of to Cuneo (Piedmont) against the "rebels." Only on February 24, 1944, did Borghese gain control over this battalion, called Maestrale.[29]

The flotilla had a submarine unit, which recovered the scuttled submarine *Aradam* in Genoa harbor and had it ready to sail in January 1944 with tubes for "pigs." It also had some midget submarines of the CB type at Pola, as part of the *Longobardo* group. A massive air raid carried out by B-17s sank the *Aradam* on September 1, 1944, at Genoa. This bombing and others also caused the loss of several other vessels, and it could be supposed that the king's Regia Marina of the south was well informed of the fact that the *Aradam* was ready with containers to bring "pigs" beyond the Allied lines. The bombing was repeated with B-26 bombers on the 23rd, causing the final destruction of the RSI Navy, which now had only some light vessels. In addition to one cruiser and two destroyers, the submarine *Ambra,* recovered after it was scuttled on the armistice, was sunk.

The surface naval unit of the X MAS was transferred to the banks of Lake Como, near Sesto Calende. The frogman unit, now called the Licio Visintini group, after the officer fallen at Gibraltar, was sent to Valdagno, north of Vicenza. The gamma men trained there, along with some German sailors, at an inside Olympic swimming pool of the Marzotto company (which produced uniforms).[30] Practical exercises also took place around the island of San Giorgio with the old tanker *Tampico.* The X MAS formed an antisubmarine unit consisting of seven small warships and one captured French corvette. Other boats were recovered and, with some MAS boats, were formed into a MAS unit.

According to Allied estimates, during the 600 days of the RSI, the X MAS raised some 50,000 men. This was in addition to the thousands of men who passed on to the San Marco Division and several specialized units that were formed. But the real strength of the flotilla was a mystery even to its commander. He explained to his captors that he used every means possible to keep these figures secret, even from the RSI government. This way, the power of the X MAS was generally overestimated.[31]

Historian Friedrich W. Deakin noted in his massive history of the German-Italian relationship that Borghese's main interests were the antiguerrilla actions on Italy's eastern border and "espionage and sabotage activities south of the Apennine front." This view has been confirmed by many sources.[32] Sabotage and commando operations as well as intelligence ones were well developed in the X MAS, which had formed the Vega battalion as a sequel to the Nuotatori Paracadutisti (NP) made up of swimmers and paratroopers. According to Sergio Nesi, a veteran of the X MAS, "These Vega squads had the typical duty, already experienced many times, of letting the enemy pass over them, and then carrying out espionage and sabotage activity."[33]

The intelligence assets of the Borghese unit were indeed highly supported: After September 8, 1943, Borghese was able to build his own intelligence and counterintelligence service with two main offices, an intelligence office and a political one. The service employed the NP battalion to send sabotage agents behind the lines, the Vega battalion for intelligence missions to the south, and from May 1944, an Operative Command O for police activity.[34]

During the winter of 1943–1944, the Germans were able to hold up the Allies at the Cassino Line south of Rome. But we should clarify that the Allies' Italian campaign was only one of the wars fought in the peninsula in 1943–1945: There was also an Italian civil war as well as a war of resistance against the Germans and another against Tito's Yugoslavian Communists—and Italy was favorable terrain for partisan-guerrilla warfare. To understand the X MAS operations, it is necessary to look inside the world of intelligence. Although conventional military operations moved at a sluggish rate, guerrilla and special operations were often carried out rapidly. Several organizations operated chaotically in order not only to win the war but also to gain the best position in the postwar organization of the country and for the future position of the country in the world system.

According to one of the most reliable sources, General Ambrogio Viviani, every armed force built up its own clandestine secret service, and every political party also organized its intelligence assets. The partisans organized by the army had their Fronte Clandestino Militare (Clandestine Military Front), which had a Ufficio Informazioni (Intelligence Office) deputy chief, the later-famous Lieutenant Colonel Giovanni De Lorenzo. The same could be said on the opposite side, where the various police forces—the Carabinieri, the Financial Guards, the Public Security (state police)—did the same, and the Ovra, the very effective secret fascist political police force, *never* ceased to operate. But what is interesting to note is that the Carabinieri remained in place and operated both in the north, in the underground, *and* in the south. There the Carabinieri immediately built up in Bari a special Contingente R (R Unit) under the command of General Giuseppe Pièche (who was later active in the Cold War). Several served in the U.S. Counter-Intelligence Corps.[35]

From this rather summarized picture it is not surprising to find that Borghese's Decima had its own intelligence unit. One of the targets of the X MAS in the north was Rear Admiral Maugeri, chief of the SIS, the intelligence service of the Royal Navy, and while he was in Rome after the armistice, Borghese's men tried several times to apprehend him.[36]

The RSI leaders were hardly satisfied with the high degree of independence displayed by the Prince and by the fact that he did not swear loyalty to the RSI government. According to Borghese, enlisting in the new Fascist Republican Party was forbidden inside the X MAS, and an unwritten rule kept the sailors from any political activity.

Therefore, the Guardia Nazionale Repubblicana (GNR, or National Republican Guard), under the command of Renato Ricci, a service with police and military police duties like the Carabinieri, kept an eye on Borghese's activities, reporting constantly to Mussolini.[37] At the same time, the Duce may have had his own private reasons for casting a suspicious eye on the X MAS. According to Ricciotti Lazzero, "Mussolini does not love those Navy officers, too young, too enterprising, too exuberant and vital, and overall unpredictable, before whom he felt himself surpassed."[38]

Tension between the X MAS and Mussolini's men continued to increase. Finally, in January 1944 Borghese was summoned to the Duce's HQ, and when he arrived there on the 13th he was arrested. He was seized in the antechamber by Colonel Fortunato Albonetti of the GNR, on Mussolini's directive and Ricci's orders, and taken to a fortress prison at Brescia. There he was interrogated by a commission of inquiry.

To understand this event it must be noted that Borghese's Decima was the only kind of navy allowed by the Germans to the Mussolini republic, as stated in Doenitz's reply to Admiral Antonio Legnani, undersecretary of the RSI Navy. Only the X MAS could employ naval resources with Italian crews and hoist the Italian flag. Other vessels would have mixed crews, and the coastal batteries also had to follow such directives.

Therefore, the RSI Navy was merely a handful of offices and officers without anything behind it, and when Admiral Legnani died in an accident, the new undersecretary, Ferruccio Ferrini, was determined to bring Borghese under his control. The event that caused the Prince to be arrested was that the GNR asked for 2,000 men of the navy to be used in antipartisan actions, and this presented both Ricci and Ferrini the opportunity to settle the question.

The tension between the navy undersecretary and the X MAS reached its climax when two navy officers, Captain Nicola Bedeschi and Captain Gaetano Tortora, were sent to La Spezia to take command of the land battalions of the Decima MAS. They were trying to group them into the San Marco Regiment and cut them off from Borghese's authority. Since Borghese was not informed, and this appeared a coup to put him aside and remove the X MAS from his control, the officers commanding the two battalions Maestrale and NP, who were seasoned warriors, arrested both the navy officers on January 9 and passed them on to the GNR.[39]

Suspecting a mutiny, the Germans sent armored cars. These rushed to the barracks. The AA guns of the X MAS were aimed at them, and the Germans withdrew. At the same time, the news of Borghese's arrest arrived at the X MAS base and provoked an emotional reaction among the ranks of the flotilla. As one remembered, "On 13 January 1944 it came about that the new fascists, jealous of the Decima, had invited Commander Borghese to Salò and then had him arrested!"[40]

Accusations against the Prince varied from lack of loyalty to the Duce and fascism to his relationship with the Allies and partisans. He was also accused of making plans to overthrow the Duce with 50,000 armed men. Interestingly, the X MAS was supposedly not Fascist enough, and informers even claimed that Borghese was the secret chief of the Christian-Democratic partisans. He was said to have met in Lugano, Switzerland, with a British count, a lord, and an American journalist.[41]

During those years, Borghese acted quite differently from other high officers and Fascist leaders. He avoided luxury, and he ate lunch with many of his officers, coming as they did from the various points where they served. At the Da Candida restaurant at Lonato, near Brescia, they discussed the war situation quite freely. Rumors reached Mussolini that they did not bother to make the ritual *saluto al Duce* to open their meetings and that Mussolini himself was barely mentioned. To the Fascists who tried to portray Borghese in a bad light, this appeared to be further proof of his lack of loyalty to the Duce.[42]

From La Spezia, X MAS officers Nino Buttazzoni and Rodolfo Ceccacci prepared to march to the prison where Borghese was held. The X

MAS men not only wanted to free their commander but also to over-throw the Salò Republic and Mussolini. According to Guido Bonvicini, a veteran of the X MAS, the Germans would have allowed the coup by the X MAS against the RSI government, but Borghese's attitude, sug-gested by a message he sent from the fortress, was to remain quiet and continue to work hard for the country while waiting the development of events.[43]

In those days, one thing that helped Borghese was the fact that the flotilla carried out its first raid behind the Allied lines, at Naples.

Borghese's independent attitude was also suspicious to the Ger-mans, or at least to some of them. The German Navy commander in Italy reported, in the second half of October 1944, "There are increas-ing reports about the existing connections [of the Italian Navy offi-cers] with the officers fighting on the opposite side." Of course, such relationships would be the target of special surveillance.[44]

The intelligence report on Borghese issued by the GNR to Mussolini was so negative that Marshal Rudolfo Graziani commented, "The Tenth must be reduced to a faint light." General Federico Magrì was sent to the Decima's headquarters at La Spezia on the 20th. His report to Mussolini was also unfavorable to the X MAS and Borghese. He said that training of the men was inadequate, that the volunteers were undisciplined, and that the unit's rules were too different from the rules of more traditional armed forces, but their morale was high. This assessment shocked the officers, who disliked Borghese because he was outside of the regular military system. Proposals to Mussolini, besides punishment for those who were fomenting revolt, included cutting off the San Marco Marine Regiment from the X MAS and limiting the lat-ter to pure naval assault duties. Magrì's report is interesting because it sheds light on the organization and personalities of Borghese's unit.[45]

Borghese sent a letter to Mussolini asking to be freed, since there were no charges yet filed against him, or for a formal military inquiry to be opened. In any case, many people intervened on his behalf, the last being Commander Grossi, who discussed Borghese's case with

Mussolini for a day and a half. Mussolini was concerned mainly with Borghese's loyalty. When he became convinced, after a meeting with Graziani, that Borghese did not want to stage a coup, he ordered his release. Grossi went to Brescia with Borghese's wife, Daria, and the Prince was released from jail on January 25. The inquiry into the X MAS, however, continued.[46]

Finally, the inquiry petered out. The undersecretary of the navy, Ferrini, was fired. But the two X MAS battalions responsible were ordered to be sent to the front line as a punitive measure: Since the NP battalion was intended for raiding behind the lines, it was the Maestrale that reached the front, while the NP remained at La Spezia.

In the meantime, military operations had been under way. The Maestrale changed its name to Barbarigo and was sent to the Anzio beachhead on former civilian buses. On March 3, the unit arrived, and its commander, Umberto Bardelli, found an unwelcome surprise. The German commander of the 715th Infantry Division, Colonel Friedrich von Schellerer, was expecting "replacements" instead of a complete unit. The Germans wanted to have the individual Italian soldiers distributed among their units. After much discussion, the companies remained intact but were dispersed among German units. The Germans had lost any kind of trust in large Italian units. For one thing, the high morale of Italian units often made the Germans suspicious.

German counterattacks and the Allies' cautious attitude had stopped the beachhead advance. The Barbarigo companies only had to carry out patrol activities—but with the heavy rain and the tremendous Allied bombardments, even this was a challenge. They hardened, however, and were later trained in antitank fighting by the Germans, learning to employ the *Panzerfaust,* an infantry antitank rocket launcher. This was certainly helpful, as the training of the units left much to be desired and the Allied troops opposite the X MAS men were highly trained forces.

After some minor attacks, on May 23, 1944, the U.S. VI Corps launched an offensive. It took three days for the VI Corps to pierce the

German defense and break out of the beachhead. The already depleted 715th Infantry Division, the parent unit of Barbarigo, suffered heavy losses, and the Italian battalion was almost destroyed.[47]

Later some of Borghese's battalions were again sent to the front line, which is what they wanted. After the operations in the east against Tito's partisans, the X MAS men retreated to the Veneto region and there partly engaged in antiguerrilla operations, a form of combat that they did not welcome. This was especially true of the NP battalion, composed of well-trained commandos, and they became so discontented that they revolted. In the trial that followed, the battalion was declared not guilty, and it was soon sent to the front against the Allies.

In February 1945, the X MAS was reorganized into two combat groups, each of three battalions plus some artillery. The Barbarigo, Lupo, and NP battalions formed the first combat group and were sent to the front against the Allies in the Imola area at the end of March 1945. The San Giorgio artillery battalion supported them. The other combat group of the Decima was built in the 2nd regiment, battalions Valanga, Sagittario, and Fulmine. This last unit included the Volontari di Francia (Volunteers from France), formed largely by sons of Italian immigrants to France.

The combat groups had little chance to take part in operations, as the end of the war was coming. They were involved in a fire brigade–style intervention on the sector of the 162nd German (Turkestan) Division to close a gap opened by British commandos in early April 1945. The two battalions at the front—NP and Barbarigo—were also involved in the last Allied offensive in Italy. When they retreated over the Po and Adige rivers, the commander of the Barbarigo battalion opened Borghese's secret orders, which instructed the X MAS troops to cut off contact with the Germans and try to reach the eastern border to protect it from the Yugoslavs. But they were encircled by Allied armored units near Padua on the 29th and surrendered to the British, who presented arms to one of the last fighting units in a dissolving Fascist republic.

The men of the NP retreated toward Venice and came into contact with their old comrades of the south. They preferred not to use arms against their former friends, so they continued to fall back on Venice, where they at first surrendered to the local CLN headed by Rear Admiral Franco Zannoni. But they quickly took up their arms again and waited for the approaching Allied troops, to surrender once and for all. The elite swimmer-paratroopers of the NP had felt uncomfortable without weapons in the midst of the various partisan militias of the CLN, some of whom may have been out for vengeance.

The kaleidoscope of warfare that erupted in northern Italy after the armistice indeed roused passions that are still felt to this day. And the Decima MAS, during this condottiere stage of Borghese's career, was at center stage in the maelstrom. Whether extending its legacy of special operations at sea, engaging in ruthless counterinsurgency actions, or fighting main force battles, the X MAS fought in all directions until the final days of the war. It remains to examine several operations in detail to understand how and why Borghese's Decima MAS, and the units and volunteers who flocked to its banner, left such a prominent mark during this terrible period of history.

CHAPTER 12

Secret Operations, 1944–1945

Those marines who sided with the Axis moved with incredible noncon-formism and independence.

Ricciotti Lazzero[1]

AS NEW, MORE AMORPHOUS BATTLE LINES WERE drawn after Italy's September 1943 armistice, it was initially assumed that the X MAS would carry out actions against Allied naval bases. But the buildup of forces proceeded slowly, and the first major action only took place in January 1944. The German Navy in Italy, especially Vice Admiral Löwisch, the German naval commander posted there, was not favorably disposed toward Borghese and his unit and feared his possible successes.[2]

"An operation of assault combat boats on the Italian eastern coast in the Ancona area does not report success," stated the German Navy report for the first half of October 1944. Indeed, the Germans were inclined to dismiss Italian efforts whenever possible. This attitude continued even though Löwisch was quite impressed by the Italian sailors in the German units. He was less satisfied with the officers, as they, in his view, "appear[ed] to be more wearing a uniform than commanders and trainers of their troops."

X MAS vessels were now placed with the light combat units, and the land forces were under the SS. But Löwisch reported that the ships were to withdraw in case of retreat at the front, and he was not yet sure how to use the "not very numerous personnel" of the Italian Navy. Talks were under way with Prince Borghese and Rear Admiral Giuseppe Sparzani, undersecretary of the RSI Navy. But the Italians and Germans clashed. The Italians said the Germans did not want an Italian Navy and refused them weapons. Löwisch held "that with the display of successful performances the buildup [of the RSI Navy] would follow."[3]

In any case, the conduct of X MAS men during assaults from the sea alongside German units was considered "positive toward the service, and they desired to fight." Löwisch was, however, always critical of the Italian Navy officer corps: "In the officer corps, it should have been reduced and purged, as intrigues can be observed. According to my observation the Italian command is not ready for employment, or at least should be kept from important duties, as there are only a few officers who have made themselves available without reservation for German service."[4]

The Germans thus remained wary of Italian capabilities, ready to intervene if the situation required. The failures of Fascist resolve in North Africa, Sicily, and especially on the Italian mainland had been disappointing, and they were always suspicious of counting too much on the "Rump State" of the RSI.

Naturally, the first priority of the X MAS was to be able to continue its special naval assaults by surface and underwater units and the gamma frogmen. The first order of business was to collect every available piece of equipment and procure any weapon the sailors could get, using every means, including salvaging, buying, or plundering. In one case, the X MAS got hold of a supply of Beretta submachine guns by supplying alcohol to the German guards at the factory. Every part of war production was German-controlled after September 13, 1943, and the low priority that the X MAS had in German eyes made it difficult for Borghese and his men to come by the needed supplies.

Borghese was nevertheless soon able to reorganize the naval units and plan attacks against the Allies. The NP battalion was also reorganized both north and south of the front line, with the northern portion under the command of Ceccacci.

On May 19 and June 22, 1944, two raids, made up of British charioteers and Italian frogmen fighting for the king, succeeded in damaging the almost completed Italian aircraft carrier *Aquila* and the heavy cruisers *Bolzano* and *Gorizia*. Participating in the second operation was Durand de la Penne, who left a message in a bottle that said "Greetings from the Decima Mas of the south."[5]

Several missions were also launched from the north. During the night of January 23, three MTSMs started from a base near Rome at Fiumicino and attacked the Allied fleet at Anzio. This attack and the additional ones launched in the following days caused little damage, and Borghese would claim that landing operations were slowed and hindered at night. On February 20 and 21, attacking boats sank a light vessel and damaged a minesweeper.[6] On April 28, 1944, a landing ship tank (LST) was sunk by a MAS attack, and several British MTBs were damaged in an encounter with the MAS two days later. The Kriegsmarine launched an attack on Allied shipping near Anzio with twenty-three *Marders* (submergible one-man midget submarines) on March 20 and repeated the attacks on April 21 with another twenty boats.[7]

Such attacks, and mine-laying operations in the Adriatic, continued to the last days of the war.[8] Sergio Nesi, a lieutenant at the time, participated in one of these operations on the night of April 13, 1945, as the Allied offensive was gaining ground to the north. The mission began with two SMAs escorted by two German MTMs, which had to refuel the SMAs before the last phase of the mission. One of the SMAs was then sighted by enemy air reconnaissance and scuttled, and the two raiders were taken prisoner by the Americans. Nesi and NCO Sergio Perbellini landed a saboteur named "Puma" near Mount Conero (where some of the enemy coastal batteries that Persano's fleet faced in the 1866 campaign of Lissa still existed). Then Nesi and his partner attacked the Ancona harbor, but their boat was spotted by radar. The defensive fire stopped the SMA, which blew up as the two jumped into the water. Later, they were rescued by British destroyers and interrogated by a British Lieutenant Edward Walter Lloyd, who said, "Welcome, Commander Nesi, I am glad to know you personally, I have been following you from the time of Anzio."[9]

But while the X MAS continued to ply its trade in naval special operations, its new, greater role unfolded on terra firma with the land operations that took place in Yugoslavia and northeastern Italy. Several of the X MAS men did not consider themselves Fascists and so were deployed on the eastern border to deal with the territorial claims of Yugoslavian partisans. There, the fighting also involved local militias because the area was under the direct control of Dr. Friedrich Rainer, the *Gauleiter,* or civilian authority, in charge of the district. Indeed, in the story of the X MAS in the north of Italy after the armistice, it may be more appropriate to speak of a "patriotic" force than a "Fascist" one. As historian Donald Gurrey wrote, "Apart from a few exceptions, none of the men were excessively pro-Fascist or pro-German; 90 percent of them were under 25 and many had come from the former 10th *Arditi* Regiment and from the *Folgore* and *Nembo* Parachute Division. Morale was high."[10]

Thus, the Italian non-Communist partisans of the Osoppo brigades and soldiers of the RSI units, especially those of the X MAS, had common interests. All of them wanted to defend Italy's eastern border from Yugoslavian claims. Such claims were being loudly made in August 1944, and considering the weight of Tito's guerrilla army on behalf of the Allied war effort, the Allies had little reason not to back these claims against Italy, which had lost the war.

In such a situation, it is not surprising that there were plans to partition the Italian peninsula into four sections to be divided among the winners of World War II. According to a plan prepared in November 1943, Italy's northeastern region would be ceded to Yugoslavia. Fortunately for Italy, it was able to mitigate such punitive views.[11]

The Yugoslavian claims grew more vociferous in the last stage of the war when it became clear that the fall of the German war machine was not far off. Combined efforts were thus made to send Slovene partisan brigades and Russian liaison officers beyond the Tagliamento River, which lies between Trieste and Venice.[12]

Interestingly enough, the core of the future Gladio stay-behind organization started with the Osoppo partisans. The Osoppo brigades were mainly formed of Alpine troops under American supervision. They wore hats with green scarves, often with the motto "Pal nostri Fogolar" (in the local mountain dialect, "for our hearth"). According to Major Thomas John Rohwort, they were more reliable, from a military point of view, than the Communist Garibaldini units, which, after the antiguerrilla actions of November–December 1944, disbanded, either handing over their arms to the Germans or joining the IX Slovene Corps.[13]

The gradual advance of Tito's Communists into Istria explains why at some point Borghese made overtures to the Allies, and more particularly to the Italian Navy of the south, prospecting the idea of changing sides. The Republican Army was strong in northeast Italy, but soon the suspicious Germans tried to convince Graziani that the X MAS units should be moved to Italy's northwest. In any case, the Allies rejected these advances, perhaps unwisely.[14]

By the autumn of 1944, the Decima units, now a division, were deployed in northeastern Italy and, having obtained the permission of Gauleiter Rainer, some battalions were transferred to the border with Yugoslavia. This area was declared the "coastal zone of operations in the Adriatic," which was a prelude to annexation to the Third Reich.[15]

On June 22, 1944, all of the Borghese units were placed under the command of Gustav-Adolf von Zangen. They totaled 4,776 men and officers.[16]

The Decima Division, from headquarters at Cividale near Udine and Gorizia, deployed the battalions Fulmine, Sagittario, Barbarigo, Valanga, and NP to control and clear the Natisone Valley. On January 19, 1945, the Fulmine battalion in the outpost of Tarnova della Selva was attacked by Yugoslav partisans estimated to number 1,300. The Italians suffered heavily before being rescued by relieving forces. Out of 214 men, 86 died and 56 were wounded.[17] Although Borghese held up the episode as a success, it was also proof that the military effectiveness of the Tito bands was becoming too great for the Decima. This view was countered, however, when two companies of the Barbarigo battalion routed Slovene partisans on the 26th on the Bainsizza plateau.

Borghese and his men were not the only ones interested in the eastern border. The area called Alpenvorland—that is, the provinces of Belluno, Trento, and Bolzano—was included in an operation area under the command of Gauleiter Franz Hofer, who would try to annex the area to Austria when the war was over.[18] The memoirs of Ezio Donà, an important anti-Fascist and partisan leader of the Trento area, revealed that two X MAS men tried to make contact with some partisan bands in order to coordinate a defense of the Italian northern border. This was to stop any form of annexation, but the partisans, who were often quite unprepared for such dealings, probably killed both.[19]

The attitude of the X MAS in the north seems to be confirmed by Borghese's memoirs, edited by Bordogna, which describe a plan to defend the "Alto Adige," as the Italians called South Tyrol and the Trentino region, from the separatist plans conceived by the Germans, and especially from Gauleiter Hofer. Borghese claimed that the X MAS gave hundreds of rifles to patriot partisans, and they were sure that such weapons would *not* be used against other Italians.[20]

Borghese displayed this same approach in Piedmont, and it is difficult to assess whether he was already in contact with the Southern Government or acting on his own initiative. But Borghese clearly did try to create a border area controlled by the X MAS and possibly partisan bands as a barrier against possible invaders.[21]

According to historian Renzo De Felice, Borghese was also requested by the Southern Government to defend the Venezia Giulia region of northern Italy. The X MAS had many contacts with the south because the unit was split in two by the armistice, and commando operations often offered possibilities for encounters. According to a letter written by Admiral de Courten to Italian Premier Ivanoe Bonomi, "The Government of the South . . . was in touch with Borghese, at least initially with the consent of the British and American secret services."[22] We have seen that this was true. It is possible that he was chosen for talks because he was known to be independent of the RSI armed forces, especially after the clashes with the Fascist authorities and his brief arrest by Mussolini.[23]

The Southern Government's attitude probably accounts for the consideration enjoyed by Prince Borghese after the fall of the RSI. The Southern Government was worried about the plans of Tito's partisans and the future of the border region and its people. In May 1944, the news coming from Bern and Paris to Minister Count Carlo Sforza was enlightening. There was talk about an agreement between Italian and Yugoslavian partisans on setting a border of operations between them at the Tagliamento River. The disappearance of many civilians at the hands of Yugoslavian partisans during the September 1943 period, when the Italian units disbanded, led the Italians to fear what could happen after the fall of Germany and its satellite republic in northern Italy.

In August, the Foreign Ministry asked the Comando Supremo to secretly ask the northern Italian military to take over the defense of the eastern border and its population. As naval historian Augusto De Toro wrote, "The southern Foreign Ministry, in order to protect the Italian population, feared much more the liberation of the northeastern provinces by Tito's forces, with which in other fields there was cooperation against the Axis forces. So even with the enemy German occupation, to this point, collaboration with the RSI was contemplated and planned."[24]

In addition, the SIS, led by Captain Agostino Calosi, had special instructions from Admiral de Courten, now chief of staff of the navy. He planned a landing in the Istria area to be carried out without Allied help so as to not disturb relations with Tito. Later, British Field Marshal Harold Alexander proposed a plan in which a landing in Istria would assist the final offensive against the German front in Italy. This plan would have included the Italian allied San Marco Marine regiment, but it was later abandoned to avoid friction with Stalin, with whom Tito was now allied.[25]

The Italian politicians turned to the Allies, that is, to an American, Vice Admiral Ellery Wheeler Stone, in the hope that Allied forces would occupy the Italian eastern provinces as soon as the German Army fell apart. Later, in March 1945, the secretary of the foreign ministry, Renata Prunas, asked Harold Macmillan, president of the Allied Commission, to have the German forces to remain in place, in case of surrender, for local security purposes.

At the same time, the navy of the south began to develop contacts (which really had never ceased) with the northern navy, which mainly consisted of the X MAS. Without informing the Allies, the SIS sent at least three officers on missions to the north. They were Lieutenant Giorgio Zanardi in September–October 1944, Engineer Giulio De Giorgis (whose brother died at Matapan) in April 1945, and Captain of Engineers Antonio Marceglia (who served in the Alexandria attack; he is also Ungarelli's cousin) in March–April 1945. Some sources list other missions, such as those of Professor Paride Baccarini, who landed with three other men on the upper Adriatic, where they were captured with money and radio equipment. They were held by the X MAS for some time. Another was carried out by navy physician Major Francesco Putzolu, who was to signal the south regarding naval facilities and related industries that were not to be bombed, but he was treated coolly in the north even though he declared himself a special envoy of Admiral de Courten.[26]

De Courten took an interest in Borghese's activities and maintained contacts with officers from both sides because he wanted to defend Italy's eastern border. But there was much fantasy surrounding the special operations forces at this time, and for many years after the war reports of their activities were colored with false details. This led some to think that Borghese had conducted these clandestine affairs to save his neck.[27]

Zanardi has published and spoken about his own experiences. In September 1944, he received orders from the commander of the SIS, Calosi, to go beyond the front line in the north, which still ran on the Gothic Line. He was to try to "understand up to what point the leaders of the RSI Navy would be ready to collaborate with Admiral de Courten in acting against the Germans when they finally began to evacuate northern Italy, in order to save what could be saved." Zanardi noted, "This was avoided when Trieste fell into Yugoslavian hands before the arrival of the Allied troops." He had already visited the north earlier and was recovering from wounds inflicted on him in a Fascist attack.[28]

Zanardi's mission was accomplished by slipping through the front lines at the Republic of San Martino. He brought two messages, one to Cardinal Ildefonso Schuster and the other to the undersecretary of the foreign ministry of the north, Serafino Mazzolini. Then, on September 24, at Montecchio Maggiore near Vicenza, he met Rear Admiral Sparzani, former commander of the battleship *Vittorio Veneto*. After Zanardi explained his objectives, the admiral replied that he was already sending several hundred sailors to Trieste, Fiume, and Pola without telling the Germans, and arming them with weapons captured by Borghese from the partisans.

Zanardi asked Sparzani to intensify this work, taking command of the area, if necessary, when the front collapsed, and they made agreements on how to exchange special signals to avoid damage and sabotages from Italian factions. Zanardi then met with the CLN members of Venezia and industrialists in the Milan area. The Southern Government was worried about the possible destruction of the factories and planned a paratroop landing to save the Milan industrial area.

Zanardi also called a cousin who was in the X MAS some miles north of Milan, at Sesto Calende, and a meeting with the Prince was arranged. Zanardi met Borghese on the 26th and tried to convince him to conclude agreements with the partisans. This had already been done in some cases in Piedmont, but reaching agreements was more difficult in the northeast. Specifically, he wanted Borghese to save the industrial plants from possible destruction. Borghese replied, "Send to me the industrialists." Neither Borghese nor Sparzani wanted to collaborate with the Anglo-American Allies, however.

On his way back from this mission, Zanardi had many adventures. He was captured twice by the Germans but escaped, and he tried four times to pass the front lines by sea before he reached the British. He was held for more than a week under custody and debriefed, but he was able to let his return be known to Capitano di Fregata Carlo Resio of the SIS (known by the code name "Salty"). He was also helped by the SIM.[29]

The X MAS sent a commando unit to watch the main Fiat plant and also to determine which factories were under German control. In fact, all the factories of any importance were now under the control of Albert Speer, according to Hitler's directive of September 13, 1943, and were considered "protected." This also (and especially) meant against the labor forces wishing to strike.[30]

Additional missions were carried out when the German front in Italy was about to collapse, thanks to news coming from the north relaying the attitudes of Borghese and Graziani. Calosi dispatched the missions at the urging of Marshal Giovanni Messe, chief of staff of the Comando Supremo and de Courten.[31]

X MAS men were sending agents south from the spring of 1944, but it was on October 12 that Borghese summoned his officers to Milan to discuss the coming action, in view of the fact that the German line on the Apennines would not resist forever. At that briefing, it was decided to reorganize the naval units into two groups, one operating in the Adriatic and the other in the Tyrrenian Sea, while the land battalions would be rounded up in the Decima Division. The latter would be sent as soon as possible to the eastern border, because "the area mostly in danger is that of the East, because the Italian character of Rome, Florenze, Milan, Turin, Venice, etc., will never be questioned, but those of Trieste, Pola, Fiume, Zara, certainly will be."[32]

Of course, to do this Borghese had to confront his German allies. He informed Mussolini of his intentions on October 26 and thereafter had talks with Rudolf Rahn and Karl Wolff, who were not very supportive. The main obstacle was Gauleiter Rainer, but he was forced to accept the presence of Italian RSI units during a party held on Hitler's birthday.[33]

Wolff declared in a postwar interview that he was well aware of Borghese's contacts with the south, and even knew that Borghese was known there as the "the man who came from the sea." He said Borghese had described his activities and promised to inform him in the future of all important results from these contacts. Wolff and Field Marshal Albert Kesselring did not oppose Borghese's desire to set up in the east, but later they, too, had to come to terms with Gauleiter Rainer, who favored some "slave workers" populating the area, which he intended to annex to the Reich.[34]

Borghese first met Wolff on January 6, 1944. He was introduced to the SS general by Rahn, with whom he was in close and friendly contact, and both seem to have always protected the X MAS's interests inside the German military.[35]

In the Friuli-Venezia Giulia area, the X MAS land forces tried to enlist some of the 12,000 Italians working for the Speer organization but met with little success. Gauleiter Rainer made life quite difficult for the X MAS in his area: At Gorizia there were clashes with the German garrison over the right to raise the Italian flag. Finally the Decima Division was allowed to deploy, but it was a hard life.

Between December 9 and 15, 1944, Borghese visited his troops in the eastern area, traveling from Venice to Pola and Fiume, where it seems that Gauleiter Rainer issued an order for his arrest. The Germans accused the X MAS of plundering in the Gorizia area and formed another unit, made up of ethnic Serbians, to replace them there.[36]

In the meantime, there were contacts between the X MAS and the "white" (right-wing, often monarchist) partisans of the Osoppo, who were opposed to any Yugoslavian takeover in the Venezia Giulia region. Lieutenant "Piave," whose true name was Cino Boccazzi, of the Mission Bergenfeld, was captured by X MAS men during combat and brought to a castle, where he was almost interrogated by a sadistic intelligence expert, Lieutenant Umberto Bertozzi, but the interrogation was canceled.

Instead he was well treated. At trial, he was acknowledged as a regular soldier, then freed to establish contact with the Osoppo partisans. Borghese was hoping that such contacts would "check the Slavonic intrusiveness and the overbearing Germans." Boccazzi accepted the mission, but both the CLNAI and the British were against this unusual cooperation. [37]

Neither the minister of the air force, Luigi Gasparotto, or Calosi, chief of the SIS, wanted to rely on RSI units to fight the Slavs, but they wanted the X MAS against the Germans. Certainly the X MAS men would fight the Slovenes, but they would fight against the Germans only in extreme cases, when Italy's interests were clearly in danger. Therefore, they most likely refused the advances made by Borghese and the southern navy.

In the meantime, tension between the Osoppo and the Communist Garibaldini reached a peak with the bloody action at Malga Porzus, where eighteen Osoppo leaders were killed by Garibaldi partisans on behalf of the IX Yugoslavian Corps.

Engineer Giulio De Giorgis was sent north to Sparzani with a message from de Courten to do everything possible on the eastern border, instructing the troops to show a white armband when the Allied soldiers arrived. De Giorgis met with Sparzani, and then on April 23, 1945, with Borghese, to deliver de Courten's message.

At the same time, Marceglia was given a mission. He had been one of the frogmen who penetrated Alexandria and knew Borghese well. His assignment was prepared by Resio, head of the D Office of the SIS, with the support of American counterintelligence. The United States was interested in infiltrating agents into the German SD, which worked closely with the X MAS, especially Captain Buttazzoni. Marceglia knew both Borghese and Buttazzoni and was the right man for the job. He also carried a message to encourage the Italians to move to protect the eastern border, since they did not feel bound by other Allied agreements, such as the one made between Tito and Alexander. Tito changed his attitude toward British support only in November 1944, after his secret visit to Stalin.

Marceglia slipped through the lines in March and reached the north, where he met in Venice with Sparzani, Borghese, and several officers of the X MAS as well as CLN members such as Rear Admiral Franco Zannoni. He also inspected the Trieste area, dressed as an X MAS officer, and conferred with local partisans.[38]

Marceglia's report of April 10, 1945, expressed disappointment about the military effectiveness of the X MAS. He said the unit was too scattered and that its best battalions were under strict German control. Marceglia noted that the unit had only 300–400 soldiers in the east, but 1,000 under the Germans. The situation was even worse with the partisans (presumably the Osoppo units), "who did not want complications," while the CLN in the Trieste area was "phantomatic" and almost "nonexistent." All was "amateurish," and there were no troops to defend the city. He invited Borghese to displace all his units to the eastern border.[39]

Borghese informed Mussolini of De Giorgis's message, and the Duce appointed Borghese as commander of all the RSI units beyond the Isonzo River, ordering him to deploy the X MAS there. But by then it was too late, as there was nothing more Borghese could do. The front had broken, and orders to X MAS units to reach the east had already been issued. Both the X MAS soldiers and the anti-Communist partisans were too few and not well enough organized to resist the advance of Tito's men. The Istria area fell under Yugoslavian occupation and was finally lost to Italy. Trieste was reached in the final days of the Allied offensive by the 2nd New Zealand Division, but the city remained under Yugoslavian occupation for more than a month before receiving special status. The details of what occurred on the border between Italy and Yugoslavia in the last days of the war are still not clear, and documents relating to war crimes are still closed.

Not everyone in the Badoglio government agreed with these missions, but they were authorized by Prime Minister Ivanoe Bonomi in agreement with Marshal Messe and Admiral de Courten. It is understandable that the CLN partisan organization did not want to deal with the Fascist side, although there are several signs that agreements were made with the Germans in certain areas.

The dealings between Borghese and the CLN had become known in the summer of 1944, as Vice Admiral Löwisch wrote that such steps— "also against the Duce and Germany"—resulted in a situation of "indecision and waiting." But Löwisch admitted, "The present government is highly unpopular."[40] Mussolini was also well informed of these contacts. The GNR secret service, always most unfriendly to Borghese, compiled a report for the Duce stating that the "man who came from the sea" had remained for two months at the gamma base at Valdagno, then left with photographs, documents, and every detail relating to the secret weapons of the X MAS.[41]

These doubts were also expressed by the commander of the Decima Division. He wrote to the undersecretary of the navy, who passed the document on to Mussolini:

> The Chief of Staff of the Division, Commander Scarelli, does not hide his sympathy for the Communists. . . . The same officer admits, and it is well known, that he gave up his submarine to the enemy and later took refuge in the RSI Navy to avoid paying gambling debts to British officers in Brindisi.
>
> There are people who suspect that he was *sent* and that after he fled London broadcasted a cover story. . . . And, always speaking of the political-military guidelines, it would be extremely interesting to go in depth in some inquiries relating what happened in Valdagno, where the past summer an envoy of the British secret service remained at the gamma group's barracks, well known to some of the officers there.[42]

In July 1944, the Germans issued orders to disarm the Italian units that proved to be unreliable, sending the men to forced labor. According to the War Diary of the German Marine Command in Italy, "In case of resistance or defection, the sharpest means had to be used." The Decima MAS, however, was an exception. German Vice Admiral Wilhelm Meendsen-Bohlken proposed to "support with every means" the efforts of Prince Borghese "to reorganize the navy, cutting out every unhelpful element."[43]

At one point, almost the entire Decima was fighting in the east, until the Germans asked it to retire to the west. Just as Borghese refused to kowtow to the RSI, so did he fail to ingratiate himself with the Germans at this stage. The German liaison officer with Mussolini deplored the "arrogant attitude of the Prince on the question of the Operation Zones."[44]

Borghese reported on his activities to Mussolini on January 29, 1945, and the next day he was appointed as undersecretary of the navy of the RSI, but he refused the position. Mussolini actually found it difficult to find anyone willing to risk his skin for such a duty. He finally ended up with an officer who transferred from the army.

Borghese, sensing the disintegration of Mussolini's power, the imminent demise of the Germans, the tentative progress of the Allies, and the aggressive dynamism of the Italian and Yugoslav Communist partisans, whom he considered his greatest enemy, preferred to go it alone. By the beginning of 1945, the X MAS numbered 10,267 men, a veritable division of fighters, flying no flag but their own.[45]

CHAPTER 13

Borghese's Rescue by the Allies

Rules of war do not stand up well in the conduct of guerrilla warfare or in the extraordinary defensive measures that have to be adopted to carry out counterinsurgency.

Max Corvo[1]

ALTHOUGH BORGHESE DECLARED MANY TIMES that he tried to avoid fighting other Italians, antipartisan operations were among the main activities of Borghese's units as the war entered its final year. In these actions the Decima MAS displayed a rather ruthless effectiveness and gained a reputation for dirty warfare.[2]

In Piedmont, Borghese arrived at a kind of "live and let live" system with the guerrilla partisans, as he was convinced that his men would lack enthusiasm for fighting fellow countrymen. He also openly criticized Mussolini's efforts to conscript local populations—and the ensuing practice of hunting for deserters—because he thought this only enlarged the ranks of the partisan bands in the hills. Units had to be formed only from volunteers, he said, and as the Italian civil war unfolded he was proved correct.

Other former members of the flotilla displayed the same point of view as Borghese toward the resistance movements, assuming that the true fight had to be continued against the Allies and Communists—especially Tito's ambitious Yugoslavians. The memoirs of Luigi Del Bono, for example, describe his surprise when partisans attacked the train on which he was traveling; it was only then that he discovered for the first time the other (Italian) side of the hill.[3]

The antiguerrilla operations originated at the outset from retaliations that followed killings of X MAS members. The Decima was ruthless in protecting, or avenging, its own. But then following the German request, forwarded by SS General Wolff, to secure the German rear lines of communications, after many other Italian security units had failed to carry out this job successfully. The administrative responsibility fell on Graziani's shoulders as commander of the RSI armed forces, but operations would be carried out under German command, namely the Southwest HQ of Field Marshal Kesselring, who in turn employed the security forces of General Wolff. This chain of command was explained by Borghese at his 1947 trial and was one of the reasons his life was saved.[4]

Wolff asked Borghese to commit his forces more to land operations against the partisans than to sea operations, which had the side effect of lessening the tension between Borghese and some German Navy officers in Italy. By the end of 1944, most of the land units of the X MAS were engaged in antiguerrilla operations.[5] Aside from the operations against Yugoslav partisans, which are considered to have been especially brutal, the operations at Borgo Ticino and the recapture of the self-proclaimed partisan Republic of Val d'Ossola stand out as particular examples of Decima MAS ruthlessness.[6]

The German antiguerrilla operations in Italy were organized on the same basis as others carried out in Western Europe, although the arrival of combat units from the Russian front caused a certain increase in viciousness. In warfare waged against and among civilians, Germans from the east were by now experienced at repression and took a cold look at their task. Kesselring himself was not overly ruthless, but his orders were quite strict and provided cover to those commanders who exceeded the limits of the field regulations on fighting partisans. This resulted, according to Gerhard Schreiber's estimate, in more than 10,000 civilian casualties, not counting the partisans who were considered *franc tireurs*. Both sides shot prisoners after capture, although in many cases important ones were held for exchanges.[7]

The summer of 1944 was the great season of antiguerrilla operations. These operations were carried out because the partisans had become numerous enough to threaten the lines of communication of the German Army in Italy, and also because the Germans needed to clean out the hills near the Po Valley in order to fortify them should their "Gothic Line" in the Apennines break.

By July 20, 1944, the X MAS had some 3,000 men in the Ivrea area, the Lupo battalion in Liguria, with 650 men, and the NP battalion resting in the Palmanova area, with 500. Another 1,500 sailors of the naval units were deployed on the lakes in Lombardia.[8]

On August 18 at Borgo Ticino, during an operation with a German unit, Lieutenant Ongarillo Ungarelli ordered a retaliatory shooting of twelve citizens in the town's central square. Seventy-five houses were also burned and looted in an orgy of revenge. The retaliation was carried out after a partisan attack on a convoy had caused the death of three German soldiers. The German officer, Waldemar Krumhar, wanted four Italians killed for every dead German, and to the twelve designated victims the X MAS added a thirteenth man. A witness confirmed this action of the Decima while testifying before the court on November 11, 1948. This is one action for which Borghese was accused, but he was declared not guilty because responsibility for the retaliation belonged to the German officer on the spot.

On November 1, the same officer ordered the shooting of five young partisans and the arrest of twenty civilians at Castelletto Ticino as a retaliation for the murder of an X MAS sailor. There were originally six condemned men, but one was too young and Ungarelli spared him while ordering the rest to be executed "on their backs as bandits, common criminals, guilty of common crimes." The inhabitants were forced to witness the shootings, which took place one after another.[9]

Toward the end of October 1944, the X MAS took part in the seizure of the Free Republic of Alba, which had been established by the "Mauri" partisans in a northern Italian valley. On this occasion, like others, the X MAS displayed its effectiveness as a cohesive unit while operating among a mixed pool of troops sent to carry out the operation.[10]

At this time, Lieutenant Umberto Bertozzi became infamous for his brutal methods of interrogation in his role as head of the intelligence office of the X MAS. His torturing of captured partisans was so severe that he was put under inquiry "for violent and sadistic acts," in addition to some "shameful accusations of a moral nature."[11]

Research on the activity of the X MAS in Treviso province stresses the personality of this Bertozzi. Though he established a record of cruelty, in some cases he seems to have treated high-ranking partisans well, as in the case of "Nino," or Gaetano Bressan, the commander of the engineer battalion of the Vicenza partisan division. After Nino's capture, Bertozzi acknowledged his status as an officer in the Italian Army.[12]

The bottom line on the guerrilla activities and antipartisan operations is that both sides summarily executed both combatants and noncombatants. The civil war in Italy raged and the casualties from it were wide. It is probable that more Italians died in World War II after September 8, 1943, than before, at least if one discounts casualties from high-altitude Allied bombing.[13] But as the Axis neared its final Gotterdämmerung, those same Anglo-American allies who had been Borghese's nemesis would now prove to be the source be his salvation.

The coming end in Italy did not mean the beginning of peace. Anti-Fascist partisans and politicians settled their quarrels not only with the Fascist armed forces, police, and administrative personnel, but clashes began to surface between the various members of the CLN, which were taking power while an Allied administration was being established. Before the Allies organized themselves, the CLNAI had full power in the north, pending the arrival of Anglo-American troops. At Milan, they only arrived on April 29, but in most of northern Italy and the large cities it was on the 25th, the day of the uprising, and this day became the national holiday of the new Italy.

At the Caserta surrender signed by the Germans on April 29, 1945, the envoys carried the full authority of the Italian republican forces that had been handed over to Wolff by the RSI armed forces commander, Marshall Rodolfo Graziani. In fact, under the terms of the surrender, "German Land Forces" meant "all German and Italian republican military or para-military forces or organizations, under the command and control of the German Commander-in-Chief-Southwest." Other Fascist units were more political than military and their fate was less lucky. The X MAS division was considered directly under the control of the Germans and was thus able to surrender to the Allies. Though some X MAS military units depended on the RSI from an administrative point of view, and although the "Black Prince," as Borghese had come to be known, was among those whom the partisans dearly wanted to execute, he was saved, like Graziani, by the intervention of the Allied and Italian secret services.[14]

As seen, Borghese was on good terms with SS Obergruppenführer Karl Wolff, who had been dismissed as Heinrich Himmler's secretary and relegated to the lesser post of Italy. Nevertheless, he had great power, being in charge of the police and security forces of northern Italy and of the German rear administration. He was then *deux ex machina* of occupied Italy, where Kesselring, and later Heinrich Vietinghoff, were the supreme military commanders. This authority led him to settle arrangements with the German ambassador, Rudolf Rahn, and to look for a separate peace in Italy. Wolff established contacts with the OSS representative in Switzerland, Allen Dulles. Then, after receiving help from the Italian industrialist Luigi Parilli and the Swiss secret service, Wolff declared, "Where the person of Borghese and his Decima Mas is concerned, I have spoken several times . . . with a representative of Mr. Dulles."[15]

According to Borghese's diary, on April 19 he went to visit his gamma group at Valdagno, where he instructed Lieutenant Eugenio

Wolk and his deputy, Lieutenant Luigi Ferraro, to save industrial plants. Then the complete Decima Division was ordered to march to the eastern border with the coming of the German surrender, in order to defend the area from the Yugoslavian advance.[16]

But the end came too early. On April 9, the Allied forces opened their final onslaught toward the Alps, although dealings between the OSS and Wolff continued until Dulles received an instruction to stop the talks. The following day, the HQ of the German OB Süd in Italy at Recoaro was bombed, but Vietinghoff and the other officers saved themselves— ironically, most of the casualties were among the local workers.[17]

With the coming end of the war, the CLNAI called on the partisans and the people to rise. The X MAS battalions were spread at various points and awaited events. Besides the HQ in Milan, others tried to surrender to the Allies so they could be considered regular prisoners of war regardless of the objections of the king's government. Falling into partisan hands would be very dangerous.[18]

The result of 600 days of this civil war was that every dawn hundreds of bodies were found in Milan's streets, killed for being Fascist or for other reasons, since for some people it was the perfect time to settle private vendettas.[19]

Other people who played important roles in the RSI were rescued only with difficulty. Many industrialists fell into Communist hands, with dire results, while others had hedged their bets. Agostino Rocca, the Ansaldo general manager, was taken by a Communist commando; however, during the German occupation Rocca had worked for the German war machine, but at the same time financed the partisans, and only the Communist ones.[20]

So how did Borghese avoid death? According to De Felice: "The Americans were interested in the Decima because they thought to employ the famous *maiali* against the Japanese. And the British also did more: a ship (but perhaps there were two) that transported weapons for the Jews from Yugoslavia to Palestine just after the war was blown up by the X."[21]

The Vatican's secretary of State, Cardinal Giovanni Battista Montini (the future Pope Paul VI), also intervened to help Borghese. On May 6, 1947, he wrote a letter to the Allied authorities on behalf of Princess Daria Borghese, the wife of the Black Prince. Montini was reputed to have been a *listener* during the war, directing an espionage network of the Vatican, certainly one of the most powerful in the world, given the global influence of the Catholic Church and the fact that people made very frank confessions to their priests. This does not mean that the future Pope Paul VI was a Fascist sympathizer: The Holy See pursued a policy that it believed would be better for the world, as well as benefit the church. It is also worth noting that on the eve of Montini's election as Pope, some politicians, such as German Chancellor Konrad Adenauer and Italian President Antonio Segni, approached the cardinals to suggest that Montini would be dangerous because he would probably be open to the Left.[22]

Returning to Borghese, at the end of 1944 the Roman aristocracy asked Vice-Admiral Ellery Stone, the new Allied military governor in Rome, to intervene in favor of the "terrible boy," Junio Valerio, who was then operating in the north. Stone had fallen in love with Baroness Renata Arborio Mella di Sant'Elia, a factor that made their approaches easier. After some days, Stone replied that legal immunity could not be assured but that he could certainly save the Prince's life. According to some authors, the Allied HQ issued instructions to hold Borghese until someone came to pick him up.[23]

On April 13, Borghese saw SS General Wolff, who updated him about the peace feelers then under discussion in Switzerland. After the war, Wolff declared that he had informed Borghese, with whom he had several meetings on Garda Lake, toward the end of February 1945 of his maneuvers with the Anglo-Americans. At the same time, Borghese went on with his discussions with the Socialist partisans Sandro Faini and Gennaro Riccio, who lived in the same palace, at place Princess Clotilde 6, Milan. He was also in contact with Lieutenant Nino Pulejo and Captain Guido Del Giudice of the royal government.

Following these agreements, the X MAS surrendered in the barracks at Fiume Square in Milan with a ceremony, hauling down their flag at 1700 on April 26, 1945, before Riccio and Major Mario Argenton of the CLN. Thereafter Borghese surrendered to Pulejo and Faini and went off with them.[24]

The X MAS surrendered to the Allied troops for two main reasons: first, because it considered them the true enemy and thus the proper party to whom to capitulate; and second, because surrendering to the partisans could mean the loss of many lives. In fact, while most of the surrendered had little problem with the CLN and the partisans, especially in Veneto, in Piedmont things were quite different. The survivors of the X MAS garrison at the Fiat plants, some seventy sailors and auxiliary women, were all summarily shot, and the same occurred to nearly all the units that surrendered to the Yugoslavian partisans.

Generally, however, the X MAS battalions were well armed and had to be treated with some caution. The NP, for example, had weapons heavy enough to temporarily stop an Allied column advancing toward Padua, destroying seven vehicles using Panzerfaust antitank weapons and heavy AA machine guns.

The gamma group at Valdagno waited for the royal southern navy and the Allies before surrendering their equipment. In the meantime, fully armed and dressed, Lieutenant Ferraro helped the local Stella partisans to stem retaliations and attacks on retreating German columns.

Ferraro remembered that the famous Commander Lionel "Buster" Crabb went to Valdagno with a Captain Marzullo of the U.S. Army to ask him to fight alongside the Allies against the Japanese, but he refused.[25] According to a contemporary document in the Vicenza State Archive: "The Royal Italian Navy did not forget the frogmen. On May 26, a little too late, as Germans, the population, and the partisans had in the meanwhile taken away many things, a mission of the navy arrived at Valdagno and recovered some explosive charges and equipment of the gamma group, but not four breathing apparatuses already taken by the Allies."[26]

On April 26, Borghese left his flat in Princess Clotilde plaza for Captain Del Giudice's home in Milan, on Beatrice D'Este Street. He arrived that night in a car. There, guarded by Pulejo of the partisan police, he waited for the navy intelligence officers who were supposedly coming to rescue him. According to his diary, he passed those hours in his friend's house in good spirits. He was visited by Sandro Faini and Corrado Bonfantini of the Matteotti partisan brigades and the Socialist Party. On May 8, he was also visited by Carabinieri Captain Giuseppe Polosa, who said that Carlo Resio and OSS agent James Jesus Angleton were in Milan looking for Borghese to give him a message from Admiral de Courten. On the 9th, Borghese met Resio and Angleton, and they said de Courten had asked for Borghese to report to him in Rome. Borghese feared a trap and was not fully convinced by the message, which was only delivered orally.

The Angletons were not unknown in Italy. James's father, James Hugh, was a former president of the Chamber of Commerce in Milan and of the Milan branch office of the National Cash Register Company. James Jesus Angleton was the chief of the OSS Operations Branch and had worked with Resio extensively, using him as his main contact with the Italian Intelligence Services.[27]

Angleton, according to Nesi, was interested in the defense of important installations, such as ports and bridges, and offered Borghese fair treatment (meaning a trial instead of summary execution) in return for his collaboration. Other services did not agree. One of them was the British counterespionage branch, which approached Angleton the evening before the rescue and told him that they asked of the Germans only two people: Valerio Borghese and the chief of the RSI Intelligence Service, the Carabinieri Colonel Candeloro Di Leo. The British planned to interrogate them and then pass them on to the partisans for immediate execution.[28]

On May 11, Resio and Angleton came to Borghese to anxiously report that the partisans were coming, having discovered Borghese's lair at Riccio's home, where he had been since May 7 or 8. The Prince went with the two intelligence officers and arrived in Rome the day after, but de Courten was not available to receive him. In his memoirs, the admiral seems to have been surprised at Borghese's arrival in Rome, but it is unclear why this would be the case, in view of the joint mission performed by the Italian Navy secret services and the OSS, which could not have happened without orders from the SIS chief and the Navy Ministry.

Borghese was held in a flat on Archimede Street in Rome, and on the 19th he was arrested by the Americans. Borghese and his wife were the only two Italian Fascists of the RSI period who were rescued by the United States. This was done essentially for his knowledge of stay-behind operations and his ability to fight Communists. The British did rescue some others.

His wife had been at Cortina with their sons. On April 22, Borghese sent his driver to rescue his family, and they were brought to Lonato, north of Milan, to the home of the Beretta family on an island in Iseo Lake. They were then rescued by a commission of partisans. One of them, Count Gavazza, was Borghese's cousin. The family was later sent south to Rome, probably in early May.[29]

The record of the Decima MAS between the armistice of September 8, 1943, and the end of World War II is unique in the annals of modern military history. Only a highly independent unit could have gathered a "company of fortune," composed of men following their commander rather than any national or philosophical symbol, in an age of highly organized total war. And in this form—last seen in Europe when warriors rode horseback and wielded swords—the X MAS could react to changing situations with great flexibility, choosing both its enemies and its friends.

Notwithstanding their achievements in battle on the sea and on land, the Black Prince and the Decima MAS fought on the wrong side of history. As Deakin pointed out, "The naval commandos of Prince Borghese had rallied directly to the Germans after the armistice." But he added, "With their high morale and voluntary recruitment [they] might have formed a model for the future regular army."[30]

CHAPTER 14

Cold War Warrior

The development of so significant a radical-right presence (of which terrorism is only a component) for such a long time in a democratic country would not have been possible without the support of elements outside the radical Right proper. . . . And there can be no doubt that for a long time many sectors representing moderate and conservative public opinion have been sympathetic toward the right-wing groups.

Franco Ferraresi[1]

B ORGHESE WAS BROUGHT TO A PRISON IN ROME in the Cinecittà area. Many German and Fascist leaders and commanders were concentrated in this mecca for the Italian movie industry. He arrived there on May 19, 1945, and the following day was instructed to prepare a summary of the wartime actions of the Decima MAS. He was debriefed by British and American intelligence officers, especially about the Vega battalion, which had operated behind the lines.

Indeed, Allied interest focused foremost on the sabotage and espionage operations carried out by X MAS units. As Giorgio Pisanò, a historian of the RSI military, who served for years in the Italian secret service and later became a member of the Italian Parliament (MP) for the right-wing Movimento Sociale Italiano (MSI, Italian Social Movement), said to Claudio Gatti in an interview: "For the Allies we were important because we had infiltrated the Communist bands, we knew their secrets and tactics and therefore developed the first antiguerrilla procedures. I was aware of this when I was briefed by them. They wanted to know how we carried out the anti-Communist war. It was clear that they knew about our experience in the war against the Communists and that they wanted to exploit that knowledge."[2]

Pisanò, a member of the Decima MAS, had twice infiltrated the Allied front in civilian clothes to gather intelligence. He was trained for parachute operations, infiltration from the sea, and intelligence operations by the Abwehr and assigned to Commando Cora under Major Jürgen von Korff. Called "Medio," he was lucky enough to save his skin; some of his friends were captured and shot as spies. After the war, he recorded his experiences.

British intelligence authorities captured Pisanò in April 1945 and wanted him to describe the details of his missions in exchange for treatment as a regular POW. He was nevertheless later held in prison by the Italian authorities as a "spy in support of the Germans," an accusation that could have meant the death sentence, but he was later transferred to Allied-controlled prisons. This kind of protection by the Allies would also save Borghese.[3]

On June 6, Borghese turned thirty-nine years old. According to his diary, British military police tried to make sure he was comfortable in prison. On the 19th, British Field Marshal Harold Alexander visited the prisoners and checked on Borghese—the Prince was probably the most famous prisoner there. Borghese complained that he had not heard news of his family, and Alexander promised to help.

In the meantime, Borghese had finished his sixty-page summary of Decima MAS activity and gave it to an unnamed British captain. The captain told Borghese that he was the same British officer who had interrogated Italian frogmen captured during earlier actions. On July 23, Borghese saw his old friend Karl Wolff, who was also imprisoned in Cinecittà.

In October 1945, the Allies released Borghese. He was found not to be a war criminal. But the Italian justice system wanted him, and therefore he was moved to the isle of Procida. From there, he was to be sent to Milan for trial, but this move was canceled. He then passed some time in the prisons at Procida, Poggioreale, Regina Coeli, and Forte Boccea.[4]

In February 1946, Marshal Graziani arrived at the island of Procida and was imprisoned in the same quarter with Borghese and other high officers, such as General Gastone Gambara, who had served in North Africa with Rommel. Life was miserable, so Graziani asked to be transferred. Graziani wrote, "Borghese could find no rest, he walked around like a caged animal."[5]

A Milan court then put Borghese on trial, prompting a series of legal maneuvers over where the Prince could get the fairest trial. The decision was made only after some delay caused by Borghese's poor health, but his political and family connections helped him.[6] The trial should normally have been held in Milan, since the Decima MAS had operated in the north, but the Court of Cassation had it transferred to Rome.

According to the prosecutor, this change of venue was of great advantage to Borghese. Many witnesses for the prosecution would have to travel to Rome for the trial, an expensive journey under the poor economic conditions of postwar Italy. In addition, the conservative forces of the aristocratic high society in Rome rallied to Borghese's support. He was a son of one of the most important families of the city and had a pope and cardinals in his family tree. The Rome courts were also more conservative than the Milan courts, in part because Rome had been declared an "open city" during the war and thus did not suffer bitter partisan fighting. Moreover, many of the old Fascist bureaucrats had remained in place after the war. Borghese could prepare a careful defense, favored by his financial situation, and would have a better chance of winning his case here than he would have in Milan.

He spent two years in prison, however. Borghese's trial finally began on October 15, 1947, before the Special Section of the Assize Court, which had been established throughout Italy to judge the Fascists who joined the Italian Social Republic and its armed forces. Two charges were brought against Borghese, the first one detailed in four points:

> The first point was to have taken the command of the X MAS and the position of deputy chief of staff of the RSI Navy; second, to have ordered the X MAS to fight at the front alongside the Germans; third, to have ordered or allowed his men to fight the partisans, who were often tortured and killed during the antiguerrilla operations; and this to free the German rear from any threat; and fourth, allowing his men to commit acts of plunder.[7]

The second charge was collaboration with the German enemy in order to help them try to win the war.

After a week, the trial was delayed until December 1 because relatives and friends of victims of X MAS retaliations had submitted further accusations. Additional investigations had to be carried out. In several cases, the charges lacked important data such as the names of the victims. The general prosecutor called the inquiry, but he was unable to find, for the most part, convincing evidence of the crimes. He concluded that there was no clear evidence of the facts and therefore asked that Borghese be declared not guilty concerning the atrocities of the civil war. But the case was not yet closed.

Moreover, the fact that Borghese could not be linked directly to any of the atrocities does not mean they did not occur. During the trial, information surfaced on several incidents in which partisans were shot after capture as *franc tireurs,*[8] and in some cases they were also tortured. One Sergio Murdaca was captured by the Germans near Novara and then apparently tortured, shot by the X MAS, and thrown into a burning house.

Other incidents involved thirty-four partisans of the Matteotti division shot between June and October 1944 in the Canavese area (Piedmont). Another twelve were killed in action and eight more shot after capture at Valmozzola, six were shot at Crocetta del Montello and others tortured, five hostages were killed at Castelletto Ticino, and twelve others were killed at Borgo Ticino. Some of the alleged acts involved female partisans who were raped as well as killed.

It is unclear how much Borghese was involved in the shootings and other brutal acts carried out by units of the Decima MAS. His units performed antiguerrilla operations according to orders issued by the Germans, who had official control over all operations in which the X MAS took part. Therefore, the main crime was that of collaborating with the Germans by helping them to free the rear from guerrilla attacks to their transportation and supply system. Moreover, there was never any doubt that the partisans also engaged in various immoral and illegal acts.

In any case, the details of the deaths were confusing enough to allow the court to declare Borghese not guilty for those crimes. The trial was dragging on, and on January 24, 1948, it was discovered that there was a plot to free Borghese. Several Fascists were arrested for this attempt.[9]

The trial resumed on November 8, 1948. The court still had to judge Borghese on the main charge of having consistently helped the enemy against the Allies and partisans. This charge was proven by the long list of antipartisan operations undertaken by the X MAS.[10]

On February 17, 1949, Borghese was at long last found guilty of collaboration with the German enemy and sentenced to twelve years' imprisonment. He was not convicted for the charges relating to war crimes. When the verdict came down, Ferraresi voiced the frustration of those who had wanted the Black Prince to suffer a stiffer punishment: "The crimes of Borghese's band were too obvious, and the verdict had to be life imprisonment. But the court, through a scandalous application of extenuating circumstances, pardons, and remissions, reduced the sentence."[11] To add to their frustration, Borghese was actually released from prison that same day to return to his estate at Artena, near Rome. The judge, taking into account various factors in his favor, and the fact that he had already spent almost four years in jail, decided he had already served his time.

This provoked an outburst of protest in the press, especially the on the Left. Certainly it was a sentence that could only have been rendered in 1948. Given the passions at the end of April 1945, Borghese probably would have been summarily shot, and in 1946 he still would have been sentenced to life imprisonment. But the factors that helped to ameliorate the judgment were actually the same as those that had saved him in April 1945.[12]

After his release, in an April 1949 letter to a former X MAS member, he claimed that the sentence was worse than he expected. However, be that as it may, he asked his former comrades to work to rebuild the country and to be ready for the day to come when the *Patria* would call upon them again.

During the coming three decades, Italy would be ravaged by acts of civil disobedience and at times by a virtual civil war between the Right and the Left in Italian politics. By no means did the majority of these actions come from the extreme Left. In fact, one work "attributes 83% of the 4,384 officially registered acts of violence between 1969 and 1975 to the extreme right." It was in this atmosphere that Borghese and his right-wing political views would fester.[13]

After being freed from jail, Borghese rather unwillingly entered the political arena as honorary president of the right-wing neo-Fascist party, the MSI, but he retained the chair for only a short time. The party was established shortly after the end of the civil war in Italy, in December 1946. It combined several right-wing movements but mostly the former followers of fascism. Because the party was a mixture of various points of view, and confrontations sometimes led to brawls, Borghese would later resign.[14]

Fascism in the postwar era was different from its prewar variety. Although it had splintered into many different factions, it had two powerful drives. One was that it was anti-Communist. It was this element that made Borghese acceptable to the mainstream parties and national secret services. He was ultimately pro-NATO, as was the rest of this wing of fascism. The other one was the realization that in the postwar environment no single European nation could stand up to the two superpowers, and hence, that *Europe* would be a third force. That is, Europe would be "opposed to the twin imperialism of international communism and international finance capitalism, both of which were perceived as being materialistic, exploitative, dehumanizing." In Italy, it was the Fascist faction that possessed the many international ties that stretched between Franco's Spain, South America, and South Africa. It was from this faction, too, that many of the acts of terrorism of the "Black International" sprung.[15]

American Ambassador James Clement Dunn, in September 1950, noted a conversation he had with a member of Italy's Interior Ministry. He stated that Borghese was reorganizing paramilitary units to be used against the Communist Party, or Partido Comunista Italiano (PCI). Dunn stated that it was his understanding that Borghese would do nothing unless there was someone who *opposed* fascism at the Ministry of Defense.[16]

In some ways, the MSI enabled Borghese's followers to receive mild treatment in the trials that followed the end of the war—trials that in any case touched only a small portion of the people who had been involved with Mussolini's regime. In the political election of 1953, the party scored 1.5 million votes, totaling thirty-eight MPs, and it remained a political factor through the following years. Much later, the Rome election in 1962 saw a big push from the MSI when a strong campaign was made to place one of its candidates as mayor.[17]

With the court cases behind him, Borghese was ready to rebuild his career. Quite simply, he yearned to return to a life of intense activity. As Jeffrey McKenzie Bale noted, "Borghese was a restless individual who chafed at the bit for action and a former military hero whose prestige other political forces sought to utilize for their own ends."[18]

The first indication of Borghese's return to the public sphere was somewhat bizarre. In an attempt to unite the MSI with the Monarchy Party (the king and monarchy had been voted out of existence shortly after the end of the war), Borghese's blue blood was suggested as a reason for him to be the next king. This occurred in 1950 at a meeting between the parties, representatives of the Vatican, and the American Embassy. The supporters of the House of Savoy immediately forced the abandonment of this "quixotic and ridiculous suggestion."[19]

The idea was put aside, but Borghese himself continued to resurface. He was someone who could rally the "patriotic" elements of Italy to the cause of NATO and other principles represented by the MSI. Moreover, those were the same elements that the CIA was trying to mobilize to fight communism, and it held a meeting with Borghese at Artena. There is no proof that James J. Angleton was at that meeting (he denies meeting with Borghese after 1945), but Angleton was assigned to Italy by CIA chief Allen Dulles.[20]

Rumors of this meeting, and that Borghese was going to establish a new right-wing organization, caused concern to the MSI leadership, which feared that the Right would be further diluted. They quickly approached him and persuaded him to come on board. He was acclaimed honorary president of the MSI on December 2, 1951, and went to the July convention of the party. There he argued for the need for a disciplined body to "reestablish the country's spiritual and material order." They could not be "conscientious objectors" in the event that the Cold War became a hot one.[21]

It was at this point, the winter of 1951–1952, that the leadership of the MSI embraced NATO. This was publicly emphasized with a pilgrimage of two top MSI leaders to the Paris headquarters of NATO in December 1951. Others, including Borghese, came out in favor of NATO because it was helping to rearm the Italian military and was resolved to fight communism. Not all were happy with this decision on the MSI's Left, and Ferruccio Ferrini, former RSI undersecretary of the navy, denounced Borghese.

But Borghese remained in the public eye. On May 15, 1952, he helped establish the newspaper *Il Secolo d'Italia*, which was founded in Rome. In 1953, he wrote the foreword to *Gli uomini e le rovine* (Men standing amid the ruins) by the Italian Fascist Julius Evola. Evola was the equivalent of a right-wing Herbert Marcuse, and his book denounced current bourgeois society. He wrote numerous books and articles and was one of the spiritual architects of the Italian Right. Evola actually met Mussolini at Hitler's headquarters shortly after Skorzeny rescued the dictator in 1943. Evola represented the party elements that did not embrace NATO, and this ultimately put Borghese at odds with him and his wing of the party.[22]

Borghese later attempted to deliver public speeches in northern Italy during the 1953 elections. He and former Marshal Rudolfo Graziani, another new MSI member, drew huge crowds. This provoked the authorities to attempt to ban his appearances. In fact, his speaking was forbidden at the Colosseum on May 24, 1953, and also at Rovigo, Bolzano, Udine, and Pescara, and he was actually held in custody by the authorities at Rovigo and Padua.[23]

His activity in the party lasted only a few years because he was unable to adapt himself to the needs of political life—he was more suited to a warrior's role. He was frustrated with the petty infighting and saw politicians as "corrupt and unprincipled." In turn, the leadership of the MSI did not appreciate Borghese's lordly and domineering manner.[24] By late 1954, Borghese had been removed from the directorate of the MSI but remained as its honorary president. He now also became president of the union of former RSI soldiers, as Graziani, who had led it, died on January 11, 1955. But Borghese would eventually leave the MSI in 1957.

Borghese's philosophy during this seven-year period had been all over the board. While a supporter of NATO, he could also embrace Evola's indictment of middle-class life. But as Bale pointed out, "Despite his frequent glorification of the principles of order and authority, the Black Prince was himself a restless, independent, and ambitious man who found it difficult to follow orders and accept advice, especially from those whom he held in contempt." This was the same bourgeois state that had imprisoned him and now had a corrupt and bribable government. But he would continue his contacts with various government representatives. He would also have contacts with "key U.S. intelligence personnel" after leaving the MSI, especially after his 1968 establishment of the Fronte Nazionale.[25]

But before resuming political activity, Borghese and his men are rumored to have performed some of the daring operations for which they had become famous. Two articles appeared, on December 18, 1991, and January 28, 1992, from the Punto Critico agency (directed by a former colleague of the murdered journalist Pecorelli). The articles claimed that Giuseppe Pella and Paolo Emilio Taviani, both future prime ministers, had delivered weapons to the clandestine forces operating under the name Committee for the Defense of Italians of Trieste and Istria. Istria, and especially the city of Trieste, had a large number of Italians, and at the end of the war it was not certain whether Yugoslavia would be allocated all of Istria or all but the Free City of Trieste. Commander Borghese had aided in infiltrating more than 500 "national volunteers" of the MSI with a cry of "To Trieste with Valerio Borghese." Armed by the army, they became actors in the bloody uprising of December 6, 1953, that Great Britain openly charged to Italian clandestine action. Trieste would be returned to Italy in 1954. In many ways, this was an attempt to recall Gabriele D'Annunzio's 1919 coup at Fiume, one of the early warning shots of Mussolini's 1922 March on Rome.[26]

But Borghese may not have been done.

The Italian battleship *Giulio Cesare*, damaged by the British battleship *Warspite* at the battle of Punto Stilo in July 1940, was turned over to the Soviet Union as a war reparation on February 3, 1949, at Valona. Before that, at Venice, Graziani's son, Clemente, was present in the right-wing demonstration against the transfer of this ship. It must be remembered that Fascists had a particularly strong hatred toward the Soviet Union and communism. Further, the surrender of their fleet in 1943 was done in part to keep it Italian and not end up as trophy warships for the Soviet Union. So this was a deeply resented act.[27]

At the time of the transfer, there was some concern, largely in the Italian press, that there were explosives on board. An army engineering unit arrived at Valona, but the men discovered that their detector could not work on a steel warship. Later, Stalin took a personal interest in the ship and every check was made to ensure that the Italians had not hidden explosive charges on the vessel.

Finally, the *Giulio Cesare* was anchored on February 26 at Sevastopol and given the new name *Novorossiysk*. The battleship underwent changes according to Stalin's personal wishes and joined the Soviet Navy in July 1949 as flagship of the Black Sea Fleet. Later this elderly battleship would become a gunnery training ship.

On October 28, 1955, the *Novorossiysk,* returning from gunnery training exercises, anchored at buoy 3 instead of its usual buoy 12. There was a strong wind, and another anchor was dropped. At 0125, a powerful explosion blew open an enormous hole (12 meters) on the bow between the forward gun turrets and the anchors. The bow began to sink, and at 0300, it was underwater. The ship was not abandoned, however, because it was thought to have only 7 meters under the keel. The fleet commander, Vice Admiral V. Parkhomenko, assumed that the ship could be saved.

Around 0410, however, just as the order to abandon ship was finally given, the *Novorossiysk* suddenly capsized and sank. The true depth of the harbor was 40 meters. The battleship sank in the mud, and many died slowly inside. The total losses were 608—the greatest Russian naval disaster in history. The news was published only in 1988, though it was known to specialists in the West at least from the spring of 1956. However, when it appeared in the press, it was not made clear which ship had sunk, or even if it was in the Baltic or the Black Sea. But a connection was immediately made with the dismissal of the conservative Admiral N. G. Kuznetsov in December 1955, who had been removed from the post of first deputy minister of defense of the USSR and commander in chief of the Soviet Navy. Later, in February 1956, he was demoted to the rank of vice admiral and forced to retire. Admiral Sergei G. Gorshkov replaced him.[28]

The loss of the *Novorossiysk* shed light on faulty harbor defenses, antimine operations, damage-control practices, and discipline issues in the Black Sea Fleet. Speculations arose about the possibility that Borghese and the Decima MAS frogmen had been involved in this act of sabotage. An alternative possibility was that old German mines laid down in the mud during the war had exploded (though there is a question of how long the mines could remain "active"). Eventually, articles appeared in the Soviet Union (and then in the West) claiming *both* possibilities. According to René Greger, the explosion of a German mine may have provoked a second explosion inside the ship in the fuel bunkers. Yet Boris Aleksandrovoich Karazhavin's book, *The Secret of the Loss of the Novorossiysk*, published in 1991, holds the mine theory as impossible.[29]

The mystery remains unsolved. On the one hand, according to Greger, the hole on the keel was only 28 square meters against 150 on the deck, and such damage could not be made by mines sunk in the mud. On the other hand, the mines might have exploded because the anchors laid down by the *Novorossiysk* were dragging along the bottom. The fact that there was a strong wind at the time of the disaster supports this view. A recent article by Captain Peter A. Huchthausen, a former U.S. naval attaché in Moscow, makes insightful points on the underground battles between Soviet admirals that partly led to the hurried inquiry and thirty-three years of silence. He concluded that there were two explosions after seeing the official statements of 1955 and interviewing Russian experts.[30]

The explosion was clearly external. Some Soviet and Russian writers have also stated that other old German mines were removed from Sevastopol Harbor after this incident. It is also important to note that the *Novorossiysk* did not anchor at its usual buoy. Huchthausen noted that the "harbor defense boom and antisubmarine netting" that protected the harbor and the *Novorossiysk* were open at the admiral's orders.

Also, the harbor's hydro-acoustic antisubmarine warfare (ASW) listening station—an instrument ideal for detecting an approaching midget submarine—was down for part of the evening.

Virgilio Ilari, in *Il generale col monocolo,* the biography of De Lorenzo, noted that in 1992 the Russian weekly magazine *Sovershenno Secretno* (Top Secret) stated that the *Novorossiysk* had an explosive hidden in the ship's hull before delivery. This would later be activated to destroy the ship.

It is alleged that the Black Prince arrived in the waters of the Black Sea employing a group of midget submarines to attack Sevastopol with two "pigs." A disguised merchant ship—one like the *Olterra* at Gibraltar, for example—could have easily supplied support for such an operation, but by this time the midget submarines had a substantial range of their own. Also, at this time, there was much monitoring of Soviet arms shipments transiting the Black Sea to the Middle East by the NATO countries.

It was alleged in some quarters that the attack was conducted by a group of four famous veterans of the Decima MAS—Elios Toschi, Gino Birindelli, Luigi Ferraro, and Eugenio Wolk—personally led by Borghese. According to this theory, the men secretly approached Sevastopol harbor and either activated the explosives placed on board before the transfer or placed an explosive charge themselves.

Birindelli would go on to become an admiral and later an MP after this incident. Toschi was at the time a consultant and designer at OTO-Melara, a major Italian defense contractor. Although sanctioned neither by NATO nor the Italian government, and impossible to publicly acknowledge, the operation may have aimed to wash away the humiliating surrender of warships imposed by the peace treaty, which all the winners had renounced except for Yugoslavia and the Soviet Union. In support of this theory is the alleged discovery of a mine set to detonate on the Soviet national holiday of November 7, 1955, at the buoy for the light cruiser *Kerch,* the former Italian cruiser *Emmanuel Filiberto Duca de Aosta.*[31]

According to the weekly magazine *Sovershenno Secretno,* the operation was both revenge against the "Reds" and a promotional stunt to show the performance of the midget submarines being produced in Italian yards (but which the Italian Navy, by terms of the peace treaty, were forbidden to own). This Cosmos type ranged from 2 to 70 tons. They had been developed from both the famous SLCs and the CB submarines produced during the war. These small ships had a range of up to 1,400 miles and a crew of four. In the 1960s and 1970s, some sixty Cosmos midget submarines would be sold throughout the world.

Very few Soviet publications in the Cold War era mentioned the *Novorossiysk* incident. *Red Star Rising at Sea* by Sergei G. Gorshkov, for example, never mentions it, even in the short biography given by John G. Hibbits at the end of the English edition of Gorshkov's work. A recent chronology of naval operations during the Cold War also omits the incident.[32]

In a letter to Captain Huchthausen dated August 4, 1999, the son of Eugenio Wolk stated that his dad had referred to "the greatest and most offensive idiocy concerning the sinking of the ex-Italian battleship." The younger Wolk went on to argue that the incident had not even occurred. Certainly, it would be difficult for the Italians to cover up a conspiracy on this large a scale, which makes the theory that they were responsible implausible.[33]

Ultimately, it is impossible to conclusively determine what happened to the *Novorossiysk,* if only because of the long time that has passed since the worst naval tragedy since World War II. Anything is possible: German mines, an explosive charge left hidden before the ship was turned over by the Italians, or a human torpedo attack led by Borghese. We suspect that a German mine was the culprit.

Even so, it has been established that Decima MAS frogmen sank a ship transporting weapons from Yugoslavia to Palestine for the Jews. This was done at the behest of the British government, which was then trying to maintain rule in Palestine.

Also, three Israeli-manned, Italian-manufactured MT explosive boats, part of what was then known as the Israeli Sea Service, attacked the Egyptian sloop *El Amir Farouk,* flagship of a small Egyptian squadron operating off the Sinai coast, on October 22, 1948. Apparently it sank, and a minesweeper may have been damaged as well; however, this attack is also shrouded in enigma. The Egyptian government carried this elderly, 17-knot, 1,441-ton sloop, armed with a 6-pounder and a few machine guns, on its registry as a Coast Guard and Fisheries Administration vessel for two more years. Haifa was "bombarded" on December 31, 1948, and it has been claimed that the *El Amir Farouk* was the attacker. There was also an MT boat used in the Dead Sea by the Israelis, most likely for running agents into Jordan, and it is now a museum ship.[34]

CHAPTER 15

Intrigue on the Far Right

. . . At the end of the 1960s as extremists on both sides collided with the status quo . . . it is hardly surprising that this period of general crisis in the West should have produced some especially shocking results in a country like Italy. During the years that followed, Italy acquired the sorry distinction of having the worst problem with terrorism in the industrialized world.

Richard Drake[1]

OVER THE NEXT TWO DECADES, BORGHESE became involved with several important organizations and individuals. Some of these would later be part of his 1970 coup attempt.

The Gladio was an Italian "stay-behind" (S/B) organization made up of military personnel and civilians. Its purpose was to set up an intelligence and resistance net behind the enemy lines in case of an invasion by the Warsaw Pact. Officially established in 1956 according to the NSC-5412/2 directive, it was part of NATO's overall program of establishing stay-behind resistance groups in nations, including neutral Switzerland, Austria, and Communist Yugoslavia, that had been invaded. Gladio was also used to defend Italy from "domestic Communist subversion." In fact, one of the key debriefs of Borghese, dated

September 23, 1945, and conducted by Major H. T. Shergold, addressed the X MAS S/B groups at the end of the war, but these groups were kept secret from the Italian public during this period.[2]

In Italy, the first Gladio recruits after the war were soldiers, many from the Salò Republic. The existence of the organization was denied by successive Italian governments, including those led by Aldo Moro and Giulio Andreotti. Finally, information about Gladio was revealed publicly in 1990. Andreotti stated that it had 139 arms caches in Italy (however, two were "lost" and ten others had been buried by new construction projects) and that the operation had been shut down in 1972. Interestingly enough, it had been funded by the CIA, the Italian intelligence agency Servizio Informazioni Forze Armate (SIFAR, Armed Forces Intelligence Service, formerly SIM) had collaborated with it, and its operatives received training from the British Intelligence Service. Its ranks were clearly made up of right-wing Italian "patriots."[3]

Gladio was controlled directly by the intelligence service and participated in NATO meetings that brought together chiefs of such organizations from various NATO countries. In recent times, Gladio has been mentioned frequently in the international press, and the Italian press is no exception. The stories tend to emphasize sinister themes and "interpret everything through Gladio"—that is, they attribute every bombing and other violent incident to the existence of the organization.[4]

By the 1970s, Gladio had only about 200 members, from the northeastern border to Bologna. Most of them were in their forties, though some were younger, and many were around fifty. The organization was composed of five sections: information and propaganda, guerrilla, sabotage, escape, and relief. Guerrilla actions were the duty of the Unità di pronto impiego (UPI, or Ready Deployment Units). Some of these men would participate in Borghese's coup attempt.[5]

There was also a parallel security organization, Organizzazione di Sicurezza (OS, Security Organization), that was divided into units called "Legions." These included the Carabinieri units. Legions were identified by numbers that were designated according to military region. For example, the one in Verona under Lieutenant Colonel Amos Spiazzi was the 5th. Thus, in the complex Cold War scenario, Gladio was the main stay-behind organization but not by any means the only one.[6]

Gladio had a secret base at Alghero near Cape Marragiu on Sardinia's west coast. Alghero was thus positioned to be of use for future Italian coup attempts as a site for processing and depositing prisoners. The base was partly staffed by U.S. military and secret service personnel and would probably have been defended by the United States in the event of war between NATO and the Warsaw Pact.[7]

The Decima MAS was also associated in the press with the "stay-behind" assets in NATO countries. The same term had also been used for an organization that the X MAS established in February 1945 for territories occupied by the advancing Allies in Italy. But these men were discovered by the OSS and neutralized. The fact remains that some specialists of the gamma group of the X MAS operated in the Agno valley, near Kesselring's HQ at Recoaro Terme north of Vicenza (where there is still an important U.S. airbase), in 1943–1945. Some of those captured were sent to the United States for interrogation or simply so the U.S. officials could draw on their experience, a fact that caused some journalists to believe that the X MAS was used by the CIA for covert operations in Italy.[8]

Another connection between the Decima MAS and Gladio was made by Peter Tompkins, a former OSS agent in Italy, who delivered a speech at a commemorative meeting held in 1994 in Venice. He said that inside the OSS there were those who "with one hand sent out democratic agents and with the other saved the *X MAS* with Valerio Borghese, to be set up with their *Gladio* to carry out the anti-Communist war."[9]

Most of the evidence on this point is circumstantial or speculative. Over the past fifty years, the story of the Cold War in Italy has been confused by journalistic reports colored by political views and written by people who can only guess at the behind-the-scenes activities. Added to this are political speculations that only make the fog of the Cold War thicker than that of the world wars.

General Gerardo Serravalle, who took over Gladio in 1971, was so disturbed by the right-wing extremism of many of his men, who wanted to crush the Italian Communist and Socialist parties *now*, that he shut down the arms caches and had them transferred to the secret base at Alghero. A plane that he was scheduled to be on for the Servizio Informazioni Difesa (SID, Defense Intelligence Service) exploded in flight on November 23, 1973, near Venice. He had canceled his plans and was not on the plane, but four crew members died. Serravalle suspected that his own men, angry at his decision, may have tried to kill him.[10]

Another part of this story involves Licio Gelli.

Gelli was born in Pistoia, Tuscany, in 1919. At eighteen he volunteered in the Spanish Civil War for Mussolini. He next shows up in Montenegro, where he was working, very probably in intelligence, for the Fascist office at Cattaro on the Adriatic coast. After the armistice, he worked, it seems, for both sides, and certainly at the end of the war he compiled the list of Fascists in the area for the winners. In 1948, he became the secretary of a Christian-Democrat MP. Later, he had a career as manager of Permaflex, a mattress company. From 1963, he entered Masonry, and in 1971 he was appointed secretary of Propaganda Lodge 2 (P2).

The lodge was disbanded because of an internal struggle among the Masonic Lodges, but it was again formed in 1976 by Gelli himself and became a powerful organization made up of some of the most influential people in the country. Gelli declared in a TV interview that he wanted to gather the best in every field to carry out his "plans of democratic rebirth." Interestingly enough, one of the first members was General Giovanni Allavena, of plan "Solo" fame (discussed below), who probably handed over to Gelli a good part of the secret files opened by General Giovanni De Lorenzo, which he could have used to blackmail people. A case of possible blackmail was described in an in-quiry that the D office of SID (the combined CIA/FBI of Italy at the time of the coup attempt) made into Gelli, as a ranking officer had a $10,000 debt to him.

Gelli was almost unknown to the public at the time but was already playing a vital role in Italian affairs. When the journalist Carmine Pecorelli, who often wrote on behalf of SID operatives, was murdered in 1979, papers from the D office of the SID were found in his office—among them some documents on Gelli and information on Borghese's 1970 coup attempt. One was a list of people whom Gelli had reported to the Sardinian counterintelligence center of SID as German collabo-rators during the occupation period 1943–1945; the other was an in-telligence note on Gelli himself, who was suspected of working for the Warsaw Pact secret services.[11]

When Gelli was discovered to be the brains of the P2 Masonic Lodge, he made front-page news in Italy. His was a secret group inside the regular Masonic Lodge. It grew to number hundreds of mem-bers—some reports say it had 2,500. Its political aims were hindering Italy's shift to the Left and, possibly, abandoning NATO. There are sev-eral Masonic groups in Italy, and the one Gelli and P2 were associated with was the Grande Orient, a secret lodge. Many on the list denied their association with the lodge, but it is known that many of the members, some from its earliest days, were from the security services of the government and political figures in Italian politics.[12]

Licio Gelli was a political "Mr. Fix-It" in Italian political circles. The P2 lodge's secrecy within the Freemasonry world abetted its signifi-cance in that its members were secret members in a secret organiza-tion. The advantage was that a Brother could receive assistance from the P2 membership for either financial or other reasons, and Gelli would expect something in return for his help. His contacts extended beyond the borders of Italy, and he had friends in the United States, mostly members of the Republican Party's right wing. Gelli was later to attend President Ronald Reagan's first inauguration.[13]

Gelli worked with the banker Michele Sindona, certainly for various reasons, but one was that Sindona was a strong anti-Communist. He also abhorred socialism and was a staunch believer in capitalism—it was through connections and hard work in the latter system that he had built his financial empire. Sindona would be known as the "Banker to God," as he would have strong financial ties with the Vatican.

So with Gelli we have a man who has a list of files that contained both true and untrue information about various individuals, some very high up in the government, that could be used to "help" them reach a decision favorable to his interests. This is somewhat reminiscent of the infamous J. Edgar Hoover files maintained in the United States by the former head of the FBI.

On March 17, 1981, as Gelli's web was becoming unraveled, agents of the Finance Guard entered his Villa Wanda at Arezzo (Tuscany) and found a list of 962 names of members of the P2. This discovery ignited a huge scandal on the political scene. His list included three cabinet ministers, forty-three MPs, the head of each branch of the military, key members of the various intelligence services, and senior business leaders in banking, the media (both publishing and broadcasting), and corporations.[14]

In September 1982, he was arrested in Switzerland (where he had a bank account worth hundreds of millions), but in August 1983 he escaped, barely ten days before his extradition to Italy. In September 1987, he reappeared in Switzerland and reported to the authorities, then was sentenced because he had entered Switzerland illegally. He was transferred the following February to Italy, then freed in April by the government led by Andreotti.[15] He was later sentenced to prison for various reasons, but at the end, after appeals, he was always found not guilty. Beyond these incidents, Gelli's organization is believed to have continued its activity in other forms.

American aid to the Italian Right also took several forms. Assistance to the anti-Communists was mainly in the form of money given monthly in *lire* to the Democrazia Cristiana (DC, Christian-Democrats) and other parties of the government, especially before elections. In some cases, the United States granted wheat to the Italian government, and the Christian-Democrats sold it to acquire the money. President Gerald Ford asked for $6 million in additional secret funds to be supplied to friendly political parties on the eve of the Italian 1975 election. A total of $10 million was spent by the U.S. government to influence the 1972 Italian election, making a total of $75 million after 1948. A $10 million spigot was turned on just for 1970—at the time of the Borghese coup. Meanwhile, of course, the Soviet Union had been bankrolling the Italian Communist Party for years.[16]

So we now arrive at the De Lorenzo–Segni "Solo" plan, which can be viewed as a forerunner to the Borghese coup. This was a counterinsurgency plot against the Left initiated by Antonio Segni, president of the Italian republic, who enlisted the help of General Giovanni De Lorenzo, commander of the Carabinieri and later head of SIFAR (though he retained some control over the Carabinieri, as he managed the budgets of both, and had men in the highest places of the Carabinieri).

The facts are that several meetings occurred during the spring of 1964 among some Carabinieri officers who were completely loyal to De Lorenzo. Other (including commanding) officers were not informed of the meetings, and those who attended came in civilian dress. Supporting the Carabinieri were politically sanitized civilians largely made up of former Decima MAS, paratroopers, and soldiers and sailors of the RSI. Interestingly, the man used to recruit some of these outside resources, Carabinieri Colonel Renzo Rocca, later lost his appointment to SIFAR's Economic Office and would be found dead with a bullet in his brain, though it was determined he had not fired the shot. The case was never solved.[17]

De Lorenzo and others attending the meetings, concerned that the government was opening to the Left, planned a coup to prevent that from happening. In fact, the Socialist Party would soon be allowed to enter the government and would even appoint a Socialist president. The Carabinieri wanted to seize control.[18]

At this point, Borghese comes into the story. According to Remo Orlandini (heir to the Orlando shipbuilding empire and one of Borghese's top men in the 1970 coup), "Borghese was De Lorenzo's friend," and he was to aid in the coup. Appropriate orders to the Carabinieri were issued. However, at the appointed time, nothing happened—for reasons that are still unclear, the coup was canceled. The next morning an angry Borghese met De Lorenzo, who was going to meet the new Socialist president. Borghese is alleged to have asked why De Lorenzo was in his dress uniform and not in battle dress.[19]

The Solo plan represented, however, a serious threat against the Left and especially the Socialist Party, which had been reluctant to accept the terms of the Christian-Democrats in the postwar government. An unnamed CIA official interviewed by Claudio Gatti commented: "It was somewhat like what happened later, in 1970, to Prince Valerio Borghese: at the last moment someone abandoned him or sold him down the river. With the difference that the Borghese coup was an act of buffoonery, the De Lorenzo one was a serious thing."[20]

De Lorenzo was meanwhile promoted to chief of staff of the Italian Army by the Christian-Democrats with the Italian Communist Party's consent. (It should be noted that he enjoyed some support from the PCI because of his role as a partisan in 1944–1945.) This was, according to Orlandini, the first aborted coup of the Italian story.

De Lorenzo would shortly be relieved of this post, in part for having created some 157,000 dossiers on political personalities and devising a counterinsurgency plan. He had also come up with a list of 731 people to be interned on Sardinia in the event that a coup succeeded. It was especially this last item that was the target of criticism from the press and political parties. He kept his post as chief of staff of the Italian Army only from February 1, 1966, until April 15, 1967.

At the beginning of 1967, an inquiry into SIFAR was established. According to the Beolchini Commission (named after commission president General Aldo Beolchini), no order to compile files had been issued (the commission probably simply did not find the order). In fact, the commission determined, it was not illegal to open files on people suspected of activity with foreign countries who could pose a threat to national security, but it was a crime to use such files as a means of pressure or blackmail. The number of files was not extraordinary. In East Germany at the height of internal security measures, the Stasi kept some 6 million files on a population of 17 million.[21]

However, De Lorenzo was fired, according to Moro, partly because he had backed the wrong Defense Ministry and political leader— Moro and not Andreotti. According to Ilari, De Lorenzo had also opposed some weapons transactions involving American M-60 tanks that were sold to Italy in those years.[22] This put him in conflict with influential leaders and was likely the main reason for his removal from power.

The U.S. point of view on the matter was, as always, that anybody who hindered the Communist PCI from coming to power deserved to be helped. But a right-wing coup would not have been in the U.S. interest in the long run. As a result of the De Lorenzo menace, Italy had formed a government that included the Socialist Party but excluded its left wing.[23]

This era of American-Italian relations was brought to an end in 1969 when Nixon became president. The policy of his national security adviser, Henry Kissinger, was against allowing the Socialist Party in the government. In his view, it was a Trojan horse bringing along the Communists. Kissinger's view of the Christian-Democrats was hardly more benign. According to Claudio Gatti, "Kissinger . . . was convinced that the Christian-Democrats would have made an agreement with hell to retain power."[24]

Nixon's policy was to reopen financial support to anti-Communist forces—which had almost closed in 1966—probably through Michele Sindona. And this money train was apparently along two separate lines, the other one being U.S. Ambassador Graham Martin and his main Italian contact, General Vito Miceli at the head of SID (appointed in October 1970). This money train delivered financial support not only to the Christian-Democrats but also to another small, pro-American party and to the MSI. Miceli would later meet with Borghese at Orlandini's home on several occasions before he became head of SID.[25]

Sindona was said to have saved the Vatican's financial situation when Pope Paul VI came to power. He was born in Patti, in Sicily, and became the primary owner of Franklin National, Continental Bank of Illinois, and other U.S. banks.[26] This banking conduit was probably used to funnel money to anti-Communist parties and military leaders in Italy. It has been established that in April 1967 the Continental Bank of Illinois transferred $4 million to one of Sindona's banks in Italy. The money was then "lent" to a Greek construction firm run by the Greek Army and controlled by Colonel George Papadopoulos.

On April 21, 1967, Papadopoulos would lead the Greek "Colonels' Coup," in which army colonels took power by force and established a military regime. Sindona is said to have planned his own Italian coup in 1972. According to one source, there was a meeting near Vicenza with Sindona and an American general about the possibility of carrying out a coup, and if the left wing reacted, American and French military forces would supposedly intervene, along with Italian civil-military units such as Gladio, to counter them. Interestingly enough, if the coup succeeded, repressive measures against the extreme wings of the Left *and* the Right would be imposed.

The Pope has a role to play in this story as well. Pope Paul VI had been a friend of Borghese's wife since the Fascist period, when he was Giovanni Battista Montini. He also knew Monsignor, later Cardinal, Francis Spellman in the late 1920s. In 1932, he joined the personal staff of the Pope's secretary of state, Cardinal Eugenio Pacelli—the future Pope Pius XII. The State Department of the church was the diplomatic arm of the Vatican, and in it were ten plus centuries of records.

Pope Paul VI's biographer has written that "Giovanni Battista Montini became the central figure of melodramatic tales and legends during the war years. He was rumored to be the chief of an espionage network, the key figure in underground organizations, and the master of Vatican Intelligence. He neither admitted nor denied anything that was said of him." In the State Department, his work included the establishment of the Information Bureau to help deliver names and information about POWs and casualties to families. In this process, information was brought to Montini's attention. It was joked that he commanded "a white Gestapo." One of his unofficial titles was "secretary of the cipher." The Vatican at the end of the war helped relocate right-wing soldiers and officials to safer nations such as Catholic Spain and Argentina, but Montini also helped to monitor the activities of some of the other, more pro-Fascist cardinals. When he became Pope Paul VI, the man who crowned him was Cardinal Alfredo Ottaviani. Ottaviani was "long regarded as on the far right of the Church . . . an arch-reactionary."[27]

Montini and Sindona would become acquainted in the 1950s when Sindona assisted Montini, now archbishop of Milan, in celebrating mass at factory sites over the opposition of PCI labor leaders. Sindona helped in this by persuading some of his clients, who owned some of these industries, to allow Montini on the premises. Some of these same labor leaders would be voted out of their positions as a result, and a bomb attempt would be launched against Montini himself.[28] So Sindona was one of the channels, perhaps one of the most important, used to back up the "coup" threats in the period 1970–1974.

Following the fall of Nixon, Sindona's bank collapsed and he immediately went to trial in the United States. He was later extradited by the Italians and died as soon as he reached an Italian high-security jail. His file in the hands of the Italian secret service was burned when his financial empire collapsed.

Sindona was also one of the main members of the P2 lodge, along with Gelli and Roberto Calvi, the director of Banco Ambrosiano. Calvi laundered hundreds of millions of dollars of dirty money for the Mafia in the United States through the financial operations of the Banco Ambrosiano and the Vatican bank Instituto Opere Religiose

(IOR, Religious Works Institute). He would also be found as a "suicide" victim, hanging from a popular bridge in London.[29]

Most of the books written on this period of the Cold War stress the part played by the military intelligence services but pay little attention to the other security agencies operating against terrorism or subversion. These include, for example, the Ufficio Affari Riservati (UAR, Office for Reserved [Confidential] Affairs of the Interior Ministry), a civilian intelligence service, and the intelligence assets of the Carabinieri, the Finance Guard, and the political police. The UAR was headed from 1968 to 1974 by Federico Umberto D'Amato, who seems never to have encountered the problems faced by his military colleagues, many of whom either mysteriously committed suicide or were fired.

This focus is not easily explained. It is true that SIFAR and SID both held enormous power. They had responsibility for a large spectrum of duties in both domestic and international affairs. This included economic matters (for example, the export of technology or control of the weapons trade). But it is quite unclear why the attention of journalists, judges, policemen, and writers have focused on the military services and their NATO connection.

The problem is that copies of documents from the military services' files apparently found their way to the CIA archives or Licio Gelli's Montevideo home. These files were gathered not just on suspected individuals but on all the members of the Italian Parliament, the clerks, and various businesspeople. Moreover, they include materials on the sexual interests of these individuals (with photos!).

In addition, SID and SIFAR have both faced controversies. For SIFAR, the death of Colonel Rocca was quite suspicious. Another SIFAR agent was found dead in a strange road accident in April 1969. An inquiry into the incident was initiated by General Carlo Ciglieri, a former commander of the Carabinieri.[30]

On December 12, 1969, a powerful bomb exploded inside the Banca dell'Agricoltura (Agriculture Bank) in Milan's Piazza Fontana, killing sixteen and wounding eighty-seven. On the same day, other bombs exploded in other banks, but they were closed and there were no reported deaths. At first, the police thought the bombs were planted by the Red Brigade, but months later, authorities began to realize that they would have to look for the terrorists in right-wing circles—in what would become known as the Black Terrorist International.[31]

SID agents were then accused of protecting the terrorists or helping them to escape abroad. Some suspected terrorists remained in foreign countries, such as Dario Zagolin, who worked for NATO intelligence services.

In October 1970, General Vito Miceli replaced Admiral Eugenio Henke as chief of the SID. It is while he was in office, with General Gianadelio Maletti as his main collaborator in domestic affairs, that the Borghese coup took place. Miceli and Maletti fought turf battles in the SID, but Miceli was an important figure for the U.S. Embassy in Italy (although not for the CIA). Through him, money was given to center and right parties, including the MSI.

Borghese had come out of semi-retirement around the time his wife, Princess Daria Olsoufieff, died in a car accident. The accident had occurred on February 4, 1963. For financial reasons, Borghese became president of the Banca di Credito Commerciale e Industriale. It had been owned by Sindona, and in fact had been his first bank. The largely ceremonial post gave the Prince a handsome salary and also kept him involved in unfolding political events. Borghese's postwar career mirrors that of the German SS commando leader Otto Skorzeny. "Scarface" (a name given to him because of his dueling scars) had escaped to Spain after World War II, and in the early 1950s, with the help of Hitler's former financial adviser Hjalmar Schacht, established an engineering firm. This firm would allow Skorzeny to represent such firms as Krupp and Messerschmidt-Werke in Spain and provide him a comfortable living. He went on to have dealings with Argentinian dictator Juan Peron and Egypt's Gamul Abdul Nassar.[32]

Jeffrey McKenzie Bale noted that Borghese's bank "became involved in an extremely complicated financial operation involving a 'vast sector' of conservative economic interests, including [the son of the Dominican Republic's dictator Trujillo, Franco's Spain], Vatican and DC circles." This venture ended with the bank's collapse. Borghese and his partners were charged with financial misdealing, but Borghese got off with a light sentence. What is significant is that Borghese clearly had many contacts on a national as well as an international scale. These connections extended to very high levels. It also appears that the financial wherewithal that he needed to survive may have come from such sources after the end of the war. One must wonder how many "strings" came with all of these financial dealings. For now it remains an unanswered question.[33]

Borghese was next involved in a crisis that arose between Austria and Italy over German-speaking inhabitants of northern Italy in the Alto Adige region of the Alps. German nationalists attacked representatives and symbols (such as post office drop boxes), and the Italian Right responded, in January 1966, by forming the Comitato Tricolore per la Italianita dell' Alto Adige (Tricolor Committee for the Italianity of Upper Adige [South Tirol]). One of the leaders was Borghese, and he spoke in public at one of the rallies organized by the Comitato Tricolore.[34]

Most likely, it was as a result of this experience that Borghese in 1967 began to consider forming a new right-wing group that would appeal to veterans, patriots, and the young. He wanted the organization to offer an alternative to communism.

The entire West was now shaken by the 1968 students' revolts, which were followed in many countries by workers' demonstrations. Political violence began to surface, which was something to which Italy was now somewhat accustomed. In 1968, Borghese resumed newspaper writing. His articles appeared in the pages of *Ordine nuovo* (ON, or New Order), a right-wing publication. He called on people to reject the democratic system and leave their ballots blank at election time.

The organization behind *Ordine nuovo* was one of several that split off from the MSI to wage a more radical political struggle against the Christian-Democratic way of life. Some of these right-wing groups employed Nazi symbols. One of the key early ON members was Clemente Graziani.

Another group was Avanguardia Nazionale (AN, or National Advanced Guard), which was close to Borghese from the outset. One of its prominent members was the notorious Stefano Delle Chiaie, consistently suspected to be a UAR agent, and a friend of Borghese's from at least the mid-1960s. Indeed, AN itself was suspected of being the creation of UAR. In any case, the movement was infiltrated by government agents. Both AN and ON were organized on two echelons: public and secret, and the latter was prepared to fight, violently, if necessary.[35]

Both enjoyed links with the armed forces, the police, and the secret services. It is difficult to say if the neo-Fascists had penetrated the secret services. Certainly there were anti-Communists inside all these organizations. But all the state security personnel had to obey orders from the government, although it is possible and probable that parallel chains of command existed, formed from men loyal to one political circle or another. The more powerful the group, the better the position of its members within the service. This allowed them to be protected from above and perhaps even from powerful agencies from *outside* the country.

On September 11, 1968, Borghese founded another right-wing movement, the Fronte Nazionale (FN, or National Front). As Borghese explained to journalist Giampaolo Pansa, the FN was not a party, and one could be a member of a party and of the FN as well, but in any case, such a member would need to follow the directives of the Borghese movement. In this way, the FN could operate in every party and organization to the common aim of the rebirth of the state according to Borghese's vision. It probably numbered almost 3,000 members at its height.

As small as it was, the FN lost some of its more moderate members in November 1969 at a meeting that led to a brief fight over tactics. One of the moderates, ex–Decima MAS member Armando Calzolari, objected to bombings designed to enrage the PCI, since they would only cause the Left to retaliate, thus forcing the Italian military to intervene and take over the country. He walked out of the meeting threatening to expose the proceedings. On Christmas morning of 1969, he went out to walk his dog and disappeared. Later, on January 28, 1970, his body was discovered in a small pond 2 miles from his home. His dog's body was nearby. It was declared an accidental death. It was not until 1976, after his mother forced the case to be reopened, that it was declared a premeditated murder.[36]

From the start, SID intelligence thought the only goal of this new Borghese organization was to bring about a takeover of the Italian government. To quote the report, it was created to "subvert the institutions of the state by means of a coup."[37]

CHAPTER 16

Madonna's Night:
Borghese's Coup Attempt

There are, however, other indications that Borghese and some of his key associates were in contact with American intelligence officials in the months leading up to the coup.

Jeffrey McKenzie Bale[1]

BASED ON OUR RESEARCH, WE THINK THE following was the reason for the Borghese coup. There was a fear in much, but not all, of the rightist ruling party in Italy, dominated by the Democrazia Cristiana (DC, Christian-Democrats) but dependent on coalition members, of allowing the powerful Partido Comunista Italiano (PCI, Italian Communist Party) into the government as part of a ruling coalition. The DC and PCI both received a little over 30 percent of the vote every election, and the PCI share had been for the most part growing over the years up to and beyond 1970.

The Italian armed forces (both military and police) supported the DC, with elements of the armed forces further to the right. The armed forces were anti-Communist and anti-PCI.

Powerful elements outside of Italy and extending to Washington, D.C., also feared the presence of the PCI in the ruling coalition. The "Solo" coup attempt had been over allowing the Socialists in, a party often viewed as "Communist lite" both inside of Italy and outside of Italy in Western circles.

By allowing the Borghese coup attempt to move forward, the ruling party delivered a warning to the PCI and leftist circles that we, the ruling party, can do this. By stopping it literally in the middle of the night, the party showed the mailed fist but did not unleash it. If the coup had been allowed to move forward, it most likely would have been crushed unless support for it emerged from elements of the Italian armed forces. We do not, though it is possible, see this simply as a Fascist plot (like the 1922 March on Rome by Mussolini) or a "generals plot" like the Colonels' Coup in Greece a few years earlier. Borghese, who saw his chance to lead Italy—always the anti-Communist—was likely a pawn on this chessboard of the world stage, and he could be expected to follow orders.

Ultimately, he would follow orders.

What follows is the story of the coup attempt that was denied by some as even having occurred. It is still wrapped in mystery. Below is the part of the story we know.

—

The philosophical goal of Borghese's Fronte Nazionale was nominally to build an honest state that was "beyond the center, right, and left." It was patriotic in a national sense, but it also called for a united Europe that would stand between the Soviet Communist empire and America's capitalist hegemony.

Borghese, known in the organization as the "Commander," established his main headquarters in Rome and then formed "action groups" throughout Italy headed by delegates who displayed qualities of leadership. These action groups were designed to respond to Borghese's Rome headquarters. In this party structure, there were two components. The "A" group was the public face of the FN. But each "A" group had a "B" group that was secret and known only to FN leaders.

Many members of the "A" group had joined for philosophical or patriotic reasons and were unaware of the subversive underside of the FN. Stefano Delle Chiaie would be made the head of the "B" groups on June 1, 1970. SID intelligence would later conclude that planning for the coup began to move ahead in July.[2]

Training of as many as 300 operatives went on during the spring and summer of 1970 at Palermo and Naples and in the central section of the Apennine Mountains. The Italian Army not only gave authorization for this training but also some logistical support. Again we see an example of the conservative military concerned about the Warsaw Pact and the Communist PCI and thus willing to train and prepare a nontraditional force. The easy cover of the Gladio stay-behind organization served to shield this training.[3]

Borghese also had the FN cooperate with other right-wing organizations, mirroring what he had done in 1944–1945 when he tried to work with the "white" partisans operating in northern Italy. This would allow him to employ more men, not just members of FN, in the coup attempt.

Although the FN had some of the trappings and ceremonies of the Fascist period, in part to appeal to older, ex-RSI members, Borghese knew that there was no returning to that past. He thought it was "pure folly" to try to rebuild Mussolini's party. But the situation now argued for a party that dominated Italy with a strong executive—who would be Borghese.[4]

Borghese argued against the distaste the Italian military was held in by much of the public and the diminished view of Italy as a nation. In 1970, he would say that it was "no longer possible to remain passive spectators of the ideological, social, and political 'stoning' of the Italian fatherland."[5] He also stated, in an interview three days before the coup, that he was hoping to establish something along the lines of Charles de Gaulle's government in France, and he professed to disdain the Greek Colonels' coup. Yet a coup is exactly what he attempted on December 7, 1970.

Borghese was moving ahead to intervene in the Italian political struggle. He started by trying on August 8 to attend a conference at

Reggio Calabria (he had made an earlier visit there on October 25, 1969). Reggio Calabria had been in disorder and a state of partial revolt because its rival city of Catanzaro had been made the provincial capital. This had only been the fuse that lit the powder of poverty and the strong MSI presence in the region. Fighting would not only be against the police, but against army units as well, and would last into 1971.

But when Borghese was forbidden to speak at a rally (as during his 1969 visit), a day of urban guerrilla activity and general disorder erupted. At the same time, organized crime in Calabria *(Ndrangheta)* was in contact with right-wing organizations such as Avanguardia Nazionale, asking for help for the popular Reggio revolt. Later, the Ndrangheta was asked to help arrest people during the "night of the Madonna"—another name for Borghese's coup attempt (since December 8 is Madonna's Day in Austria, Italy, and Spain).

This unrest, Borghese thought, might indicate a time for him to strike. Just a quick, forceful coup might be enough to bring the rotten Italian state down by forcing the military to intervene and take over the government. Borghese thought that the situation of 1922, when Mussolini marched on Rome, was available to him in 1970.

Several witnesses would argue how deeply Borghese's movement was or was not involved in the coup over the following years, but recently more information has surfaced with the fall of communism and the Berlin Wall. Several contacts took place between Borghese, whose heroic charisma was intact, and armed forces officers, plus old comrades who had fought with him. Such contacts also involved other organizations and circles and were aimed at strengthening the state in view of a dangerous opening to the left—at this point the left-wing of the Christian-Democrats were willing to work with the PCI in a new government.

Borghese began to contact army officers and old comrades in order to know "how they would think" about the imposition of military rule. This would be a change in internal politics to avoid a turn of the country toward the Left and the danger of drifting to the eastern side of the Iron Curtain.

It came to light in 1976 that many members of the FN, ON, and AN had been trained in disinformation and guerrilla warfare at the special camp at Alghero in Sardinia. At the time, the information made little sense, since the general public did not know about the existence of Alghero. It was only later that the significance of the base was understood.

One of Borghese's friends, who was sometimes linked to the coup attempt, was General Diulio Fanali, who had been a wartime fighter pilot for Mussolini and was now a member of the Christian-Democrats. The American Air Force had pushed his career over the years, in part because of his virulent anti-communism. At the time, he was the chief of staff of the Italian Air Force. Later, the MSI wanted to run him in 1972 as a parliamentary candidate. He would later fall in the mid-1970s for being involved in the Lockheed bribery scandal over the purchase of new aircraft, a scandal that reached far up and deep into the Christian-Democrat government. Also implicated for giving some limited support to Borghese's efforts were other members of the military, including those who belonged to the P2 Freemasonry lodge.[6]

It is still difficult to assess the events of the past fifty years, and the Borghese coup attempt is no exception. Sources vary in their estimation of events and the situation, and assessments are often written inside an ideological and political battle. Several books tend to "guess" what existed behind the curtain of lies that protected for so many years the authors of so many acts of political atrocity. Frequently, poor knowledge of the complex military organizations led easily to wrong assessments. To give an example, Sergio Flamigni quoted the discovery of the "Field Manual" in Gelli's daughter's suitcase without knowing that there are *hundreds* of Field Manuals. Another example in an otherwise excellent book has the 3rd Army Corps HQ being mistaken for the 3rd Army HQ, which are quite different in location and area of responsibility.[7]

Therefore we are bound to quote as much as possible from official documents produced by Italian authorities, whenever possible, or from personal memoirs, with the obvious caution that, again, there could be a "bodyguard of lies" in this "game of mirrors." Moreover, certain secondary sources appearing both in Italy and the United States have been of help. While in Italy books published in the United States are of great interest, an important work such as Philip Willan's *Puppetmasters* was not translated into Italian and is generally ignored.[8]

Of course, the part played in this changing game by several of the players remains somewhat in the shadows, and there are many gaps in this story of the Cold War in Italy. We have virtually nothing on the KGB or Warsaw Pact secret service operations in Italy, on the French secret services, which were certainly quite active in Italy; of the British MI6 and German BND; or of the Mossad and PLO turf battles on Italian soil. The fact that no study explains the part played by these nations severely restrains our angle of view and therefore our analysis. We know, for example, that, according to the Italian civilian secret service (the Servizio Informazioni Sicurezza Democratica, SISDE), the PCI feared at the beginning of the 1980s the types of operations carried out by Cuban and Czechoslovak intelligence. Moreover, the Chilean secret service (after the coup against Allende) traveled to Europe, and in some cases PLO members were found with Soviet weapons on Italian soil.[9]

Results from many trials and investigations located a NATO organization in Lisbon under the name of Aginter Press led by Yves Gueric Serac, a Catholic anti-Communist who was an expert in unconventional war and had long experience in various campaigns. Aginter Press was a news agency that supported right-wing movements and also issued false stories for disinformation reasons. According to Vincenzo Vinciguerra, his main agent in Italy was Delle Chiaie.[10]

Unfortunately, this underground world that "doesn't exist" still remains very much in the dark.

When contemplating Borghese's final act, one must keep in mind that to the American public the coup would have been a tree falling in a forest. What NATO through Gladio, or Nixon's foreign policy team, might have done or not done, as well as the inter- and intra-government connections within Italy, were largely ignored by a U.S. citizenry concerned

with Vietnam and other matters at the time. Unless they were particularly worldly or had family or business connections to Italy, it was unlikely the typical American even knew what was going on, and it was certainly an underreported incident in any non-Italian newspaper.

The coup attempt also has to be placed in the context of the Cold
War. Italy was the southern flank for NATO, and clearly the United
States and NATO, as well as the conservative political Right of Italy, did
not want the Communists to come to power in Italy and would pull
out all the stops to keep this from occurring. Also in this equation was
the strong U.S. support for Israel. Bases in Italy were key to this continued support. Copious amounts of money to buy elections, which
both the Soviets and the United States supplied to political parties
during the Cold War, was only one tool.

The U.S. government, with Henry Kissinger running American foreign policy alongside Nixon, funneled money to the Italian MSI during this period. This occurred under the ambassadors Graham Martin,
John Volpe, Richard Gardner, and others. The money funneled to
Martin came through the Vatican banker and Borghese's friend and
patron, Sindona.[11] Ambassador Martin was appointed to Italy by
Nixon in September 1969. A former army colonel, he had just come
from Thailand, where he had helped steer that nation into close support of the American war effort in Vietnam. He was considered a hard-
line hawk.[12]

Ambassador Martin was able to obtain $800,000 (this represented
about 10 percent of the American funds made available to help Italian
politicians at this time to defeat the PCI) for a neo-Fascist leader in
1972, though over the objections of the CIA. Martin insisted that this
would be required "to demonstrate solidarity for the long pull" and to
help stave off the powerful Italian Communist Party coming to power.
At one point the CIA so disagreed with Martin that he threatened to
put the CIA operative in Rome on an airplane home.[13]

Martin maintained nonofficial contacts with various right-wing
Italians, including Sindona. He was also in contact with a Fronte

Nazionale man, Pier Talenti, who owned a bus touring service that would play a role in the attempted coup, and Hugh Fenwich, an American who was a manager at Selenia, an electronics firm that produced items of military value. Fenwich lived in Italy and was probably a CIA operative.[14]

Nor must it be forgotten that the American and British secret services in the 1970s were establishing electronic eavesdropping methods against the NATO allies. This continues to this day, though on economic warfare lines more than for security or military reasons. The extent of this network is not known at this time.[15]

Also in this picture is the fact that Italy from 1943 until the end of the Red Brigade era had been racked with one right- or left-wing coup, attack, or terrorist act after another. There was an atmosphere of disruption.

Finally, as Jeffrey McKenzie Bale has stated:

> It would be a major error to consider the Black Prince and his men apart from the far more powerful political forces which they claimed had promised to lend support to their action. Whatever else Borghese may have been, he was not an operational novice when it came to military affairs. No one with significant experience in military and paramilitary activities would have been foolish enough to believe that a total force consisting of a few thousand civilian activists would be able to carry out a successful *coup d'etat* in Rome without the support of elements from the regular security forces.[16]

Borghese first established a political headquarters—"Command Post A"—at an office in Rome. An operational "Command Post B" was set up at one of Orlandini's shipyards. At Post A was Borghese, Mario Rosa, an army general and colonel, and a Carabinieri captain, Salvatore Pecorella. Mario Rosa was a commercial adviser and one of the prominent figures in the FN. Assembling at the shipyard were men armed and dressed as Carabinieri and a small fleet of tour buses supplied by Pier Talenti's business. The buses were to transport the men into Rome at the propitious time.

Other concentrations of men took place through the day and into the night of December 7–8, including a right-wing university group called the Fronte Delta, or Delta Force. Orlandini later stated that he had a battalion of police under his command in Rome during the coup.[17]

On the evening of December 7, 1970, several groups of military, paramilitary, and political supporters of the Right began to move in various parts of Italy to assemble in specific locations. The signal had been given by Borghese with the words "Tora, Tora," a shortened version of the Japanese signal on December 7, 1941. There were bands ready to occupy vital points of the nation, such as TV and radio networks, ministries, policy centers, power plants, and the like.

Documented movements carried out that night were:

1. A group of fifty men of Avanguardia Nazionale, led by Stefano Delle Chiaie, penetrated the Interior Ministry's armory, took some 200 submachine guns, and prepared them for transport. (A portion was to be sent to Orlandini's shipyard.) They had gained entry with an "alleged" authorization from General Domenico Barbieri, the former head of the Public Security training center. A police captain allowed them in at the ministry. This was a particularly important action because if the Interior Ministry was seized it contained a communications system to all of Italy's police facilities.

2. A group of 197 heavily armed forest rangers with fourteen trucks moved under the command of Major Luciano Berti toward Rome with the objective of reaching the TV stations. They approached to within some hundreds of meters of the stations. Berti later on the early morning of the 8th took the entire expedition back to its training camp.

3. At the same time, groups of *mafiosi* in Calabria were told to prepare to receive uniforms of Carabinieri policemen in order to arrest trade unionists and adversaries on the political Left.

4. An AN commando arrived to arrest the chief of the police, Angelo Vicari. They entered his building but became trapped in an elevator until the following day. It would not have mattered, as Vicari was visiting Palermo at the time. Members of the Mafia later stated that Borghese had tried to recruit them for such an action as well as for other strikes.

5. At a meeting in the sporting club of the parachutists national association at Rome, some 200 right-wing activists remained waiting for orders with Sandro Saccucci, who would later become an MSI member of Parliament. In addition, by midnight several other groups remained in bands throughout Rome, possibly waiting for the guns liberated from the Interior Ministry.

One of the raiders, probably Delle Chiaie himself, under the cover name of Alfredo Di Stefano, later told (with some exaggeration) the Chilean DINA (Chilean secret police under Pinochet) agents in Rome that he "had led a group of fifty neo-fascist commandos in a midnight takeover of the Italian Interior Ministry in the Viminale Palace." What appeared to Chileans as "seasoned warriors" remained there waiting for "the military uprising in other parts of the city that never came." So they left in the morning with "180 submachine guns."[18]

Delle Chiaie would later state that he did not participate in the failed coup. He angrily rebutted this accusation though his story leaves some question marks. That secret services (Italian or not), Carabinieri, and police used right-wing activists as informers is quite obvious, since they offered themselves for the job, and therefore the police authorities knew all about these movements. Interestingly, when the band occupying the Interior Ministry received orders to give up and return weapons, one of them retained a submachine gun in order to have proof of the state authorities' involvement and thus avoid any of the following investigations. The security services tried to replace the stolen one with another weapon made up of parts, but it lacked the correct serial number.[19]

At the same time, 0845, the artillery unit under Lieutenant Colonel Amos Spiazzi based at Verona received an order via the military wireless net, preceded by a correct password, to carry out the *Esigenza Triangolo* (Triangle Exigency) plan. The order went out on the military line from the Regimental HQ. But the order was not followed by the word *esercitazione* (training exercise), and it was therefore an *operational* order. Confirmation of the order was asked, and it came again—therefore, Spiazzi mobilized a 105 mm gun battery with ammunition and drove toward Milan, where he had to deploy according to plans at Sesto San Giovanni. Similar military operations were undertaken elsewhere that night. According to Spiazzi, the message to undertake this anti-insurgency plan came not through standard military channels, but from SID, the intelligence service.

Spiazzi's column was about to arrive at its objective when the order was transmitted again followed by the word *esercitazione,* repeated three times, and this meant that the order was a training exercise (although strange) and the artillery had to return to Verona. He had already moved about 100 miles from his barracks; because he had the ammunition already on the trucks, he was well on his way before being recalled. Other columns that had received the same order moved very little or were called off before having exited their barracks.[20]

In fact, that night many army columns moved to one place or another following activation orders for the *Esigenza Triangolo.* At Modena, the military academy was alerted and sandbagged machine-gun nests were set up. At the end, many of those who participated thought it really was a training exercise. Spiazzi was not so sure because through his contacts with the Monarchists (he was a Monarchist as well as a member of the FN) he was aware of a big demonstration that Borghese's Fronte Nazionale would hold in Rome on December 8 to protest Tito's visit to Italy. The Monarchists wanted to send people to Rome to show how the right-wing organizations could mobilize and show their muscles.

Spiazzi began to suspect a trap and phoned a friend connected to Borghese to warn him. The friend, in turn, warned Borghese and later put Spiazzi in direct touch with the Prince, who was inclined to think that Spiazzi was a provocateur and found it difficult to believe him. Spiazzi's conversations remained unknown for a long time, while another phone call of the same kind was widely known in the army. It may have been Colonel Giuseppe Claudio Condò who warned Borghese of the trap. Condò was a military magistrate but was operating with SID when the coup attempt occurred.[21]

While these movements were in progress, just after midnight a counterorder came to cancel the operation. This may have resulted from the mysterious phone call Borghese received from Condò. After speaking for a bit, he turned to his fellow conspirators and told them that the coup would not receive the external military support it required. The Italian military would not back him.

The next frantic hours were spent in contacting the various action groups and putting everything into reverse. The people rounded up at the sporting club were told to go back home. Some wanted to continue, and Captain Salvatore Pecorella, who by now was on the scene, threatened them with a gun. The Forest Guard also returned home, and the people assembled at the Orlandini factory were told that the police had surrounded the place, and they later dispersed.

This entire misfire of a coup created many bitter feelings among those involved, and much of the anger was directed at Borghese. He never spoke on the matter other than to say that he had "obeyed superior orders."[22]

The U.S. Ambassador, Graham Martin, was well informed through Hugh Fenwich, who was in contact with Remo Orlandini. A member of the AN had put Orlandini in touch with Fenwich. Orlandini would meet with Fenwich several times to try to gain American support for Borghese's future actions. The ambassador denied this support after some inquiries about the plan and the men behind them, whose act had resulted in failure.

Fenwich had previously lived in South Korea and Vietnam and was alleged to have direct access to President Nixon. In the inquiry following the coup attempt, Orlandini claimed that he was present once at

Fenwich's home when he called Nixon. Fenwich, however, was not carried on any official list of American agents. Captain Antonio Labruna of SID contacted the CIA, and one of his regular contacts refused to discuss Fenwich's status—note not deny, but simply not discuss. Labruna later decided that he was a "CIA 'resident'—an intelligence operative who conducted normal business activities abroad but secretly carried out delicate intelligence tasks."[23]

Therefore, before the famous night of December 7, Orlandini had to be well informed of the American attitude, but Fenwich probably left things somewhat foggy, and Orlandini could have believed he had some degree of support from the American government and NATO.[24]

In case of a successful coup, Borghese had prepared a proclamation to be read on TV. He would say that the time in which the men of order and the military could no longer be "ridiculed, insulted, injured and killed with impunity" had arrived. Those, in fact, were difficult times in which to wear a uniform. According to a confiscated document, the political program would have called for close cooperation with NATO and a possible Italian intervention into the Vietnam War. The latter would have been a token but powerfully symbolic force—the only European power to commit troops to Vietnam.[25]

It is interesting to note that Borghese's old friend James Angleton is said to have arrived in Rome before the coup and left afterward, although this journalistic news remains unconfirmed.[26]

The coup triggered a Carabinieri (and army) counterinsurgency plan, but it was stopped before any further movement. The subsequent early inquiries about the "coup" appeared to make it out as a less-than-serious enterprise. Hence the claim by some that this was a "buffoon" coup.

In March 1971, the press finally revealed the story, after inquiries made by the Ministry of Interior intelligence services got the first news of these events in February 1971. Giovanni De Rosa, Mario Rosa, Sandro Saccucci, and Remo Orlandini were arrested on March 17 and 19. Clearly, however, General Miceli tried to "prevent the exposure of the operation and, in the process, protect the conspirators."[27]

CHAPTER 17

The Prince in the Shadows

The most helpful coup is one that isn't successful.

Paolo Cucchiarelli and Aldo Giannuli[1]

AFTER HIS FAILED COUP, BORGHESE WAS COM-pelled to flee to Franco's Spain along with some fellow plotters. It seems that the police (and possibly the navy), as in other similar cases, covered up his flight so that he could remain in touch with his friends.[2] There in Spain he may have met his fellow exile, Otto Skorzeny.

The few arrested were released on December 1, 1973, and Prince Borghese's arrest warrant was also canceled, but he did not publicly return to Italy. He probably clandestinely returned before his death in 1974.

Borghese's flight from Italy was followed by the 1972 elections in which the MSI made an alliance with the Monarchists to gather 8.7 percent of the votes. This created many problems for the Christian-Democrats, who feared a migration of votes toward the Right and placed Andreotti as premier in a center-right government without the MSI. In 1973, U.S. Ambassador Martin left Italy for Saigon, and the new ambassador, John Volpe, suspended financial support to the Right, while in October the PCI leader, Enrico Berlinguer, began to promote an agreement with the Christian-Democrats. The following year, there would be another opening to the Left.

More information about the coup attempt was now coming out. According to the information that reached Spiazzi in those days, a former Italian defense minister had asked Borghese to organize a great protest against the visit of Tito. Tito had come to Italy to discuss the assets of the Istria and Trieste areas.[3] Spiazzi spoke about this during a TV interview and his statements were later published in a book, then repeated in his memoirs published in 1995, and nobody thought to comment on it, which is at least bizarre.

But in 1974, the inquiry was resumed when Spiazzi was arrested in January. The reaction among the armed forces was quite emotional, and the officers' class reacted to being under fire from leftist judges. As a result, General Miceli was fired on July 31, 1974, and replaced with the more acceptable Admiral Mario Casardi. Toward the end of the previous year, Miceli had instructed the chief of the counterintelligence centers, Colonel Federico Marzollo, to send agents to Tuscany to investigate Gelli. The report was sent to Gianadelio Maletti, chief of the counterintelligence office, and Miceli had to suffer for his initiative with Gelli's revenge. As Viviani wrote: "An intermediary organized a luncheon meeting between Andreotti, who knew Gelli for many years, and Maletti, whose quarrels with his chief Miceli were well known."[4]

Toward the end of the year, the government changed yet again, and Maletti was fired on December 22, 1975. On March 27, 1976, General Maletti and Colonel Labruna were both arrested and found guilty, and Maletti, upon being sentenced to four years in jail, fled Italy. Maletti was recently interrogated by the Stragi Commission in South Africa, where he moved after his unfortunate judicial ventures, and he declared that what happened was a politician's fault, since the secret service received orders from them.

As for Miceli, he went to jail on October 31, 1974, and was freed on May 7, 1975 (receiving a telegram of congratulations from Aldo Moro). He became an MP in the MSI, and during a confrontation in Parliament with Andreotti, he revealed that SID had investigated politicians *with the support* of NATO. He refused, however, to go into detail on the subject and claimed parliamentary immunity over the revelation.

The fact that the arrest warrant against Borghese was suspended was not enough to persuade him to come back to Italy. He had learned that his experience as a warrior had not prepared him to face the Byzantine machinations of Italian politics. But the Prince probably did visit Italy to see a woman with whom he was in love, and when in 1974 the inquiries were resumed after the SID report was sent to the magistrates, the secret service tried to capture him. But Borghese died before this could happen.

After the coup attempt, Borghese was also spotted in Corfù, Zante, and Athens at various times. Borghese, with Delle Chiaie, later visited Chile in April 1974. On April 29, he met with General Pinochet. Present at the meeting was the head of Chilean police intelligence, Colonel Jorge Carrasco.[5]

Borghese died in Spain, at Cadiz, on August 26, 1974, at the age of sixty-eight.

According to Viviani, "One Roman prince named B" died in Spain on August 24, literally in the arms of a woman. She was a Roman princess, the lover of this "prince B," and was contacted by SID through the friends of a Romanian princess, the widow of an Italian nobleman, who still worked as a spy for Romania, the Vatican, and others.

Borghese's death seems to have happened quite naturally, and from some points of view, in the best possible way. Viviani commented that the princess was able to "create a stress stronger than those caused by the defenses of the port of Alexandria, where the prince B. during a daring and courageous enterprise had sunk during the war two British battleships, gaining a gold medal." He went on to say that it was *not clear* whether this stress was natural or prompted by a specific action.[6]

In this story related by Viviani we can reasonably detect the demise of the Black Prince. Apparently, he died in the arms of the Roman princess, and the latter fled after "having found the time to empty two glasses of Dom Perignon still full on the night table."[7]

It is also true that a lot of people were relieved by this providential departure of Borghese, just before a report by SID agents was presented for a case in September on Andreotti's instructions.[8]

It remains to note that General Spiazzi declared in an interview that he felt sure that Borghese was murdered, and Ilari wrote that the Prince "died in Spain in circumstances that lead one to suspect poisoning."[9]

Just twelve days previously, an SID agent named Guido Giannettini, wanted by justice, had presented himself to the police. Borghese died, General Viviani wrote, "in rather obscure circumstances and with lucky coincidence." If Borghese had come back to be a witness at the trial, he could have embarrassed some politicians. Correct in our view is the connection made by Ferraresi to the Vinciguerra declarations before the district attorney of Venice, Felice Casson. He said that it was Borghese who "held contacts with persons of the State (Italian and other) organizations and with hidden circles of power."[10]

We are clearly unable at this time to fully investigate the hows and whys of Junio Valerio Borghese's death. Perhaps in years to come, someone will find interesting evidence on this. But the consequences of the SID's report are intriguing. It is viewed differently by various authors. The Commissione Stragi report, signed by Senator Giovanni Pellegrino, held the view that the SID report was sound and proved the conspirators' intentions to carry out the coup, and that they were protected by officials of the secret service.

Interestingly, the SID presented three reports. One was on Borghese's coup, one on the Rosa dei Venti organization, (which co-opted the compass symbol that NATO uses as its logo), and one on a coup that had been planned for 1974, sometimes called the "white coup," by the famous partisan and anti-Communist Edgardo Sogno. Of these reports, the one on Borghese was mainly the result of confidential talks held by Captain Labruna and Colonel Giorgio Genovesi, who worked with a special unit called NOD of the famous D Office, with Remo Orlandini. These discussions took place at Lugano, Switzerland, where Orlandini had fled.[11] Orlandini spoke freely because he thought the

SID would help him, but he was speaking to the wrong side of the service—those who wanted to fire General Miceli.

Maletti first presented the report on Borghese to the Defense Ministry, and only later to the chief of the service, Miceli. The Defense Ministry instructed him to reduce the size of the report. Some parts were deleted, and names were removed (including Gelli's name and references to NATO). So the famous journalist Pecorelli wrote of a *malloppo* (booty gained by a thief) and *malloppino* (little booty); in other words, the final report was sanitized before it was given to the judges.[12]

There was a strong rivalry between the chief of SID, the pro-Arab General Miceli, and the chief of the D Office of the SID, General Maletti, whose collaborator, Labruna, gathered the material to make the case. Maletti was against a pro-Arab policy and was a supporter of Andreotti, who became minister of defense on March 15, 1974. As a first act, in June 1974 the new minister gave an interview to the magazine *Il Mondo* in which he burned an SID extreme right-wing confidant, Guido Giannettini. Giannettini was also the coauthor of some pamphlets and an interesting handbook for unconventional war and was allegedly associated with the Piazza Fontana massacre group.[13]

Andreotti encouraged the deep rivalry between Miceli and Maletti. The latter presented a dossier on the Borghese coup to Defense Minister Andreotti and to his chief, Miceli, who considered it too vague. Maletti then got the dossier to several other authorities, and eventually it was given over to the magistrates. In a newspaper interview Andreotti stunned everyone by announcing the Miceli firing without giving prior warning to other members of the cabinet. At the same time, the Padua district attorney, Giovanni Tamburino, accused General Miceli, who was the main target of the Borghese affair.

General Viviani, former commander of the D office, wrote that as a consequence of that report, Miceli was first fired and replaced with General Casardi, then indicted for having taken part in a coup against the state. He was arrested in October 1974 and released in May of the following year (when a new government came to power). In the end he was found not guilty, partly because the "events did not reflect a true armed insurgency" and partly because the coup in "fact did not happen."[14]

Other high officers were also arrested and indicted but later found not guilty. But for some time, a consequence of the public scandal was that both the SID and the intelligence service of the Interior Ministry were forced into a "lull period in their activity . . . and later into another reorganization." In other words, politicians exploited the Borghese coup in various ways. Andreotti would take advantage of the coup attempt to adopt an anti-Fascist tone to prepare for an "opening to the left."[15]

Doubt about the seriousness of Borghese's coup is unavoidable. The attempt has been called "buffoonery," and that was indeed the evaluation of the Rome judges in 1984, although it is possible that they had been persuaded to take that view by intelligence authorities. But the seriousness of the coup has been questioned by others as well, including the Parliamentary Committee on the secret service[16] and the Stragi Commission, formed to investigate the various bombings that took place in Italy around the same time.

Given the known facts, the coup was likely doomed to failure from the start. The claims of Orlandini—that the plotters had a direct connection with the White House through Talenti and Fenwich—cannot be confirmed. Nixon could have ordered a covert action of this type, but the notion that he would have personally followed it, leaving the vast U.S. intelligence network out of the loop, is difficult to accept. It is more likely that he would have remained behind the scenes. Yet one left-wing publication has written that four U.S. Navy vessels left Malta to head north on the night of the coup. We could not confirm this information.[17]

Moreover, it is unclear who made the decision to stop the operation. According to Spiazzi, DC lawyer Filippo De Jorio, later an MP, had some knowledge of this because he spoke with Borghese about it. It might have been a former defense minister or Colonel Condò.[18]

The famous list of people who were to be interned afterward in the Eolian isles off Sicily is yet another mystery. Its contents are still unknown, but according to the New York Times, it may have contained

1,617 names. Another list, ominously called the "Death List," is also rumored to exist; supposedly found in the home of Dr. Paolo Porta Ca-
succi, it is said to include the names of left-wing and center-left individuals, and also the leader of the MSI.

Some political adversaries, many from the Communist Party, were
to be taken away by airplane or by ship. Captain Labruna revealed to
the prosecutor, Guido Salvini, that the owner of the ships that were to
be used had told him this during a weapons transport operation in
Sardinia on behalf of the D Office of the SID.[19]

According to Pellegrino's commission, the "coup that never was"
might simply have been intended as a "menace" by Licio Gelli and his
unnamed associates. That is, they wanted to warn the politicians and
the Italian government that they could mount a credible threat. Under
that scenario, Borghese was a puppet in the hands of superior forces. If
this is not the case, then at some point the conspirators must have been
deprived of the fundamental approval of the United States and the support of the Carabinieri, without which the coup could not succeed.[20]

The left-leaning nation of Chile, of course, did suffer an American-
supported coup in 1973. In 1967, the Greek Colonels' Coup also succeeded with American aid, and the ringleaders subsequently cooper-
ated with the right wing of Italian politics, including members of the
FN. At the time of the Greeks' one-year anniversary, fifty-one right-
wing Italian extremists visited Greece and were "formally wined and
dined at two military barracks."[21]

While these rightist governments took the occasion to punish their
extreme right wings (and this was among Gelli's intentions), in a few
years the regimes fell one after another. It is therefore much more
probable that the political and strategic maneuver in Italy had not
been meant to succeed. It was enough to show muscle, and after the
"night of the Madonna," the PCI activists were quite aware that something dangerous was in the air.

Most of the investigations into the coup point out the extent of the
organization that it required and the huge number of people involved

in it. Although no blood was shed that night, there is surprisingly little interest in the fact that some people may have died for it later. Borghese's mysterious death is an example, as is that of Colonel Condò, the officer who called Borghese on the night of December 7 to warn him that he was about to walk into a trap. At age forty-two Condó died of a heart attack just before Turin Prosecutor Luciano Violante could interrogate him.[22] According to his memoirs, Spiazzi also felt for some time that he was in great danger. While in custody, at one time he was left in the open country with the possibility of escape, but he understood that he would be risking his life if he attempted to run away.[23]

Gelli was strongly connected with the United States and had ready access to American politicians and intelligence agents at the highest levels, at least in the FBI, if not in the CIA. Indeed, his powerful position was not fully understood until the 1980s, when the commission investigating the activities of the P2 lodge filled some 200 volumes. CIA and FBI involvement has been rumored but not documented, and the FBI, which theoretically operates only in domestic matters, could have operated in the shadows in Europe or within other parts of the U.S. and NATO intelligence communities.[24]

According to several sources, Gelli was in contact with Borghese, since he joined the Fronte Nazionale early on. But although he was a close friend, he did not admit to participating in the affair, calling it "a prank" because "it started to rain and they all went home."[25]

Prosecutor Salvini's inquiry brought witnesses to the surface who said that Gelli's role in the coup was to personally arrest the president of the republic, as he had access to the president's residence. In fact, Gelli seems to be the real power behind the whole operation. As late as 1998, the president of the republic denied permission for access to a special investigative unit of the Carabinieri, the Reparto Operativo Speciale (ROS). The guest list for the president's residence on the evening of December 7, 1970, has thus never been examined for clues.[26]

The responsibility for the coup, attempted or only threatened, cannot be placed solely on the right wing. The individuals on the Right clearly enjoyed some protection from the state agencies of intelligence. As Salvini wrote, "More probably, the involvement of state organizations in the development of right-wing terrorism should not be considered a deviation, but instead normal activity, part of their institutional functions."[27]

Nor should Italian (and NATO) secret services be blamed for the strategy of tension. Intelligence services cannot operate in the long term without a high degree of collaboration and planning. But the appearance of chaos ensures "plausible denial" to the political leadership. That is, there is a method to their madness, which is to pretend the political leadership didn't know what the secret services were doing.[28]

Salvini concluded that many events "could not have been repeated if they were part of a common political and strategic plan, most probably to maintain our country in the Atlantic Alliance." In other words, such a "strategy of tension," although making use of many organizations of the right wing, did not aim to put a Fascist regime into power but instead to "destabilize to stabilize" the country in order to avoid changes in Italy's strategic position.[29]

Vinciguerra, in a penetrating analysis, proposed that right-wing movements such as AN or ON were not only connected with Italian and NATO secret services but manned by them.[30] It is true that people who were compelled to take cover abroad found help in France and Franco's Spain, as well as in Portugal and London.

On August 28, 1974, the Italian newspaper *Il Corriere della Sera* published Borghese's obituary: "Valerio Borghese Dead in Spain at Sixty-Eight." "Sunday evening, while on vacation at Conil between Gibraltar and Cadiz, he was hit by very strong pains and the friends who were with him accompanied him to the hospital." Borghese had used up his ninth life. The newspaper stated that Borhese's body was transported from the hospital to the cemetery of Cadiz, where only one son was present at the funeral ceremony, and that it would be transported to Italy after preparation.

Even his death is shrouded in mystery. On August 31, the same paper reported that the dead Borghese had arrived the previous evening at 1930 on Iberia flight 351. His sons Livio and Paolo and his daughter Maria arrived on the same airplane.[31]

Borghese did not want a great ceremony. He wanted his gravestone to simply read, "This is a soldier who has served his country well." According to the last of Borghese's wishes, there were to be no public demonstrations, although several thousand former Decima MAS men were present.[32]

The paper published another article on Borghese's death on September 1. The burial ceremony was to take place the following day. The Prince was to be buried in the famous basilica of Santa Maria Maggiore, in the Vatican near Pope Paul V, who was also a Borghese. The Vatican had to explain that the burial was to be done in the Santa Maria Maggiore because the Borghese family had buried their relatives there from 1611.

On September 2, 1974, the paper referred to the final ceremony, which took place at 1100 in a chapel of the basilica and not in the central aisle. After the ceremony, several young members of right-wing movements—there were some 2,000 people present—overcame the weak resistance of the Vatican's Swiss guards, took up the coffin, and carried it around outside the basilica shouting, "Italy, Italy, up with the X MAS." They then returned it to the chapel.

Borghese was ever the warrior, always willing to put his life on the line for what he thought was best for his country. His impact was far-reaching, influencing some of the most important people and events of his time. But World War II, the Cold War, and the passage of time had taken their toll. And there lies the warrior who fought for the past and not the future.

The unit that he is so identified with, the Decima MAS, is still in existence today in the Italian Navy with three special force units. One is for training, one is for research, and the other is for operations.[33]

NOTES

CHAPTER 1

1. Franco Maugeri, *From the Ashes of Disgrace* (New York: Reynal and Hitchcock, 1948), 240.
2. R. O'Neill, *Suicide Squads* (London: Landsdowne Press, 1981), *passim*.
3. On the large and decisive use of torpedo boats in this war, see Jack Greene and Alessandro Massignani, *Ironclads at War* (Conshohocken, Penn.: Combined Books, 1997), 349 *ff*.
4. Erminio Bagnasco, *M.A.S. e mezzi d'assalto di superficie italiani*, 2d ed. (Rome: Ussmm, 1996).
5. For the narrative of the events, we are referring to Paul Kemp, *Underwater Warriors* (London: Arms and Armour, 1996), 19–20, and to standard works on the naval war in the Adriatic such as A. Ginocchietti, *La guerra sul mare* (Rome: Libreria del Littorio, 1930); Guido Po, *La guerra marittima* (Milan: Corbaccio, 1934), 290–302; and Ettore Bravetta, *La Grande Guerra sul mare*, 2 vols. (Milan: Mondadori, 1925).
6. Technical data in Bagnasco, *M.A.S. e mezzi d'assalto di superficie italiani*, 399–406.
7. From the report of Captain Raffaele Rossetti. Paolucci's and Rossetti's reports are printed in Ezio Ferrante, *La Grande Guerra in Adriatico nel LXX anniversario della vittoria* (Rome: Ussmm, 1987), 183–201.
8. From the Paolucci report.
9. Also see Jack Greene and Alessandro Massignani, *The Naval War in the Mediterranean, 1940–1943* (London: Chatham, 1998), 167–168, and René Greger, *Austro-Hungarian Warships of World War I* (London: Ian Allan, 1976), 25. The Italian Navy claimed, probably rightfully, to not know of this changeover in ownership.
10. Marco Spertini and Erminio Bagnasco, *I mezzi d'assalto della X Flottiglia Mas, 1940–1945* (Parma: Albertelli, 1991), 15. This is an excellent book that should be a candidate for an English version, especially with its numerous illustrations.

CHAPTER 2

1. Junio Valerio Borghese, *Sea Devils* (Chicago: Regency, 1954), 18.
2. Cavagnari was the de facto head of the Italian Navy until 1940, as Mussolini held the portfolio of secretary of the navy. A conservative "battleship" admiral, he would be one of the key reasons for the Italian Navy's poor combat performance in World War II.

3. The research of Fortunato Minniti on the issue resulted in a series of articles, and later he summarized these results, publishing *Fino alla guerra: Strategia e conflitto nella politica di potenza di Mussolini (1923–1940)* (Naples: ESI, 2000).

4. As governor of the Africa Orientale Italiana (AOI, Italy's empire in the Horn of Africa), Duca Amedeo D'Aosta would surrender at Amba Alagi in 1941 and would die as a POW.

5. This method of attack would succeed against the British heavy cruiser *York* at Suda Bay but later fail in an attack against Malta.

6. It should be noted that MT was a later abbreviation. For the first two prototypes, the abbreviations were MA for *Motoscafo Assalto* (assault motorboat) and MTA for *Motoscafi Avio Trasportati* (air-transported motorboats). See Erminio Bagnasco, *M.A.S. e mezzi d'assalto di superficie italiani*, 2d ed. (Rome: Ussmm, 1996), 412.

7. This estate lies near the coastal town of Viareggio, about midway between Leghorn and Spezia on the Gulf of Genoa.

8. Borghese, *Sea Devils*, 12–19, and Robert Mallett, *The Italian Navy and Fascist Expansionism, 1935–1940* (London: Frank Cass, 1998), 58–59.

9. Emilia Chiavarelli, *L'opera della marina italiana nella guerra italo-etiopica* (Milan: Giuffré, 1969), 61. For the naval aspects of the Ethiopian crisis between Italy and Great Britain, see also the first chapter of Mallett, *The Italian Navy and Fascist Expansionism, 1935–1940*.

10. Major Al Williams, *Airpower* (New York: Coward-McCann, 1940), 19–20. Williams, from the United States, was taken in quite well by the Italians; he thought they had 7,000 to 10,000 warplanes in 1938 when the real total was 3,000, including obsolete aircraft.

11. Jack Greene and Alessandro Massignani, *The Naval War in the Mediterranean, 1940–1943* (London: Chatham, 1998), 17, and sources quoted there.

12. We use the terms "Republican" and "Loyalist" interchangeably. They represented, in large part, the left wing of Spanish politics and the legitimate government. In Spain today, the Nationalists are seldom referred to as Fascist (though clearly a portion were—just as a portion of the Loyalists were Marxists and Communists) but instead are called Nationals, insurgents, Franquists, or rebels (letter to authors from Jose Luis Arcon Dominguez).

13. Erminio Bagnasco, *Submarines of World War Two* (Annapolis, Md.: Naval Institute Press, 1977), 153, and P. M. Pollina et al., *I sommergibili italiani, 1895–1971* (Rome: Ussmm, 1971), vi–vii, 164–168. Special thanks to Andrew Smith on the incident with HMS *Havock*.

14. Giorgio Giorgerini, *Uomini sul fondo: Storia del sommergibilismo italiano dalle origini a oggi* (Milan: Mondadori, 1994), 198–199, 626–628. Giorgerini quoted a witness, Commander Teucle Meneghini, who was embarked with Borghese at the time.

15. Sonar can be classified as "active" because it locates the target by emitting a sound pulse and receiving and analyzing the returning echo. The type carried was Type 124 Asdic. Asdic was the British name for sonar until 1943. The hydrophone, first employed in World War I, is a "passive" device, as the operator listens for sounds and then analyzes them. Hydrophones were the standard equipment at the time in most nations for detecting underwater sounds. Sonar equipment was much better; however, it performed poorly at high speeds when there were varying density "layers" of water, such as near mouths of rivers or in heavy seas. Also, until 1943 British sonar did not recognize the *depth* of the object it was pinging. For British prewar development of sonar, see G. D. Franklin, "A Breakdown in Communication: Britain's Overestimation of ASDIC's Capabilities in the 1930s," *The Mariner's Mirror* 84, no. 2, 204–214.

16. Additional British forces arrived on 1 and 2 September, but the bird had flown by then.

17. Jack Greene and Alessandro Massignani, *The Naval War in the Mediterranean, 1940–1943*, 22–24; the British report is in PRO, ADM 116/3534-123288, Report Admiral J. F. Somerville to the commander in chief of the Mediterranean Fleet of 4 September 1937; for the Italian de-

scription, see Franco Bargoni, *L'impegno navale italiano durante la guerra civile spagnola (1936–1939)* (Rome: Ussmm, 1992), 309–310.

18. Letter to Admiralty dated 4 September 1937. It is ironic to think of a might-have-been if the British captain had been more effective in his depth-charging.

19. See Ciano diary under 4 September 1937, in Galeazzo Ciano, *Diario, 1937–1943,* edited by Renzo De Felice (Milan: Rizzoli, 1980). In *L'impegno navale italiano durante la guerra civile spagnola (1936–1939),* Bargoni claimed that the *Woodford* was flying under a false flag and that it crewed Rumanians and others. Actually, it had recently undergone a change from Greek to British registry. The ship did not have a British master, however, which violated British merchant shipping law.

20. The reports of Rear Admiral Moriondo on both conversations are published in Bargoni, *L'impegno navale italiano durante la guerra civile spagnola,* 305–316.

21. Bargoni, *L'impegno navale italiano durante la guerra civile spagnola,* 316.

22. Ibid., 314. But Filippo Sinagra said this code was introduced later and was never penetrated. See also his *Dalla scitala all'Enigma, etc., etc.,* private manuscript, 1998. We are indebted to Sinagra for his courtesy and great competence in cryptology. F. H. Hinsley et al., in *British Intelligence in the Second World War,* vol. 1 (London: HMSO, 1979), 52–53, 199–202, explains that the British read most of the Italian cypher books, especially "the most secret and general book cyphers" from 1937 on, as well as one of the two naval attaché codes. Also, the Enigma and Hagelin cypher machines received from the Germans were broken, but these were not used for the submarines. The situation in this sphere was quite good for the British on the eve of the war. The British GC&CS was located in London (during World War II it would move to the famous Bletchley Park site) and was subordinated to the British Secret Intelligence Service—best known as MI6.

23. Patrick Beesley, *Very Special Intelligence* (London: Hamish Hamilton, 1977), 14.

24. According to Giorgio Giorgerini, *Uomini sul fondo,* 626–628, quoting Teucle Meneghini as a witness. Common Italian war medals, in order of lowest to highest, are the War Cross *(Croce di Guerra),* the Bronze Medal, the Silver Medal, and the Gold Medal *(Medaglia d'Oro al Valor Militare).* There were also various military orders, such as the Colonial or Savoy orders. One criticism concerning Italian medals is that they were awarded for bravery more than for brilliant performance.

25. See Bargoni, *L'impegno navale italiano durante la guerra civile spagnola,* 343, and Giorgerini, *Uomini sul fondo,* 202.

26. This point is stressed by Brian R. Sullivan in his essay "Fascist Italy's Military Involvement in the Spanish Civil War," *Journal of Military History* 59, no. 4 (October 1995), 697–727, and NA, T1022 roll 3015, "Report of the Naval Attaché of 16 June 1937."

27. Bargoni, *L'impegno navale italiano durante la guerra civile spagnola,* 332–341.

28. Ibid., 342.

CHAPTER 3

1. James J. Sadkovich, *The Italian Navy in World War II* (Westport, Conn.: Greenwood, 1994), 25.

2. See Carlo De Risio, *I mezzi d'assalto,* 4th ed. (Rome: Ussmm, 1992), 12–13.

3. Several episodes are recalled in Beppe Pegolotti, *Uomini contro navi* (Florence: Vallecchi, 1967).

4. Quoted in Junio Valerio Borghese, *Sea Devils* (Chicago: Regency, 1954), 26–27. The original writer's name is not given. See below on the actual weights of the warhead charges and their evolution.

5. Pegolotti, *Uomini contro navi*, 32.

6. Besides Marco Spertini and Erminio Bagnasco, *I mezzi d'assalto della X Flottiglia Mas, 1940–1945* (Parma: Albertelli, 1991), see the article written by Junio Valerio Borghese, "Tecnica costruttiva dei mezzi d'assalto," in *La scienza illustrata* (December 1950), 36–41. One can be seen at the Comsubin (Commando) Museum at the small town of Atvari Gnano near La Spezia.

7. Nipolit was a compound of PETN, NC (nitrocellulose), DEGDN, and stabilizers. Thanks to Andrew Smith for his research on this.

8. The *jeune école*, or young school, advocated cruiser warfare and torpedo-craft over the battleship. See Jack Greene and Alessandro Massignani, *Ironclads at War* (Conshohocken, Penn.: Combined Books, 1997), 190–192.

9. The *Ametista* would survive twenty-seven war missions and be scuttled after the armistice on 12 September 1943. Recovered by the Germans, the submarine was transferred to La Spezia and never employed, as it was bombed and sunk by the U.S. Air Force.

10. The *Ametista* was laid down in 1931 and completed in 1934. The submarine had a displacement of 700 tons surfaced and 842–860 tons submerged, and it was almost 200 feet long. With a maximum speed of 14 knots on the surface and 7.5 submerged, and with a crew of about 45 men, it had a range of 72 miles submerged at 4 knots and a surface range of 2,280 miles at 12 knots. The name means "Amethyst" in English. See Erminio Bagnasco, *Submarines of World War Two* (Annapolis, Md.: Naval Institute Press, 1977), 148.

11. De Risio, *I mezzi d'assalto*, 20. Goiran was in command of the upper Tyrrhennia naval station, which included La Spezia and the area where the 1st MAS worked. Much of the Mediterranean is actually rather deep, but the water is quite clear, and near harbors the water does become shallow. We thank retired British submariner Captain R. F. Cannon on this point.

12. Borghese, *Sea Devils*, 20.

CHAPTER 4

1. Peter Kemp, "Decima Mas," *Quarterly Journal of Military History* 7, no. 1 (Autumn 1994), 81.

2. We rely on Erminio Bagnasco, *M.A.S. e mezzi d'assalto di superficie italiani*, 2d ed. (Rome: Ussmm, 1996), and Marco Spertini and Erminio Bagnasco, *I mezzi d'assalto della X Flottiglia Mas, 1940–1945* (Parma: Albertelli, 1991).

3. René Greger, "I CB nel Mar Nero," *Storia Militare*, no. 21 (June 1995), 45–48.

4. "CC" would mean Costiero Caproni (Coastal Caproni) and "CM" would be for Costiero Monfalcone (Coastal Monfalcone), since the yards Cantieri Riuniti dell'Adriatico were at Monfalcone, near Trieste.

5. Erminio Bagnasco and Achille Rastelli, *Sommergibili in guerra: Centosettantadue battelli italiani nella seconda guerra mondiale*, 2d ed. (Parma: Albertelli, 1994), 178–179, 294–295. See also Paul Kemp, *Underwater Warriors* (London: Arms and Armour, 1996), 58, a pioneering book on the topic of clandestine naval action.

6. Fortunato Minniti, "L'industria degli armamenti dal 1940 al 1943: i mercati, le produzioni," in Vera Zamagni, ed., *Come perdere la guerra e vincere la pace* (Bologna: Il Mulino, 1997), 55–148, 137.

7. We rely mainly on Erminio Bagnasco, *The Submarines of World War Two* (Annapolis, Md.: Naval Institute Press, 1977), and Bagnasco and Rastelli, *Sommergibili in guerra*.

8. But see Greger, "I CB nel Mar Nero," who discusses the doubt about the claimed sinking of Soviet submarines, and also J. Rohwer, *Axis Submarine Successes of World War Two* (London:

Greenhill Books, 1999), 218–219. We conclude that only one of three possible Soviet submarines was actually sunk.

9. Junio Valerio Borghese, *Sea Devils* (Chicago: Regency, 1954), 33.

10. Franco Maugeri, *From the Ashes of Disgrace* (New York: Reynal and Hitchcock, 1948), 32. Maugeri's memoirs were published abroad and not in Italy, as statements he made caused others to consider him a traitor.

11. This point was stressed to us by Giovanni Montagna, a SIM agent in Albania and later in Yugoslavia during World War II. He recalled turf battles between Axis secret services—and sometimes also between Italian ones. In one case on 8 September 1942, one year before the armistice, his chief major, Antonio Scaramuzza, met Admiral Wilhelm Canaris in the Danieli Hotel in Venice, and Montagna gave orders to penetrate into the hotel to free his chief if he was not out by a certain time. All went well, but later he learned that there had been three boats full of counterespionage agents ready to intervene. The Abwehr was the German intelligence service.

12. Ambrogio Viviani, *I servizi segreti italiani, 1815–1985* (Rome: And Kronos, 1985), 212. See the very good essay of Brian Sullivan's.

13. Montgomery Hyde, *The Quiet Canadian* (London: Hamish Hamilton, 1962), 106–107; William Stevenson, *A Man Called Intrepid: The Secret War* (New York: Harcourt Brace Jovanovich, 1976), 314.

14. Ezio Ferrante, "L'ammiraglio Lais, Roosevelt e la 'beffa' delle navi," *Storia delle Relazioni Internazionali* 7 (1991/1992), 375–397, who quotes the literature in which Admiral Lais appears. Lais managed to organize the sabotage of the Italian ships being requisitioned in U.S. ports on 19 March 1941, but he was not presented to the king upon his return, most likely because he was under a cloud of suspicion.

15. Franco Maugeri, *Ricordi di un marinaio: Diari e memorie* (Milan: Mursia, 1980), 74, 76–78.

16. Giuseppe Pesce, "Spie in libertà ad Algesiras: Racconto del Cap. Venanzi," *Rivista storica* (January 1996), 32.

CHAPTER 5

1. Junio Valerio Borghese, *Sea Devils* (Chicago: Regency, 1954), 46.

2. Beppe Pegolotti, *Uomini contro navi* (Florence: Vallecchi, 1967), 41; part of Giorgini's report appears in Carlo De Risio, *I mezzi d'assalto*, 4th ed. (Rome: Ussmm, 1992), 22.

3. For the role of the aircraft carrier in the Mediterranean, see Jack Greene and Alessandro Massignani, *The Naval War in the Mediterranean, 1940–1943* (London: Chatham, 1998), 109–114.

4. The *Calipso* was one of the *Spica* class of thirty ships all laid down between 1934 and 1937. They weighed in at almost 800 tons, much more than the 600-ton limit imposed by the London Treaty. Each was crewed by about 118 men, armed with three 3.9-inch guns capable of only a 45-degree elevation, a light AA armament and limited depth charge capability, and four 17.7-inch torpedoes in twin mounts, and they were fitted for mine-laying and designed for 34 knots. These little ships would be workhorses in the war, and over two-thirds of them would be lost, primarily while working as convoy escorts.

5. See Antonello Biagini and Fernando Frattolillo, eds., *Diario storico del Comando Supremo*, vol. 1 (Rome: Ussmm, 1986), for 20–22 August 1940. The war diary does not mention whether Cavagnari explained the details of the plan.

6. The Italians thought they came in at 60–70 meters altitude in the attack. The 30-foot height was noted in a report by the commander of the subflights. This discrepancy points out the inability of either side to correctly get all the facts "right" in a combat situation.

7. Quoted in Michael Simpson, ed., *The Cunningham Papers* (Bodmin, U.K.: Naval Records Society, 1999), 137–138.

8. F. H. Hinsley et al., *British Intelligence in the Second World War,* vol. 1 (London: HMSO, 1979), 211.

9. The 1943 armistice would see Borghese remain with the Axis, while de Courten would be the chief of naval staff for the Italian fleet that joined the Allies. This may be why Borghese made his charge—they were enemies.

10. Jack Greene and Alessandro Massignani, *The Naval War in the Mediterranean,* 65–81.

11. De Risio, *I mezzi d'assalto,* chapter 2. De Risio published the order of operation and the battle report of the *Gondar* commander, Brunetti.

12. It was the Sunderland L 2166 of 230 Squadron.

13. Besides De Risio's account, see also Greene and Massignani, *The Naval War in the Mediterranean,* 95–96. Most British accounts list two dead.

14. G. Hermon Gill, *Royal Australian Navy, 1939–1942,* vol. 1 (Reprint, Sydney: William Collins, 1985), 224, and Alberto Santoni, "L'intelligence e la 'Decima,'" *Storia Militare* 11, no. 120 (September 2003), 18–27.

15. Ibid. Cunningham's signal is not carried in *The Cunningham Papers* published by the Naval Records Society.

16. Ibid., 224.

CHAPTER 6

1. Junio Valerio Borghese, *Sea Devils* (Chicago: Regency, 1954), 82.

2. Ibid., 46.

3. Gino Birindelli, "Le imprese dei mezzi d'assalto nella seconda guerra mondiale," *Bollettino d'Archivio dell'Ufficio storico della Marina Militare,* December 1987, 197–211 (quotation, 200); March–June 1988, 179–193; and September 1988, 207–216. Birindelli was born in Pescia, Tuscany, and was awarded both the Silver and Gold Medals for bravery at the actions at Alexandria and Gibraltar. After the war, he continued his career in the navy until reaching the rank of vice admiral. His last appointment was commander of the NATO naval forces of South Europe. He retired in 1973.

4. See Susan Rose's article "Islam Versus Christendom: The Naval Dimension," *Journal of Military History* 63, no. 3, 561–563.

5. Birindelli, "Le imprese dei mezzi d'assalto nella seconda guerra mondiale," *Bollettino d'Archivio,* December 1987, 208.

6. William Schofield and P. J. Carisella, *Frogmen First Battles* (New York: Avon, 1989), 57.

7. Partly printed in Carlo De Risio, *I mezzi d'assalto,* 4th ed. (Rome: Ussmm, 1992), 57–60.

8. Erminio Bagnasco, "Gli inglesi sapevano . . . ," *Storia Militare* 11, no. 120 (September 2003), 18–27.

9. Birindelli, "Le imprese dei mezzi d'assalto nella seconda guerra mondiale," *Bollettino d'Archivio,* June 1988, 190–192.

10. Besides his memoirs, already quoted, see Birindelli, "Le imprese dei mezzi d'assalto nella seconda guerra mondiale," *Bollettino d'Archivio,* September 1988, 207–216, especially the letter of his rescuer: "You were to die"; see also his interview with Paul Kemp in Kemp, *Underwater Warriors* (London: Arms and Armour, 1996), 23.

11. For the de la Penne report, see De Risio, *I mezzi d'assalto,* 60–62.

12. This is based on the Tesei report, excerpted in De Risio, *I mezzi d'assalto,* 62–63.

13. Maurice Harvey, *Gibraltar* (Staplehurst, U.K.: Spellmount, 1996), 154.

14. For Matapan, see Jack Greene and Alessandro Massignani, *The Naval War in the Mediterranean, 1940–1943* (London: Chatham, 1998), 141–160.

15. Besides De Risio, *I mezzi d'assalto,* our account is based on the excellent study of the Istituto di guerra marittima, "L'azione dei mezzi d'assalto di superficie a Suda il 26 marzo 1941," *Bollettino d'archivio,* March 1994, 43–67.

16. After the war, Faggioni continued the career in the navy and became admiral. He was also appointed to command the diver school at Varignano.

17. Michael Simpson, ed., *The Cunningham Papers* (Bodmin, U.K.: Naval Records Society, 1999), 307. On 29 April the *York* was officially abandoned; it was not worth salvaging because of repeated air attacks. Several British divers died in the air attacks.

18. De Risio, *I mezzi d'assalto,* 67–72. The X MAS order of operation and the after-action report are printed in the study of Istituto di guerra marittima, "L'azione dei mezzi d'assalto di superficie a Suda il 26 marzo 1941."

19. Bagnasco, "Gli inglesi sapevano . . . ."

20. Beppe Pegolotti, *Uomini contro navi* (Florence: Vallecchi, 1967), 101–103, quoting an interview with Faggioni. The concept of a speedboat loaded with explosives, first developed by the Italians, is not dead. In May 2002, the Moroccan secret service, acting on a tip from the United States, began surveillance operations against three Saudi members of Al Qaeda. Their plan allegedly was to launch speedboats loaded with explosives and operated by suicide bombers against warships crossing through the Straits of Gibraltar. They were arrested and the Al Qaeda cell was broken up. See Anthony Tucker-Jones, "Between the Rock and a Hard Place," *Warships International Fleet Review* (December 2003), 9–11.

21. The MTS would be a type that is considered to have been a failure.

22. See the Visintini report in De Risio, *I mezzi d'assalto,* 80–81.

CHAPTER 7

1. Letter a to friend before the Malta action, quoted by Beppe Pegolotti, *Uomini contro navi* (Florence: Vallecchi, 1967), 107.

2. The *Diana* was envisioned as Mussolini's yacht when laid down in 1939 but was used primarily as a fast transport. It was armed with two 4-inch guns and six 20 mm AA guns. The Maltese name for Marsa Muscetto is Marsamxett. Twenty sea miles are equivalent to about 37 km. Point B was 9 sea miles distant—see J. Caruana's letter in *Warship International* 29, no. 4 (1992), 331, and J. Caruana's "Decima MAS Decimated," *Warship International* 28, no. 2 (1991), 331.

3. Quoted in Junio Valerio Borghese, *Sea Devils* (Chicago: Regency, 1954), 21.

4. Jack Greene and Alessandro Massignani, *The Naval War in the Mediterranean, 1940–1943* (London: Chatham, 1998), 179. See also Christopher Shores and Brian Cull, with Nicola Malizia, *Malta: The Hurricane Years, 1940–1941* (London: Grubb Street Press, 1996), 260–266.

5. F. H. Hinsley et al., *British Intelligence in the Second World War,* vol. 2 (London,: HMSO, 1981), 328–329.

6. Borghese, *Sea Devils.*

7. Joseph Caruana, Malta 26 luglio 1941, "Una nuova ipotesi sulla morte di Teseo Tesei," *Storia Militare* no. 6 (March 1994), 4–9, includes a picture of Tesei's recovered SLC. Also, the Costa SLC was recovered, but in pieces some miles from the entrance to Valletta.

8. Quote from Adm223/460 and Adm1–11872, PRO Kew Garden, London.

9. Michael Simpson, ed., *The Cunningham Papers* (Bodmin, U.K.: Naval Records Society, 1999), 497. It is interesting to note that Cunningham overestimated the size of the attack by a factor of almost two. James J. Sadkovich's account in *The Italian Navy in World War II* (Westport, Conn.: Greenwood, 1994), 167–168, is a bit confused, putting Tesei on an MT, and Borghese's account in *Sea Devils*, 106, reduces the MT force to eight. One MT was found anchored the next day and is on display at the small Maltese military museum at St. Elmo. It is most likely MT Number 5.

10. Erminio Bagnasco, "Gli inglesi sapevano . . . ," *Storia Militare* 11, no. 120 (September 2003), 4–17. The actual MT now on display at the Malta Naval Museum is the MT16.

11. Crabb would go on to mysteriously disappear in the 1950s while diving around a Soviet light cruiser on a visit to Great Britain.

12. T. J. Waldron and James Gleeson, *The Frogmen: The Story of the Wartime Underwater Operators*, 2d ed. (London: Evans Brothers, 1955), 13–15.

13. Andris J. Kursietis, *La Regia Marina, 1919–1945* (n.p.: Ark Publications, 1995), 63. This is one of those small semi-self-published works that populate the landscape today that usually treat an obscure topic, in this case an order of battle for the navy and a listing of admirals, and are always welcome. The authors of this work have hiked on this trail, too! It must, however, be treated with some caution.

14. Michael Simpson, ed. *The Somerville Papers* (Aldershot: Naval Records Society, 1995), 307.

15. Borghese, *Sea Devils*, 129.

16. Bundesarchiv-Militärarchiv (hereafter BA-MA), RM7/233, Skl Iop 1639/41 of 2 October 1941, "Angriff italienischer Sturmboote auf Gibraltar."

17. BA-MA, RM7/233, Skl Iop 1646/41 of 3 October 1941, "Italienische Sturmboote."

CHAPTER 8

1. As quoted in C. E. T. Warren and James Benson, *The Midget Raiders* (New York: William Sloane, 1954), 15. Warren and Benson present a good, though older, account of the British activities in this realm, including the 3 January 1943 attack on the small light cruiser hull of the *Ulpio Traiano*, which had been launched but was incomplete at the time of the attack.

2. Viscount Cunningham of Hyndhope, *A Sailor's Odyssey* (New York: Dutton, 1951), 433, and Renato Sicurezza, "A cinquant'anni dalla notte di Alessandria," *Bollettino D'Archivio dell'Ufficio storico della Marina Militare*, December 1991, 58, an article on the fiftieth anniversary of the attack containing excerpts from the war diary. Also see Alberto Santoni, "'L' Intelligence e la 'Decima,'" *Storia Militare* 11, no. 120 (September 2003), 18–27.

3. The *Mohawk* had been lost during the destruction of the *Tarigo* convoy bound for North Africa with supplies, mostly German, for the Axis army. After the battle, a gamma team of divers had been sent to try to retrieve the destroyer's radar equipment and papers. See Greene and Massignani, *The Naval War in the Mediterranean, 1940–1943* (London: Chatham, 1998), 161–164.

4. William Schofield and P. J. Carisella, *Frogmen First Battles* (New York: Avon, 1987), 37, and Junio Valerio Borghese, *Sea Devils* (Chicago: Regency, 1954), 135–166.

5. Also in this vein, all SLC crews received regular R&R at a mountain resort, usually just before and after an operation, and this crew was no exception. It was a special arrangement that Borghese had been key in obtaining.

6. William Schofield and P. J. Carisella, *Frogmen First Battles*, 112–118. Alexandria has two harbors; one, to the east, was purely commercial.

7. Commander Luigi Durand de la Penne, "The Italian Attack on the Alexandria Naval Base," *United States Naval Institute Proceedings* 82, no. 2 (February 1956), 126. Earlier, but after the war had begun, the X MAS was able to draw on any personnel with a strong swimming or diving background from throughout the military, even getting volunteers from the Alpini (Alpine) troops.

8. Quotation from de la Penne, "The Italian Attack on the Alexandria Naval Base," 130.

9. Ibid.

10. Ibid., 132.

11. Ibid., and Mario Sposito, "Alexandria—December 1941," *Amici nel Mondo Association Militaria Italian Collectors International* 10, issue 2, 13–16.

12. Renato Sicurezza, in *Bollettino D'Archivio,* December 1991, 55–70.

13. See ADM116 4555, PRO Kew Garden, London, and Frank Wade, *A Midshipman's War* (Vancouver: Cordillera Publishing Company, 1994), 125. Wade has the French cruisers on the far side of the harbor, but the Admiralty report shows two of them stationed near the *Lorraine.* A "torch" is a British term for flashlight. Wade was a Canadian serving in the British Navy and one of those lucky men often at the scene of momentous events during the war. His book is a must-read for anyone interested in the Mediterranean theater.

14. De la Penne, "The Italian Attack on the Alexandria Naval Base," 135.

15. Wade, *A Midshipman's War,* 119–122.

16. G. G. Connell, *Mediterranean Maelstrom* (London: William Kimber, 1987), 145–146. *Jervis* was the flagship of the 14th Flotilla.

17. Alan Raven and John Roberts, *British Battleships of World War Two* (Annapolis, Md.: Naval Institute Press, 1978), 360–361.

18. Wade, *A Midshipman's War,* 122. Cunningham said he was thrown in the air 5 feet, which was probably an exaggeration.

19. Frank Wade, who was on board, stated that about fifty engine personnel died on the *Queen Elizabeth,* while the official historian I. S. O. Playfair stated a total of eight casualties. See Wade, *A Midshipman's War,* 124; I. S. O. Playfair et al., *The Mediterranean and Middle East,* vol. 3 (London: HMSO, 1960), 115. The War Diary states that there were no reported casualties on the *Queen Elizabeth*—see Renato Sicurezza, in *Bollettino D'Archivio,* December 1991, 66. In conversations with Andrew Smith on 26 September 1999, he pointed out that a salvage expert and one other source indicated that some engine personnel had been lost in the attack on the *Queen Elizabeth.* Reports show that the *Queen Elizabeth* was less prepared for the explosion than the *Valiant* was, in part owing to the presence of two of the Italian frogmen on board.

20. The quotation is from William Schofield and P. J. Carisella, *Frogmen First Battles,* 118. Some British sources have stated that the damage to the British battleships were kept from the Italians for an extended period, but it required only a few days for confirmation.

21. Other members of the SLC teams gave additional details, such as their departure from La Spezia. This tendency to talk about one's exploits was not, by any means, limited to the Italians. Otto Kretschmer, the famous U-boat commander who has posters about his victories printed to this day for public consumption, discussed details of his tactics with his British interrogators. See Peter Padfield, *War Beneath the Sea* (New York: John Wiley and Sons, 1998), 116.

22. ADM 116 4555, PRO Kew Garden, London.

23. Bernd Stegemann, *Germany and the Second World War,* vol. 3 (Oxford: Oxford University Press, 1995), 724; quotation from Renato Sicurezza, *Bollettino D'Archivio,* December 1991, 61.

24. Richard Ollard, *Fisher and Cunningham: A Study in the Personalities of the Churchill Era* (London: Constable, 1991), 123. It has been argued elsewhere that Cunningham did not want to spend additional money for recommended harbor defense improvements. Cresswell's name is given sometimes with only one "s."

25. Michael Simpson, in Michael Simpson, ed., *The Cunningham Papers* (Bodmin, U.K.: Naval Records Society, 1999), 458–459.

26. Wade, *A Midshipman's War,* 119.

27. Erminio Bagnasco, "Gli inglesi sapevano . . . ," *Storia Militare* 11, no. 120 (September 2003), 4–17.

CHAPTER 9

1. Franco Maugeri, *From the Ashes of Disgrace* (New York: Reynal and Hitchcock, 1948), 38. Vittorio Tur, *Plancia Ammiraglio,* vol. 3 (Rome: Canesi, 1963), 478, points out that Maugeri, thought by some to be a traitor to Mussolini's government, had obtained much of the information for the Alexandria attack.

2. At the time of their capture at Alexandria, the frogmen told their captors that there was a MAS unit (or large ship) named the *Vittorio Tur.* They had also placed the dead Moccagatta as the commander of the X MAS.

3. He was awarded with the Gold Medal by the Regia Marina. He is featured in the movie *Malta Story* (1953). Italian intelligence on Malta during the war was abysmal.

4. Junio Valerio Borghese, *Sea Devils* (Chicago: Regency, 1954), 208; Carlo De Risio, *I mezzi d'assalto,* 4th ed. (Rome: Ussmm, 1992), 149–150.

5. Giorgio Pitacco, "La X Mas ad Algeciras e i mezzi R," *Storia Militare,* no. 31 (April 1996), 44–50, and Borghese, *Sea Devils,* 208–209; Beppe Pegolotti, *Uomini contro navi* (Florence: Vallecchi, 1967), 154–157. A picture of Ramognino's design is on p. 46 in the *Storia Militare* article.

6. According to some sources the name was given after the war. See Luigi Emilio Longo, *I reparti speciali italiani nella seconda guerra mondiale* (Milan: Mursia, 1991), 71, and Giuseppe Pesce, "Spie in libertà ad Algeciras," *Rivista storica* (January 1996), 32–39. According to Pesce, the binoculars were 64 power—a sort of mini-telescope.

7. Pegolotti, *Uomini contro navi,* 158–159.

8. Aldo Cocchia, quoted by Livio Del Pino in "I fratelli Visintini," *Rivista storica* (April 1996), 56–60.

9. De Risio, *I mezzi d'assalto,* 224–225.

10. Pitacco, "La X Mas ad Algeciras e i mezzi R," and Marshall Pugh, *Commander Crabb* (London: Macmillan, 1956), Prologue; Pegolotti, *Uomini contro navi,* 142–144.

11. Maugeri, *From the Ashes of Disgrace,* 66–67.

12. F. H. Hinsley et al., *British Intelligence in the Second World War,* vol. 2 (London: HMSO, 1978), Appendix 15, 719 *ff.,* and F. H. Hinsley and C. A. G. Simkins, *British Intelligence in the Second World War,* vol. 4 (London: HMSO, 1990), 202–206.

13. Hinsley and Simkins, *British Intelligence in the Second World War,* vol. 4, 204.

14. T. J. Waldron and James Gleason, *The Frogmen: The Story of the Wartime Underwater Operators,* 2d ed. (London: Evans Brothers, 1955), 24–27.

15. Marco Spertini and Erminio Bagnasco, *I mezzi d'assalto della X Flottiglia MAS: 1940–1945* (Parma: Albertelli, 1991), 214–219.

16. Ibid., 54; Marcello Bertini, *I sommergibili nel Mediterraneo,* vol. 2, (Rome: Ussmm, 1968), 73–74. Some sources incorrectly have this attack as by the SLCs.

17. This account is based on De Risio, *I mezzi d'assalto,* 155–156, and Erminio Bagnasco and Achille Rastelli, *Sommergibili in guerra: Centosettantadue battelli italiani nella seconda guerra mondiale,* 2d ed. (Parma: Albertelli, 1994), 90–91.

18. With improvements in Sigint, the British began to gather a large amount of intelligence on the Abwehr in Spain and Portugal but had less knowledge of the Italians.

19. Pugh, *Commander Crabb,* 37.

20. Ibid., 42.

21. Of 1,050 tons, incorrectly given as torpedoed by a German E-Boat by Jünger Rohwer and Gerhard Hummelchen, *Chronology of the War at Sea, 1939–1945,* rev. ed. (Annapolis, Md.: Naval Institute Press, 1992), 160. Moreover, the Italians claim the *MTSM 228* was sunk by Stukas, and according to the British it was by Swordfish.

CHAPTER 10

1. Marshall Pugh, *Commander Crabb* (London: Macmillan, 1956).

2. The grenadiers made up the division considered to be the King's Guard. Bersaglieri are light infantry.

3. Marco Spertini and Erminio Bagnasco, *I Mezzi D'assalto della Xth Flottiglia MAS: 1940–1945* (Parma: Albertelli, 1991), 58, incorrectly has the *Ocean Vanquisher* also being sunk. It would be damaged, repaired, and then lost on 19 March in Tripoli harbor to German bombers (Ju-88s). In *Underwater Warriors* (London: Arms and Armour, 1996), Paul Kemp does not credit the *Berto* as being sunk.

4. F. H. Hinsley et al., *British Intelligence in the Second World War,* vol. 3 (London: HMSO, 1984), Part 1, 194.

5. Pugh, *Commander Crabb,* 58.

6. The after-action reports of the three human torpedoes are partly printed in Carlo De Risio, *I mezzi d'assalto,* 4th ed. (Rome: Ussmm, 1992), 240–246, and Kemp, *Underwater Warriors,* 45. Neither I. S. O. Playfair et al., in *The Mediterranean and Middle East* (London: HMSO, 1960), nor Jünger Rohwer and Gerhard Hummelchen, in *Chronology of the War at Sea, 1939–1945,* rev. ed. (Annapolis, Md.: Naval Institute Press, 1992), mentioned this successful Italian attack.

7. De Risio, *I mezzi d'assalto,* 246.

8. According to an initial report by Vice Admiral H. M. Burrough at Gibraltar on the recovery of the damaged SLCs from the *Olterra,* "Olterra was towed across from Algeciras to the commercial anchorage at Gibraltar on October 11, 1943, being released by the Spanish at Italian request. She was then examined, and we found out what she had been used for. By this time the only Italian left aboard was her chief engineer, who provided a lot of information. The Decima MAS working areas had been wrecked on 23rd September 1943 by a Signor D-something and two men from the 'Spanish [*sic*—Italian?] consulate,' who threw a good deal of material overboard, and set to detonate the scuttling charges in two of the three SLCs aboard before leaving late on the 23rd. A party of a petty officer and two ratings, survivors from *Ugolino Vivaldi,* were sent from Cartagena to finish the job on the 26th, but sent back by the Spanish authorities before they could do anything. The initial sabotage was conducted immediately after a Spanish naval guard party had left the ship." Special thanks to Andrew Smith for locating this. ADM 1/12939, "Italian Torpedo Attacks on Shipping at Gibraltar" (Admiralty file M.055194/1943), letter 4211, 16 November 1943.

9. In the same period, there was a gamma action against Allied ships at Huelva, but the British were alerted and inspected the ships there and the action had no consequences.

10. *British Vessels Lost at Sea, 1939–1945* (Cambridge: Patrick Stephens, 1976), 83.

11. The transport *Fernplant* is not listed in the British merchant losses in this period.

12. Junio Valerio Borghese, *Sea Devils* (Chicago: Regency, 1954), 193.

13. The *Leonardo Da Vinci* was sunk on 23 May 1943 by the destroyer HMS *Active.*

14. De Risio, *I mezzi d'assalto,* 198–200. See also Giulio Raiola and Carlo De Risio, "Attacco all'America," *Storia illustrata* (March 1969), 22–33.

15. Pugh, *Commander Crabb*, 76.

16. Borghese, *Sea Devils*, 260.

17. Pugh, *Commander Crabb*, 76.

CHAPTER 11

1. Dennis Mack Smith, *Mussolini* (New York: Knopf, 1982), 308.

2. On the German countermeasures, the standard work is by Joseph Schroeder, *Italiens Kriegsaustritt 1943: Die deutschen Gegenmassnahmen im italienischen Raum: Fall "Alarich" und "Achse"* (Göttingen: Musterschmidt, 1969), but see the in-depth analysis of Gerhard Schreiber, *Die italienischen Militärinternierte im deutschen Machtbereich, 1943–1945: Verraten, verachtet, vergessen* (München: Oldenburg, 1989). The Italian edition has an updated bibliography; See *I militari italiani internati nei campi di concentramento del Terzo Reich, 1943–1945* (Rome: Ussmm, 1992). Hitler's criminal order of 9 September was mainly accepted without question. As an example, see RM7/952, 32, "Behandlung ital. Truppenteile, die Waffen an Aufständische abliefern bzw. mit Aufständischen verhandeln," 1421, of 12 September 1943.

3. Joseph Schroeder, *Italiens Kriegsaustritt, Die deutsche Gegenmaßnahmen im italienischen Raum: Fall Alarich und Achse* (Göttingen-Zürich-Frankfurt: Musterschmidt, 1969); *Akten zur deutschen Auswertigen Politik*, Serie E, vol. 6, doc. 311 (Göttingen: Vandenhoeck and Ruprecht, 1979), 533–535. The Führer's order was published by Karl Stuhlpfarrer, *Die Operationszonen "Alpenvorland" und "Adriatisches Küsterland," 1943–1945* (Wien: 1969). (Italian edition: *Le zone d'operazione Prealpi e Litorale Adriatico, 1943–1945* [Gorizia: 1979], 193–195.)

4. *Kriegstagebuch der Seekriegsleitung, 1939–1945* (hereafter KTB/Skl), edited by Werner Rahn and Gerhard Schreiber, with Hansjoseph Maierofer, vol. 49 (Berlin: Mittler and Sohn, 1994), note on 3 September 1943.

5. The Borghese 1943–1945 diary was published recently by his aide-de-camp: Mario Bordogna in *Junio Valerio Borghese e la X Flottiglia Mas: Dall'8 settembre 1943 al 26 aprile 1945* (Milan: Mursia, 1996), 23 *ff*.

6. Zara Algardi, *Processo ai fascisti*, presented by Ferruccio Parri, with a Foreword by Domenico Peretti Griva (Florence: Parenti, 1973), 197–198. Algardi takes for granted that Borghese received the orders.

7. National Archives and Record Services, Washington, D.C., RG 226, Entry 119A, Folder 1824, Box 71, OSS London-X-2-PTS-35, "Second Detailed Interrogation Report on Capitano di Fregata Borghese, Valerio," 17 October 1945. The Alto Dige is the area of the Alps bordering Tyrol.

8. Bordogna, *Junio Valerio Borghese e la X Flottiglia Mas*, 35.

9. McGregor Knox, "Borghese, Junio Valerio," in Philip V. Cannistraro, ed., *Historical Dictionary of Fascist Italy* (Westport, Conn.: Greenwood, 1982), 87–88.

10. ACS, SPD, CR, RSI, bundle 73, "Promemoria per l'eccellenza Ferrini," 4 pages, n.d., part of documents collected for the inquiry against Borghese by RSI officials.

11. Ibid.

12. Bundesarchiv-Militärarchiv (hereafter BA-MA), RM7/952, 33. The message is dated 12 August 1943, but this is clearly a printing error. It arrived from Abwehr to the submarine HQ, where Borghese had good relationships; also Joseph Schroeder, *Italiens Kriegsaustritt 1943*, 309–310, note. "Borghese offered already on 13 September to employ without reserve the flotilla on the German side" (BA-MA, RM7/237, "Marine-Nachrichten-Dienst," no. 1/Skl Im 28032/43 of 16 September 1943, to Deutsche Marinekommando Italien).

13. Donald Gurrey, *Across the Lines: Axis Intelligence and Sabotage Operations in Italy, 1943–1945* (Tunbridge Wells, U.K.: Parapress, 1994), 68.

14. Bordogna, *Junio Valerio Borghese e la X Flottiglia Mas,* 41–42. See also Guido Bonvicini, *Decima marinai! Decima Comandante! La fanteria di marina, 1943–1945* (Milan: Mursia, 1988), 15–17; Ricciotti Lazzero, *La Decima Mas: La compagnia di ventura del "Principe Nero"* (Milan: Rizzoli, 1984), 18; Sergio Nesi, *Decima Flottiglia nostra . . . I mezzi d'assalto della marina italiana al sud e al nord dopo l'armistizio* (Milan: Mursia, 1986; 2d ed., 1987), 95.

15. Giampaolo Pansa, *Borghese mi ha detto* (Milan: Palazzi, 1971), 56.

16. KTB/Skl, vol. 50, note on 3 October 1943, 42–43. Wolff's postwar statement is in Ricciotti Lazzero, *La Decima MAS,* 20, 22 (nn. 11, 17).

17. BA-MA, RM7/237, "Marine Nachrichten Dienst to Marinekommando Italien," 28032/43 for 16 September 1943. With the same message, stating the intention of Grossi to continue to fight alongside "German comrades without conditions," the documents also reported the Borghese situation. On Commander Grossi, see also the critical assessment of Paolo Ferrari, "L'Italia tedesca del dicembre 1943," *Storia militare* (January 1998), 33–41, a long report on Grossi.

18. Erminio Bagnasco and Achille Rastelli, *Sommergibili in guerra: Centosettantadue battelli italiani nella seconda guerra mondiale,* 2d ed. (Parma: Albertelli, 1994).

19. KTB/Skl, vol. 49, note on 28 September 1943, 550.

20. Bordogna, *Junio Valerio Borghese e la X Flottiglia Mas,* 45. Bordogna wrote that the daughter of Borghese recalled Mussolini's cool attitude toward him; the king, in contrast, was always very nice to him. This may be due in part to Borghese's "royal blood."

21. Among the considerable list of works on the Resistance, recent ones such as Claudio Pavone's *Una guerra civile: Saggio storico sulla moralità della Resistenza* (Milan: Bollati Boringhieri, 1991), and Massimo Legnani and Ferruccio Vendramini, eds., *Guerra, guerra di liberazione, guerra civile* (Milan: Angeli, 1990), should be mentioned.

22. Of course figures change considerably, especially in Italian historiography. According to some estimates, about 50 percent of the fighting partisans were Communists or under their control. The figures for the latter are obviously quite difficult to assess. The Allies estimated about 40 percent. For a study from a military point of view of the Resistance, see Antonio Pietra, *Guerriglia e controguerriglia: Un bilancio militare della Resistenza, 1943–1945* (Valdagno: Rossato, 1997). See also the review by Giorgio Rochat in *Italia contemporanea,* no. 213 (December 1998), 925–926. For an estimate of the Italian guerrilla operations, see the classic John Ellis, *From the Barrel of a Gun: A History of Guerrilla, Revolutionary and Counter-Insurgency Warfare, from the Romans to the Present* (London: Greenhill, 1995), 171–173.

23. Luigi Del Bono, *Il mare nel bosco: X Flottiglia MAS, 1943–1945,* 2d ed. (Savona: Liguria, 1989), 22. Of the memoirs of former members of the X MAS, those of Del Bono are generally considered among the best.

24. For Parri's witness at Borghese's trial, see Algardi, *Processo ai fascisti,* 220.

25. Bonvicini, *Decima Marinai! Decima Comandante!,* 18, 19.

26. Bordogna, *Junio Valerio Borghese e la X Flottiglia Mas,* 52.

27. As examples we could quote Aussmm, titolo F, the Armed Forces Ministry letter of 15 February 1945, no. 02/976, "X Flottiglia MAS," on the discipline of the sailors at Imperia under naval bombardment on 15 January 1945 and population claims against wild gunshots and prepotency in Aussmm, fondo RSI, bundle I-1.

28. See ACS, SPD, CR, bundle 73, Mussolini letter of 28 December 1943, the undated General Chirieleison's Memorandum for the Duce about the navy infantry, and the Meendsen-Bohlken letter of 20 December, no. G.4454. The force really available on 14 December 1943 included 106 officers and 1,000 sailors, all volunteers. See Aussmm, titolo F, "Notizie relative alla costituzione dei reggimenti fanteria di marine," 3 pages, n.d.

29. Aussmm, titolo F, Ferrini to Mussolini, 24 January 1944, no. 140043/SSB, and Aussmm, titolo C, no. 873, 24 February 1944, "Dipendenza Fanteria Marina," signed by Sparzani.

30. This swimming pool was already in use by gamma men in 1940 before the war.

31. Gurrey, *Across the Lines,* 68, and National Archives and Record Services, Washington, D.C., RG 226, Entry 119A, Folder 1824, Box 71, OSS London-X-2-PTS-35, "Second Detailed Interrogation Report on Capitano di Fregata Borghese, Valerio," 5. For the specialized units, see Appendix.

32. Friedrich W. Deakin, *The Brutal Friendship: Mussolini, Hitler and the Fall of Italian Fascism* (New York: Harper and Row, 1962), 658.

33. Nesi, *Decima Flottiglia nostra,* 113. The Vega battalion X MAS was disbanded on 4 April 1945. Interestingly enough, some of these documents on the X MAS were at last declassified in 1990.

34. Ambrogio Viviani, *I servizi segreti italiani, 1815–1985* (Rome: And Kronos, 1985), 306–307. This was also noted by intelligence reports gathered against Borghese. See ACS, SPD, CR, RSI, bundle 73.

35. Viviani, *Servizi segreti italiani,* 263–290. A detailed account of the war fought in the RSI by various agencies is written by Franco Fucci, *Spie per la libertà: I servizi segreti della Resistenza italiana* (Milan: Mursia, 1983), who devoted chapter 23 to the German intelligence organizations but unfortunately did not deal with the X MAS.

36. This is what Admiral Franco Maugeri wrote in his memoirs, *Ricordi di un marinaio* (Milan: Mursia, 1980). This book is not a translation of the more famous *From the Ashes of Disgrace* (New York: Reynal and Hitchcock, 1948) and does not repeat many sensitive statements made in *Ashes.*

37. Luigi Bonomini et al., eds., *Riservato a Mussolini: Notiziari giornalieri della Guardia Nazionale Repubblicana, novembre 1943–giugno 1944* (Milan: Feltrinelli, 1974), published a selection of these reports.

38. Ricciotti Lazzero, *La Decima Mas: La compagnia di ventura del "Principe Nero"* (Milan: Rizzoli, 1984), 225–226.

39. The highest officers at the base were Lieutenant Commanders Umberto Bardelli and Aldo Lenzi.

40. Aldo Bertucci, *Guerra segreta oltre le linee: I "Nuotatori Paracadutisti" del Gruppo Ceccacci (1943–1945)* (Milan: Mursia, 1995), 16.

41. For a summary of the accusations, see Deakin, *The Brutal Friendship,* 658–659; Bordogna, *Junio Valerio Borghese e la X Flottiglia Mas,* 74.

42. Lazzero, *La Decima MAS,* 201. There were several inquiries carried out on Borghese and the X as a possible danger for Mussolini and fascism.

43. Bonvicini, *Decima marinai! Decima Comandante!,* 52. This also proves that the X MAS worked with the Abwehr. See also Nesi, *Decima Flottiglia nostra,* 128–129, who is also more detailed on this aspect.

44. Deakin, *The Brutal Friendship,* 785–786; Rahn summarized the Italian situation with the Duce; see his report of 31 March 1944, BA-MA, PG 33969, "Auszug aus dem Kriegstagebuch des deutschen Marinekommando Italien–1, Juni 1943–31 August 1943 und 1 November 1943–31 Oktober 1944," 95. For this and other documents from the German archives we are very grateful to Pier Paolo Battistelli for his generous help.

45. ACS, SPD, CR, RSI, bundle 73: "Rivolta al San Marco e 10th Flottiglia," 28 January 1944. Graziani had been known as "Mussolini's Marshal," largely because of his successes before the war in Libya and Ethiopia. Disgraced in his defeat in North Africa in 1940–1941, he had gone north and strongly supported the Salò Republic; after the war, he would join with Borghese in helping the MSI—the Fascist Party of the postwar era.

46. ACS, SPD, CR, RSI, Job 153, 044968-9: "Domanda," 19 January 1944, and ACS, SPD, CR, RSI, Job 153, 044970-92. The report of General Semandini, "Relazione sui fatti verificatisi a La Spezia, in seno al reggimento San Marco il mattino del 9 gennaio 1944-XXII," was sent on 18 January to Mussolini with Borghese's statements and interrogation minutes.

47. The Barbarigo story is covered by Marino Perissinotto, *Duri a morire: Storia del battaglione fanteria di marina Barbarigo, Decima Flottiglia Mas, 1943–1945* (Parma: Albertelli, 1997), with an English summary inside. See also Bonvicini, *Decima marinai! Decima Comandante!*, chapter 6, and Ernest F. Fisher, Jr., *Cassino to the Alps* (Washington, D.C.: Center of Military History, 1977).

CHAPTER 12

1. Ricciotti Lazzero, *La Decima Mas: La compagnia di ventura del Principe Nero* (Milan: Rizzoli, 1984), 11.

2. Eitel Friedrich Moellhausen, *La carta perdente: Memorie diplomatiche 26 luglio 1943–2 maggio 1945* (Rome: Sestante, 1948), 403–407, described Löwisch as "stupid."

3. See the Löwisch report in Bundesarchiv-Militärarchiv (hereafter BA-MA), PG 33969, "Auszug aus dem Kriegstagebuch des deutschen Marinekommando Italien—1 Juni 1943–31 August 1943 und 1 November 1943–31 Oktober 1944," 88–89. Nevertheless, according to Borghese, Löwisch would never forget the Prince's "attitude held in the Loewemberg-Fellner affair" (Mario Bordogna, ed., *Junio Valerio Borghese e la X Flottiglia Mas: Dall'8 settembre 1943 al 26 aprile 1945* [Milan: Mursia, 1996], 166). Despite his name, Loewemberg was an Italian Navy officer shot by the Germans without just cause; this incident marked the lowest point of a bad relationship between the two navies.

4. BA-MA, PG 33969, "Auszug aus dem Kriegstagebuch des deutschen Marinekommando Italien—1 Juni 1943–31 August 1943 und 1 November 1943–31 Oktober 1944," 95.

5. In *Decima Flottiglia nostra . . . I mezzi d'assalto della marina italiana al sud e al nord dopo l'armistizio* (Milan: Mursia, 1986; 2d ed., 1987), 292–294, Sergio Nesi contended that the *Aquila* was not damaged and that the explosive charge did not blow up.

6. These failures were often the result of the intelligence work of the SIS of the Regia Marina of the south. Some of the men hated Borghese, but others would help rescue him at the end of the war. See *La marina italiana nella seconda guerra mondiale*, vol. 14, *La Marina dall'8 settembre 1943 alla fine del conflitto* (Rome: Ussmm, 1962), 496.

7. Bordogna, *Junio Valerio Borghese e la X Flottiglia Mas*, chapter 8, and Nesi, *Decima Flottiglia nostra*. At least 300 *Marders* were built during the course of the war.

8. It is impossible to list all these missions here; however, Sergio Nesi has written a detailed account of these actions. See Nesi, *Decima Flottiglia nostra*.

9. Nesi, *Decima Flottiglia nostra*, 283.

10. Donald Gurrey, *Across the Lines: Axis Intelligence and Sabotage Operations in Italy, 1943–1945* (Tunbridge Wells, U.K.: Parapress, 1994), 68.

11. Vanna Vailati, *1943–1944: La storia nascosta; Documenti inglesi segreti che non sono mai stati pubblicati* (Turin: GCC, 1986), 290 *ff*. Marshall Pietro Badoglio is Vailati's uncle. The plan set up by the Foreign Office and the War Office would give the southern boot to Greece; Sicily, Calabria, and Sardinia to Britain; and Piedmont and Milan to France, while Rome would go the United States, which would have probably organized the remainder under the Pope. Dwight D. Eisenhower and Bedell Smith showed little sympathy for such a plan. This idea was somewhat similar to American calls from some circles to turn postwar Germany into an agricultural nation.

12. PRO, WO 204/7031, 39706, Report on Zone of Operation "Bergenfield" between 24 October 1944 and 24 February 1945, by Major Rohwort, 6.

13. Ibid., 10. For Alerio, see chapter 6.

14. Richard Lamb, *War in Italy, 1943–1945: A Brutal Story* (New York: Da Capo Press, 1996), 7, 252. The feelers were first put out by Borghese beginning in December 1944 and brought forward to March 1945, but they were rejected by the Allies because of the X MAS's reputation, which had been tarnished by its reckless antiguerrilla activity.

15. See the interesting political-military report on the poor situation for Italian interests on the eastern border by the commander of the San Giusto battalion, Lieutenant Commander Enzo Chicca, in Aussmm, Marina RSI, F, no. 1977, 22 December 1944, "Situazione battaglione *S. Giusto.*"

16. Aussmm, Titolo F 13, letter 1228 of the 22nd from liaison officer Heggenreiner to RSI Armed Force Ministry. Figure is from allegato 4.

17. See the order signed by SS General Globocnik, who was responsible for rear security of the zone of operation, published in Nicola Cospito and Hans Werner Neulen, *Salò-Berlino: l'alleanza difficile. La repubblica Sociale Italiana nei documenti del Terzo Reich* (Milan: Mursia, 1992), 154–155, and Aussmm, Marina RSI, F, *Comando divisione Decima,* 1/284 of 23 January 1945, "Relazione sull'operazione conseguente all'attacco partigiano su Tarnova della Selva." See also Bordogna, *Junio Valerio Borghese e la X Flottiglia Mas,* 161. The document relating the rescue of the *Fulmine* is published in Cospito and Werner Neulen, *Salò-Berlino,* 156–157. A detailed account using Yugoslavian sources is in Ricciotti Lazzero, *La Decima MAS,* 153 ff. See also Maurizio gamberini and Riccardo Maculan, eds., *Battaglione Fulmine X Flottiglia MAS, 1944–1945: Documenti ed immagini,* (Bologna: Lo Scarabeo, 1994).

18. Italy acquired Bolzano and Trento provinces, plus a part of the Belluno province, with its victory in World War I in 1918. Of these, the Bolzano province was largely German speaking (with an ancient but significant "native" portion) until the Fascist regime planted Italian citizens in the area.

19. Enno Donà, *Tra il Pasubio e gli altipiani: Ricordi della Resistenza* (Rovereto: Museo storico italiano della Guerra–Memorie 4, 1995). Professor Giuseppe Acerbi, who was in the CLN of Valdagno, where the gamma group was stationed, explained to us that the partisans were mainly the "operative branch," while the intellectuals were in the CLN, and therefore the former were often not able to understand such sensitive political aims.

20. Bordogna, *Junio Valerio Borghese e la X Flottiglia Mas,* 145–146. During his interrogation, Borghese remembered that there were 500 rifles delivered and the deal took place with one Bortolotti.

21. This point led the Turin Fascist federal secretary to report to Mussolini that Borghese did not trust the RSI government. See Friedrich W. Deakin, *The Brutal Friendship: Mussolini, Hitler and the Fall of Italian Fascism* (New York: Harper and Row, 1962), 741.

22. Renzo De Felice, *Il Rosso e il Nero,* ed. Paquale Chessa (Milan: Baldini and Castoldi, 1995), 132.

23. Fabio Andriola, "1944–1945: la strana alleanza tra marinai del Sud e della RSI per difendere Trieste e le terre dell'Est," *Bollettino d'archivio dell'Ufficio storico della Marina militare* 12 (March 1998), 119–142.

24. Augusto De Toro, "La Marina del Sud e la difesa della Venezia Giulia (1944–1945)," *Rivista storica* 8, no. 8 (August 1995), 48–53.

25. This relationship began in November 1944, when Tito chose between the British support given him up to that point and Stalin's support after secretly visiting Stalin in Moscow.

26. Nesi, *Decima Flottiglia nostra*, 100–101, 110. Writing in 1986, ten years before the publication of the de Courten and Zanardi memoirs, Nesi referred to personal talks with Borghese and Forza.

27. As an example, see Giorgio Bocca, *La repubblica di Mussolini* (Bari: Laterza, 1978), 323.

28. Giorgio Zanardi, *Il problema della Venezia Giulia: I contatti fra l'ammiraglio de Courten e il comandante Borghese*, in *La Marina nella Guerra di Liberazione e nella Resistenza*, atti del convegno di Studi, Venezia 28–29 aprile 1995 (Rome: Ussmm, 1997), 115.

29. The report and the explanation are printed in Giorgio Zanardi, "Il problema della Venezia Giulia: I cointatti fra l'ammiraglio de Courten e il comandante Borghese," *La Marina nella Guerra di Liberazione e nella Resistenza*, meeting held at Venice on 28–29 April 1995 (Rome: Ussmm, 1996), 115–127. Some of Zanardi's declarations at the Borghese trial and Borghese's notes are in Bordogna, *Junio Valerio Borghese e la X Flottiglia Mas*, 131–132. The book speaks of several missions of this kind sent by the navy secret service SIS on behalf of Admiral de Courten. See also Timothy J. Naftali, "ARTIFICE: James Angleton and X-2 Operations in Italy," in George C. Chalou, ed., *The Secrets War* (Washington, D.C.: National Archives and Records Administration, 1992), 220–221.

30. On the organization of the war effort in northern Italy during the German occupation, and the aim of exploiting Italy's most industrialized area and avoiding unrest in the population, see Paolo Ferrari and Andrea Curami, with Alessandro Massignani, "Lavorare fino all'ultimo," *Italia contemporanea*, 1997–1998.

31. Messe was the most famous of Italy's generals in World War II. He had served in the Soviet Union and surrendered in Tunisia after the Germans.

32. Bordogna, *Junio Valerio Borghese e la X Flottiglia Mas*, 136.

33. According to Nesi, *Decima Flottiglia nostra*, 106, this was forced by the local Fascist secretary, who publicly attacked Rainer for his anti-Italian attitude.

34. Quoted by Ricciotti Lazzero, *La Decima MAS*, 62; Moellhausen, *La carta perdente*, 409.

35. National Archives and Record Services, Washington, D.C., RG 226, Entry 119A, Folder 1824, Box 71, OSS London-X-2-PTS-35, "Second Detailed Interrogation Report on *Capitano di Fregata* Borghese, Valerio," 15.

36. Aussmm, Marina RSI, F, no. 659/R/F 56 16 February 1945, "Reparti della *X MAS* nella zona del Litorale Adriatico."

37. In his memoirs, *Col di luna* (Treviso: Canova, 1947), Cino Boccazzi left much to guess about the part he played in the contacts between X MAS and the Osoppo, probably because the book was written too near the end of the war. According to Nesi, *Decima Flottiglia nostra*, 101, Boccazzi remained three months with the X-MAS and his treatment was "brotherly." See Bordogna, *Junio Valerio Borghese e la X Flottiglia Mas*, 155–158; Pier Arrigo Carnier, *Lo sterminio mancato: La dominazione nazista nel Veneto orientale, 1943–1945* (Milan: Mursia, 1982), 181–182.

38. Augusto De Toro, "La Marina del Sud e la difesa della Venezia Giulia," 52.

39. Marceglia's report is reprinted in *Antonio Marceglia*, privately published by his relatives in Venice in 1977; see "Missione al Nord," 43–50. The report was rewritten in 1956 at Admiral de Courten's request because the original 1945 report was missing. A special thanks to Antonio Sema for having located this book, as his family was friendly with Marceglia's. A different account, in Lazzero, *La Decima Mas*, 236–237, states that it was J. J. Angleton who instructed Marceglia.

40. BA-MA, PG 33969, "Auszug aus dem Kriegstagebuch des deutschen Marinekommando Italien—1 Juni 1943–31 August 1943 und 1 November 1943–31 Oktober 1944," 85, note relating to the second half of September.

41. Lazzero, *La Decima Mas,* 224–225.

42. ACS, SPD, CR, RSI, bundle 73, General G. Corrado report, 7–8. We could not confirm the story of the submarine.

43. BA-MA, PG 33969, "Auszug aus dem Kriegstagebuch des deutschen Marinewkommando Italien—1 Juni 1943–31 August 1943 und 1 November 1943–31 Oktober 1944," 54, note of the period 1–15 July 1944. The German admiral was well impressed by the fact that Borghese placed units not employed at the front with Wolff for the struggle against the partisans in the Milan area.

44. NARS, T311, roll 10, fr. 7010373: Report of 31 March 1945, 5.

45. Aussmm, Marina RSI, F 13, Relazione riassuntiva circa attività, forza e dislocazione dei reparti della decima Flottiglia MAS, 1 January 1945.

CHAPTER 13

1. Max Corvo, *The OSS in Italy, 1942–1945: A Personal Memoir* (New York: Praeger, 1990), 260.

2. As an example, see in Aussmm, Marina RSI, F, "Ministero delle forze armate," no. 06835 of 30 September 1944, transmitting the letter of the German military city command in Piacenza to the Modena SS and police commander in order to not move from Piacenza an X MAS unit "much esteemed by German collaborators" in order to carry out operations against partisans.

3. Luigi Del Bono, *Il mare nel bosco: X Flottiglia MAS, 1943–1945,* 2d ed. (Savona: Liguria, 1989), 23 *ff.*

4. Giorgio Bocca, *La repubblica di Mussolini* (Bari: Laterza, 1978), 106; Friedrich W. Deakin, *The Brutal Friendship: Mussolini, Hitler and the Fall of Italian Fascism* (New York: Harper and Row, 1962), 662.

5. Aussmm, Marina RSI, F, "Relazione riassuntiva circa attività forza e attuale dislocazione dei reparti della Decima Flottiglia MAS," 1 December 1944.

6. In *La repubblica di Mussolini,* 280, Bocca wrote: "So the Tenth mops up, shoots, hangs up like a German unit, on German's orders."

7. Gerhard Schreiber, *Deutsche Kriegsverbrechen in Italien: Täter, Opfer, Strafverfolgung* (Munich: Bech, 1996).

8. Aussmm, Marina F, X Mas to Army General Staff, no. 867, 20 July 1944, "Gruppi di combattimento Decima."

9. Zara Algardi, *Processo ai fascisti,* presented by Ferruccio Parri, with a Foreword by Domenico Peretti Griva (Florence: Parenti, 1973), 210–211. This form of cruelty, it must be said, especially underlined in the trial against Borghese and Ungarelli, was not uncommon: Spies of the X MAS caught in southern Italy were shot in the same manner. A wartime movie series made by U.S. reporters, released in Italy under the tile *Combat Film* (1994), shows several executions of X MAS commandos carried out in southern Italy by the same procedure.

10. For this episode, see Ricciotti Lazzero, *La Decima Mas: La compagnia di ventura del "Principe Nero"* (Milan: Rizzoli, 1984), 118, and Guido Bonvicini, *Decima Marinai! Decima Comandante! La fanteria di marina, 1943–1945* (Milan: Mursia, 1988), 101–104. There were no Germans involved, as the republic did not threaten any line of communication. Both sides suffered four casualties.

11. ACS, SPD, CR, RSI, bundle 73. The report of Brigade General Giuseppe Corrado is dated 29 March 1945 and was sent to Mussolini by the undersecretary of state for the navy on 10 April, just a few days before the end of the war. This general, under the command of Borghese, reported directly to the navy's undersecretary and therefore to Mussolini *against* Borghese.

12. Federico Maistrello, *La Decima Mas in provincia di Treviso* (Verona: Istituto per la storia della Resistenza e della Società contemporanea della marca trevigiana, 1997); Benito Gramola and Annita Maistrello, *La divisione partigiana Vicenza e il suo battaglione Guastatori* (Vicenza: La Serenissima, 1995), 50. This witness confirmed that one of the sailors assigned to Bertozzi's staff defected in order to avoid sexual harassment by Bertozzi.

13. David T. Zabecki, ed., *World War II in Europe,* vol. 1 (New York: Garland, 1999), 33. The deaths to the civilian population through Allied bombing may keep the losses *before* 8 September 1943 higher than those occurring *after* this date.

14. Article 1 of the Orders for German Land Forces, published as Appendix A in the Ph.D. dissertation of Charles Wayne Smith, *S.S. General Karl Wolff and the Surrender of the German Troops in Italy, 1945,* University of Southern Mississippi Press, 1970, 168.

15. Wolff was probably referring to Gero von Schultze-Gaevernitz. Wolff's words are from Lazzero, *La Decima Mas,* 223, and quoted by Claudio Gatti, *Rimanga tra noi: L'America, l'Italia e la "questione comunista": I segreti di 50 anni di storia* (Milan: Leonardo, 1990), 22.

16. Mario Bordogna, ed., *Junio Valerio Borghese e la X Flottiglia Mas: Dall'8 settembre 1943 al 26 aprile 1945* (Milan: Mursia, 1996), 190.

17. The latest contribution on this is by Maurizio Dal Lago and Giorgio Trivelli, *1945: La fine della guerra nella valle dell'Agno* (Valdagno: Lions Club, 1999).

18. The question was raised by the Germans through the Red Cross in Swiss as they captured Italian soldiers fighting with the Allies. They asked the same treatment for the captured Italian soldiers of the RSI. The Allies agreed, and the Italian Comando Supremo (Marshal Messe) accepted, although the RSI soldiers were considered by the king's government to be "rebels and traitors." Messe proposed to judge the cases after the war, when the status of POW would be over. Hopes that the Italian internees captured on 8 September 1943 would be treated as POWs were disappointed. Nor would the Germans consider the partisans regular combatants if they wore the three-color band on their breast. Vietinghoff said this was impossible because the partisans did not fight according to international laws of war. We warmly thank Dr. Paolo Battistelli for procuring documents on the question. See also Nicola Della Volpe, "I soldati della RSI e la loro sorte," in *L'Italia in guerra: Il sesto anno, 1945* (Rome: Ussmm, 1996), 211–225.

19. Pier Paolo Battistelli, "Il 'buco nero' nella storia della RSI. Analisi storiografica dell'apparato militare della repubblica di Salò," *Storia contemporanea* 26, no. 1 (February 1995), 101–132.

20. Sandro Setta, *Profughi di lusso* (Milan: Angeli, 1993), 79.

21. Renzo De Felice, Il *Rosso e il Nero,* ed. Paquale Chessa (Milan: Baldini and Castoldi, 1995), 133.

22. William E. Barrett, *Shepherd of Mankind* (Garden City, N.Y.: Doubleday, 1969); see also Giuseppe Alberigo, ed., *Storia del Concilio Vaticano II* (Bologna: Il Mulino, 1998), quoted in *Famiglia Cristiana,* 31 May 1998, 153, n. 21. It is interesting to note that Major Rowarth, whose report about the dealings of Borghese with the Osoppo partisans was already discussed above, was sent on a mission to northeastern Italy in August 1944 after training in southern Italy. He spoke Italian and escaped from a POW camp after the Italian armistice, and when he took cover in the Vatican he had contacts with Montini. See Lazzero, *La Decima Mas,* 128.

23. Franco Bandini, *Vita e morte segreta di Mussolini* (Milan: Mondadori, 1978), 294.

24. The name of Fiume Square has been changed to Piazza della Repubblica.

25. Sergio Nesi, *Decima Flottiglia nostra . . . I mezzi d'assalto della marina italiana al sud e al nord dopo l'armistizio* (Milan: Mursia, 1986; 2d ed., 1987), 314–315; Ferraro was still alive at the time of this writing.

26. Archivio di Stato di Vicenza (Vicenza State Archive) CLNP, bundle 11, f. 18, "Relazione sulla ricognizione eseguita a Vicenza," 12. We thank Maurizio Dal Lago, who drew our attention to this document.

27. George C. Chalou, ed., *The Secrets War* (Washington, D.C.: National Archives, 1992); Timothy J. Naftali, "Artifice," 220.

28. Lazzero, *La Decima Mas,* 244, quoting a magazine interview.

29. Ibid., 240–241.

30. Deakin, *The Brutal Friendship,* 602.

CHAPTER 14

1. Franco Ferraresi, *Threats to Democracy* (Princeton: Princeton University Press, 1996), 3–4.

2. Claudio Gatti, *Rimanga tra noi: L'America, l'Italia e la "questione comunista": I segreti di 50 anni di storia* (Milan: Leonardo, 1990), 23.

3. Giorgio Pisanò, *Io fascista, 1945–1946: La testimonianza di un superstite* (Milan: Il Saggiatore, 1997).

4. All this is from his diary, part of which was published by Mario Bordogna, his aide-de-camp, in *Junio Valerio Borghese e la X Flottiglia Mas: Dall'8 settembre 1943 al 26 aprile 1945,* (Milan: Mursia, 1995), 218 *ff.*

5. Alessandro Cova, *Graziani, un generale per il regime* (Rome: Newton Compton, 1987), 267.

6. This would be known as the Corte di Cassazione, or "Court of Cassation."

7. Zara Algardi, *Processi ai fascisti,* presented by Ferruccio Parri, with a Foreword by Domenico Peretti Griva (Florence: Parenti, 1973), 147–148.

8. On irregular combatants, see Bob Newmann, *Guerrilla in the Mist: A Battlefield Guide to Clandestine Warfare* (Boulder: Paladin Press, 1997), 140. For a detailed discussion on trials, see Mimmo Franzinelli, *Le stragi nascoste. L'armadio della vergogna: l'impunità e rimozione dei crimini di guerra nazifascisti, 1943–2001* (Milan: Mondadori, 2002).

9. Annibale Paloscia, *Storia della polizia* (Rome: Newton Compton, 1989), 125.

10. Algardi, *Processi ai fascisti,* 209–210.

11. Ferraresi, *Threats to Democracy,* 19–20.

12. Borghese's *Sea Devils* (Chicago: Regency, 1954) notes his imprisonment for three years and his work as a civilian writing for several papers on naval affairs during the postwar years; the 1995 Naval Institute Press edition ignores his postwar career.

13. Jeffrey McKenzie Bale, Ph.D. dissertation, *The "Black" Terrorist International: Neo-Fascist Paramilitary Networks and the "Strategy of Tension" in Italy, 1968–1974* (University of California at Berkeley, 1994), 4. Bale displays an excellent grasp of the period.

14. Piero Ignazi, "The Changing Profile of the Italian Social Movement," in Peter H. Merkl and Leonard Weinberg, eds., *Encounters with the Contemporary Radical Right* (Boulder: Westview Press, 1993), 75–92.

15. Bale, *The "Black" Terrorist International,* 52. Note that race and racism underlay some, but not all, of the Fascist factions.

16. National Archives and Record Service (NARA), 765.00/9-1950.

17. Dennis Eisenberg, *The Re-emergence of Fascism* (New York: A. S. Narnes, 1967), 140 *ff.*

18. Bale, *The "Black" Terrorist International,* 257.

19. Ibid., 259.

20. Ibid., 258–260.

21. Ibid., 262.

22. Ferraresi, *Threats to Democracy,* 47–48.

23. Bale, *The "Black" Terrorist International,* 265.

24. Ibid.

25. Ibid., 268–270.

26. Virgilio Ilari, *Il generale col monocolo: Giovanni De Lorenzo 1907–19* (Ancona: Nuove Ricerche, 1994), 70, and Bale, *The "Black" Terrorist International,* 266. Ilari wrote that the uprising happened on 6 November 1953 and that the British press acknowledged the Italian action as a cause.

27. See Jack Greene and Alessandro Massignani, *The Naval War in the Mediterranean, 1940–1943* (London: Chatham, 1998), 297–306.

28. *New York Times,* 25 April 1956.

29. Boris Aleksandrovoich, *The Secret of the Loss of the* Novorossiysk (St. Petersburg: Isdatelstvo, 1991). See also René Greger, "Quando la 'Giulio Cesare' affondò a Sebastopoli," *Rivista storica* (March 1994), 52–58; *Warship International,* no. 3 (1991), 297–298; and review of Karazhavin's book in *Warship International*, no. 4 (1992), 363–364. In "Navi italiane all'Urss," *Storia militare* (August 1995), 24–33, Sergey Berezhnov supports the view that the sabotage was a fabrication of the regime, but it should be noted that the sabotage theory began to appear with the winds of *Glasnost.* Most recently, the Soviet who handled the salvage operation, in an interview with Captain Peter A. Huchthausen, never came to a conclusion as the evidence did not weigh significantly either way.

30. Peter A. Huchthausen, "Espionage or Negligence? A Sinking Mystery, *Naval History* 10, no. 1 (February 1996), 19–24.

31. Ilari, *Il generale col monocolo,* 57, and Huchthausen, "Espionage or Negligence?"22.

32. Sergei Gorshkov, *Red Star Rising at Sea* (Annapolis, Md.: Naval Institute Press, 1974), 142–146. Hibbits seemed to be unaware of all the details concerning the replacement of Admiral Nikolai G. Kuznetsov by Gorshkov. He did note that Gorshkov was from the Ukraine and supported Khrushchev in his desire to downplay large surface craft and promote the submarine force—and that Kuznetsov opposed this. Robert Waring Herrick's *Soviet Naval Strategy* (Annapolis, Md.: Naval Institute Press, 1968) does not mention the loss but does note the new "deterrent-defensive naval strategy" adopted by Khrushchev. He saw the Soviet turn away from an ocean strategy as partly fueled by the high price of an ocean navy. David Fairhall's *Russian Sea Power* (Boston: Gambit, 1971) also does not discuss the incident. The recently published naval chronology by Norman Polmar omits all mention of the loss of the *Novorossiysk.*

33. Peter Huchthausen was kind enough to send this letter to us along with three Italian newspaper articles from April 1992. The elder Wolk would continue working on SLCs and midgets up to 1960, when he retired after working with the Argentines on similar projects.

34. Renzo De Felice, *Il rosso e il nero,* ed. Paquale Chessa (Milan: Baldini and Castoldi, 1995), 132–133. See W. Vincent Arnold, *The Illusion of Victory* (New York: Peter Lang, 1998), *passim.* Also from conversations between Paul Silverstone, who is working on a book concerning the Palestine Blockade with Andrew Smith, and a letter from Smith dated 7 March 1995. Also see *The Daily Telegraph,* 20 June 1994 obituary for Major General Yohai Bin-Nun. Dr. David Nicolle, in an e-mail dated 20 September 1999, noted that the *Farouk* may not have been sunk. Yohai Bin-Nun, who is credited with the sinking, went on to lead the Israeli naval commando Seal Team 13.

CHAPTER 15

1. Richard Drake, *The Aldo Moro Murder Case* (Cambridge: Harvard University Press, 1995), 28.

2. Philip Willan, *Puppetmasters: The Use of Political Terrorism in Italy* (London: Constable, 1991), 146–159 (quotation, 146). RG226, Entry 119A, Folder 1812, Box 70, OSS London-X-2-

PTS-34, 2–12; Olaf Goebel, "*Gladio* in den Bundesrepublik," in Jens Mecklenburg, ed., *Gladio: Die geheime Terrororganisation der NATO* (Berlin: Elefant Press, 1997), 48–89.

3. Willan, *Puppetmasters,* 146–147.

4. Claudio Gatti, *Rimanga tra noi: L'America, l'Italia e la "questione comunista": I segreti di 50 anni di storia* (Milan: Leonardo, 1990); Commissione Stragi, Proposal of Relation by Senator Giovanni Pellegrino, 1994; Giovanni Fasanella and Claudio Sestieri, with Giovanni Pellegrino, *Segreto di Stato: La verità da Gladio al caso Moro* (Turin: Einaudi, 2000), 20 *ff.*

5. Paolo Inzerilli, *Gladio: La verità negata* (Bologna: Analisi, 1995), 14, 20. According to the Venice district attorney, Felice Casson, there were also different levels of security and capability in the Gladio. See Sentenza Ordinanza of 10 October 1991, printed as an appendix in the magazine *Avvenimenti,* no. 21 (1991), 69–95.

6. Amos Spiazzi di Corte Regia, *Il mistero della Rosa dei venti* (Verona: Centro Studi Carlomagno, 1995), 142–144, and Gatti, *Rimanga tra noi,* 25, 28. Annibale Paloscia, *I segreti del Viminale* (Rome: Newton, 1994), 370, published a Carabinieri document estimating that the most extreme Left of the PCI also formed a "red" Gladio and was preparing for possible guerrilla operations in the Tuscany mountains. The strength estimate is most likely exaggerated.

7. Jeffrey McKenzie Bale, Ph.D. dissertation, *The "Black" Terrorist International: Neo-Fascist Paramilitary Networks and the "Strategy of Tension" in Italy, 1968–1974* (University of California at Berkeley, 1994), 302–303.

8. *L'Espresso* of 5 January 1995, quoted by Virgilio Ilari, *Il generale col monocolo: Giovanni De Lorenzo 1907–19* (Ancona: Nuove Ricerche, 1994), 70. Valdagno saw much new construction of public works during Mussolini's regime and is home today to one of the authors.

9. Peter Tompkins, "The Origins of the O.R.I.," in *Fondazione corpo volontari della Libertà-Veterans Association of O.S.S., Gli americani e la guerra di liberazione in Italia. Office of Strategic Service (O.S.S.) e la Resistenza,* atti del convegno internazionale di studi storici, Venezia, 17–18 ottobre 1994 (Rome: Presidenza del Consiglio dei ministri, Dipartimento per l'informazione e l'editoria, 1995), 325–327.

10. Willan, *Puppetmasters,* 45, 153–154. Some have argued that this was an attempt by the Israeli Mossad to get revenge for Italy's leniency with Palestinian terrorists. The Venice prosecutor accused the chief of Mossad of the bombing, but the court found him not guilty for lack of evidence. Nevertheless, Maletti was plotting with the Mossad to kill Palestinian terrorists on an Argo 16 flight organized by Miceli. They did not succeed in this attempt. See Fasanella and Sestieri, *Segreto di Stato,* 83. Clearly, however, the Italian right wing did not have many scruples about using murder as a weapon.

11. "Comitato parlamentare per i servizi di informazione e sicurezza e per il segreto di Stato," *Primo rapporto sul sistema di informazione e sicurezza* (Bari: Laterza, 1995), 80–83, and Ambrogio Viviani, *I servizi segreti italiani, 1815–1985* (Rome: And Kronos, 1985), 360. See also Francesco Pecorelli and Roberto Sommella, *I veleni di OP: Le "notizie riservate" di Mino Pecorelli* (Milan: Kaos, 1994), *passim.* On 17 November, former Prime Minister Giulio Andreotti was sentenced on appeal to twenty-four years in prison for ordering the 20 March 1979 murder of journalist Carmine Pecorelli. The eighty-three-year-old senator for life cannot be imprisoned, however, and announced his decision to appeal the sentence. He had been cleared of the murder on 24 September 1999 by a Perugia court, but the local prosecutor's office appealed. The Perugia court also jailed Mafia boss Gaetano Badalamenti for twenty-four years for the murder of Pecorelli, editor of the magazine *Osservatorio Politico (OP),* who was about to publish material linking Andreotti with the Mafia. At www.rsf.org/article.php3?id_article=6521. The *New York Times* of 31 October 2003 reported that the conviction was overturned and Andreotti is cleared of the crime.

12. Larry Gurwin, *The Calvi Affair: Death of a Banker* (London: Macmillan, 1983), xii.

13. Nick Tosches, *Power on Earth* (New York: Arbor House, 1986), 4, and Gurwin, *The Calvi Affair,* 51–52. Gelli would later fall during the Michele Sindona scandal involving international banks, the Vatican of Pope Paul VI, the Mafia, and various corporate giants. He had some Teflon qualities, as his fall was well cushioned. Sindona's empire began to unravel in 1974 with the bankruptcy of Franklin National Bank in New York. Also see Richard Hammer, *The Vatican Connection* (New York: Holt, Rinehart and Winston, 1982), who supplied details on the Mafia connection to this entire episode.

14. Gurwin, *The Calvi Affair,* 65–66. One of the authors had lunch in April 2000 with an American security expert who recalled meeting an Italian member of the P2 Lodge at a security training session in the United States. Shortly after his return, he was arrested in the fallout from Gelli's arrest warrant.

15. One of Italy's police forces is the Finance Guard, which consists of uniformed officers with their own equipment and bureaucracy. These officers may stop people on the street, and people who are found to be carrying an excessive amount of cash or personal checks may be questioned. They literally guard Italy's money so that illegal amounts are not taken out of Italy, though with the advent of the Euro procedures have been modified.

16. Philip Agee, *On the Run* (Secaucus, N.J.: Lyle Stuart, 1987), 138; John Prados, *President's Secret Wars: CIA and Pentagon Covert Operations from World War II Through the Persian Gulf* (Chicago: Ivan R. Dee, 1996), 323; Willan, *Puppetmasters,* 90–120; and *CIA: The Pike Report* (Nottingham: Spokesman Books, 1977), 16. The Pike Commission conducted a congressional inquiry into the CIA. Philip Willan wrote for the *Sunday Telegraph*—a conservative organ similar to the *Washington Times.*

17. Franco Ferraresi, *Threats to Democracy* (Princeton: Princeton University Press, 1996), 78–79. On Rocca, see also Carlo Bonini and Francesco Misiani, *La toga rossa: Storia di un giudice* (Naples: Marco Tropea Editore, 1998), 37–39.

18. The president in Italy is not a strong position—most power lies with the prime minister.

19. Bale, *The "Black" Terrorist International,* 272.

20. Gatti, *Rimanga tra noi,* 71.

21. The best source on the Italian secret service is always Viviani. See his *Servizi segreti italiani,* 335–338. On this case, see also the proposed report of "Commissione parlamentare d'inchiesta sul terrorismo in Italia e sulle cause della mancata individuazione dei responsabili delle stragi," n.d. [1996?], chapter 3, section 1. The Stasi also provided supplies to the Red Army Faction, a terrorist organization operating in West Germany.

22. Virgilio Ilari, *Storia militare della prima repubblica, 1943–1993* (Ancora: Nuove ricerche, 1994), 484; Ilari, *Il generale col monocolo,* 288 *ff.*

23. Gatti, *Rimanga tra noi,* 55. See also pp. 62–63 for a discussion of the Kennedy policy, which favored the coming to power of the socialists but would not accept a communist government in Italy. For a different view, see the pioneering work of Marco Fini and Roberto Faenza, *Gli americani in Italia* (Milan: Feltrinelli, 1976), *passim.*

24. Gatti, *Rimanga tra noi,* 123.

25. Bale, *The "Black" Terrorist International,* 300. Interestingly enough, the CIA chief in Rome, Howard Stone, was cut off from this special relationship.

26. The movie *Godfather Part III* features Sindona and some of the men he was surrounded with (most notably Calvi). In the movie, Pope John Paul I replaces the dying Pope Paul VI.

27. William E. Barrett, *Shepard of Mankind: A Biography of Pope Paul VI* (Garden City, N.Y.: Doubleday, 1964), and J. P. Gallagher, *Scarlet Pimpernel of the Vatican* (New York: Coward-McCann, 1967), 24 (quotations, 155, 175–176). See also Bale, *The "Black" Terrorist International,* 48–60. Ironically, Borghese was a descendent of the medieval Pope Paul V!

28. Bale, *The "Black" Terrorist International*, 444–445. The bomb attempt that blew up Montini's office has never been officially resolved.

29. In Britain, Calvi's death has recently been declared an unsolved murder.

30. "He was in civilian clothes, without personal documents, driving a civilian car which was the property of his HQ. . . . Apart the personal documents, taken away by a thief or by somebody who wanted to delay the recognition of the man, also a briefcase appearing in a photograph taken after the accident which also disappeared" (Viviani, *Servizi segreti italiani*, 352).

31. *New York Times*, 29 March 1971.

32. The Borghese family had been well established in the seventeenth and eighteenth centuries and were known as patrons of the art in Rome. The family lost much of its wealth in the nineteenth century. We appreciate the help of Christina Huemer of the American Academy in Rome for this information. It should be noted that unconfirmed rumors made the rounds that Daria's death was not an accident.

33. Bale, *The "Black" Terrorist International*, 270.

34. Ibid., 276.

35. Quoted by Ferraresi, *Threats to Democracy*, 244, n. 7, and Stuart Christie, *Stefano Delle Chiaie* (London: Anarchy Magazine/Refract Press, 1984), 6. He probably was not an agent of the UAR. Allegedly, Delle is an incredibly nasty right-wing terrorist who later, while in exile, would be involved in Argentina's "Dirty War," in Franco's Spain fighting the ETA, in Chile helping Pinochet to shoot members of the opposition, and even the Bolivian "Cocaine Coup" of 1979. He would freely come and go from Italy in the post-Borghese coup environment with the connivance of the Italian security services. When finally brought to Italy as a prisoner, he would be declared not guilty after being brought to trial. See Ferraresi, *Threats to Democracy*, 226–227, and Bale, *The "Black" Terrorist International*, 145–146, 172–174.

36. Giampaolo Pansa, *Borghese mi ha detto* (Milan: Palazzi, 1971), 79–80, and Bale, *The "Black" Terrorist International*, 310–315, 472.

37. Bale, *The "Black" Terrorist International*, 284.

CHAPTER 16

1. Jeffrey McKenzie Bale, Ph.D. dissertation, *The "Black" Terrorist International: Neo-Fascist Paramilitary Networks and the "Strategy of Tension" in Italy, 1968–1974* (University of California at Berkeley, 1994), 303.

2. Ibid., 276–277, 287–288, 306–307.

3. Ibid., 308.

4. Ibid., 280, 293.

5. Ibid., 281.

6. David Boulton, *The Grease Machine* (New York: Harper and Row, 1978), 148–151, and Bale, *The "Black" Terrorist International*, 298–299.

7. Sergio Flamigni, *Trame atlantiche: Storia della Loggia massonica segreta P2* (Milan: Kaos edizioni, 1996), and Paolo Cucchiarelli and Aldo Giannuli, *Lo Stato parallelo* (Rome: Gamberetti, 1997), 282.

8. Philip Willan, *Puppetmasters: The Use of Political Terrorism in Italy* (London: Constable, 1991). See also Franco Ferraresi, *Threats to Democracy* (Princeton: Princeton University Press, 1996), and Claudio Gatti, *Rimanga tra noi* (Milan: Rizzoli, 1990).

9. Many of the witnesses in the inquiries led by Salvini or other magistrates spoke of French training experts of OAS origins and an underground organization in France with probably the same aim as Gladio in Italy. The OAS was said to be secretly financed by the CIA through the

same channel probably used to funnel money through Permindex in Italy. The CIA was also active in Italy with the Centro Mondiale Commerciale (World Trade Center). This was managed by people later connected with the JFK assassination, such as Clay Shaw, a CIA agent in Rome in the early 1960s. See Jim Garrison, *On the Trail of the Assassins: My Investigation and Prosecution of the Murder of President Kennedy* (New York: Sheridan Square Press, 1988), 86–89. See also Paris Flammonde, *The Kennedy Conspiracy: An Uncommissioned Report on the Jim Garrison Investigation* (New York: Meredith Press, 1969), 224. Flammonde noted that the name of Princess Marcella Borghese, a member of the Black Prince's family, was found in Shaw's personal phone book. Although Aldo Moro was not directly involved with military matters, in his memoirs, which he wrote while a prisoner of the "Brigate Rosse," he said he was convinced that "in Europe all in the military field is under American guidance, while one could imagine a certain degree of German presence, on behalf of the US, in the field of intelligence." See *Aldo Moro: Ultimi scritti 16 marzo–9 maggio 1978,* ed. Eugenio Tassini (Casale Monferrato: Piemme, 1998), 71. An inquiry was made by Italian counterintelligence over a presence of Israeli weapons depots to serve "Israeli's interests in Italy." See "Sentenza-ordinanza del giudice istruttore Guido Salvini of 18 March 1995" (hereafter referred to as "Salvini"), 330. On this occasion, SID Captain Santoni upset Maletti because he had found evidence about Gelli's strange operations. Also see Willan, *Puppetmasters,* for an international view of Italian affairs and good insight into them. On at least two occasions, the Italian press published parts of SISMI and SISDE documents obtained by the judiciary and referring to espionage against political parties. For the PCI reports, see *Taci, il Sisde ti spia: I rapporti dei servizi segreti sui partiti, 1978–1981,* supplement to *L'Espresso,* especially pp. 78–79. Other files of the SISMI are commented on (but not published) in Gianni Cipriani, *Lo spionaggio politico in italia* (Rome: Editori Riuniti, 1988).

10. Bale discussed this agency in *The "Black" Terrorist International,* 125–128. He concluded that Delle Chiaie worked with Aginter Press.

11. Ibid., 446; Richard Drake, *The Aldo Moro Murder Case* (Cambridge: Harvard University Press, 1995), 214–216. Some of this came out during the Pike Commission hearings in the U.S. Congress.

12. Bale, *The "Black" Terrorist International,* 381–383.

13. *CIA: the Pike Report* (Nottingham: Spokesman Books, 1977), 16. It is interesting to note that the Republican administration dragged its feet in supplying documents and appearances of key individuals, reminding one of much of the foot dragging that took place under the Clinton administration for more mundane matters.

14. Bale, *The "Black" Terrorist International,* 387–388. (Fenwich may be an alias.)

15. These are called "those perfidious Anglo spies" in *The Economist,* 29 April–5 May 2000, 53–54. Former CIA Chief James Woolsey claimed that the United States needs to continue this to counteract the bribes offered by European companies to secure large foreign economic orders, such as for aircraft and defense contracts.

16. Bale, *The "Black" Terrorist International,* 345.

17. Ibid., 327–329, 331.

18. John Dinges and Saul Landau, *Assassination on Embassy Row* (New York: Pantheon Books, 1980), 159. Curiously enough, Delle Chiaie was interviewed on Italian TV about his life abroad when an arrest warrant had been issued for him.

19. See, for example, the discussion in Salvini, 314. For the serial number (#Q/2041, manufactured by Beretta), see Bale, *The "Black" Terrorist International,* 331. Interestingly, in the "thorough investigation" that the Italian security services later had to carry out, none of those who were on "guard" that day and night at the Interior Ministry were interviewed.

20. Amos Spiazzi di Corte Regia, *Il Mistero della Rosa dei venti* (Verona: Centro Studi Carlomagno, 1995), 150–151.

21. On this officer, see the summary of Pecorelli's well-informed articles in Francesco Pecorelli and Roberto Sommella, *I veleni di OP: Le notizie riservate di Mino Pecorelli,* (Milan: Kaos, 1994), 78–80; Cucchiarelli and Giannuli, *Lo Stato parallelo,* 339–340; and Spiazzi, *Il Mistero della Rosa dei venti,* 151.

22. Bale, *The "Black" Terrorist International,* 340.

23. Ibid., 303–304. Selenia would later be caught up in the Lockheed scandal and had eleven retired high-ranking Italian officers on staff as experts—not an unusual practice for a defense contractor.

24. Patty Anderson at the Nixon Presidential Materials Project could not confirm the existence of any phone calls from Italy or Malta about this coup attempt, but it is unlikely they would be "official."

25. The full proclamation appears in Bale, *The "Black" Terrorist International,* 324.

26. Quoted by Willan, *Puppetmasters,* 118.

27. *New York Times,* 21 March 1971, 29, and Bale, *The "Black" Terrorist International,* 301.

CHAPTER 17

1. Paolo Cucchiarelli and Aldo Giannuli, *Lo Stato parallelo* (Rome: Gamberetti, 1997), 247.

2. Ibid., 278, and Jeffrey McKenzie Bale, Ph.D. dissertation, *The "Black" Terrorist International: Neo-Fascist Paramilitary Networks and the "Strategy of Tension" in Italy, 1968–1974* (University of California at Berkeley, 1994), 341.

3. Amos Spiazzi di Corte Regia, *Il Mistero della Rosa dei venti* (Verona: Centro Studi Carlomagno, 1995), 148–149; Zavoli, *La notte della Repubblica* (Milan: Mondadori, 1992), 152; and letter to the authors, 6 June 1998.

4. In *La toga rossa: Storia di un giudice* (Naples: Marco Tropea Editore, 1998), Carlo Bonini and Francesco Misiani discuss a personal experience of a left-wing member of the judiciary. Quotation from Ambrogio Viviani, *I Servizi segreti italiani, 1815–1985* (Rome: And Kronos, 1985), 360.

5. Magnus Linklater et al., *The Nazi Legacy* (New York: Holt, Rinehart and Winston, 1989), 212.

6. Ambrogio Viviani, *Manuale della controspia* (Milan: Mondadori, 1988), 46.

7. Ibid., p. 45.

8. Ibid., 44–46.

9. Also in a letter to the authors of 6 June 1998 and Ilari, *Il generale col monocolo: Giovanni De Lorenzo, 1907–19* (Ancona: Nuove Ricerche, 1994), 274, n. 9.

10. Viviani, *Servizi segreti italiani,* 363. Quotation in Italian edition: Franco Ferraresi, *Minacce alla democrazia: La destra radicale e la strageia della tensione in Italia nel dopoguerra* (Milan: Feltrinelli, 1995), 224, n. 12.

11. According to one officer of the organization, Amos Spiazzi, he simply executed the orders received to alert against Communist insurgency. His organization was declared illegal, and he was imprisoned for six years but later found not guilty. He did not say anything about Gladio, although at some point he revealed some of these assets. See his memoirs, *Il mistero della Rosa dei Venti.* Nevertheless Claudio Gatti, in his *Rimanga tra noi: L'America, l'Italia e la "questione comunista": I segreti di 50 anni di storia* (Milan: Leonardo, 1990), 131, defined the "Rosa dei Venti" as "another operetta plot conceived by unreliable characters who claim contacts with NATO." He stated, "But in our research we have found nothing that shows a US involvement."

This conclusion is suspect in our view, because similar training at the international level was organized by Radio Free Europe, a CIA creature.

12. Francesco Pecorelli and Roberto Sommella, *I veleni di OP: Le notizie riservate di Mino Pecorelli* (Milan: Kaos, 1994), 311–312. The file that Pecorelli had in his office when he was murdered was entitled "Coup attempt under the name of Junio Valerio Borghese."

13. Giannettini had a warrant of arrest on his head, and Andreotti probably sacrificed him in the maneuver to hit the right wing of the Christian Democrat Party and form the center-left government.

14. Viviani, *Servizi segreti italiani,* 367.

15. Ibid., 363–364, 368; Eugenio Tassini, ed., *Aldo Moro: Ultimi scritti 16 marzo–9 maggio 1978* (Casale Monferrato: Piemme, 1998), 117; and Gatti, *Rimanga tra noi,* 134–135. It should also be taken into account that the De Lorenzo case was opened in a turf battle between Moro and Andreotti.

16. Comitato parlamentare per I Servizi di informazione e sicurezza e per il segreto di Stato, *Primo rapporto sul sistema di informazione e sicurezza* (Bari: Laterza, 1995), 80.

17. Bale, *The "Black" Terrorist International,* 377. Bale tends to accept Orlandini's statement at face value. When we made an inquiry to the U.S. Navy on this matter through the Freedom of Information Act, we were informed that we would need to submit the names of the ships!

18. Pietro Calderoni, ed., *Servizi segreti* (Naples: Tullio Pironti, 1986), 68. Pecorelli wrote in his magazine *OP* (10 April 1975) that Andreotti used other people to communicate with Borghese, whom he knew.

19. *New York Times,* 15 November 1973. The Eolian islands are off Sicily; the reference to Sardinia could be the NATO secret base at Alghero.

20. Commissione Stragi, Proposal of Relation by Senator Giovanni Pellegrino, chapter 6, "Il c.d. Golpe Borghese," 1996.

21. The Greek colonels had several trips arranged for right-wing Italians to visit Greece and prepare for a coup in Italy. See Bale, *The "Black" Terrorist International,* 156–157. Note that President Clinton apologized to Greece on his trip in November 1999 for U.S. support of the colonel's regime.

22. In 1999, he was president of the Chamber in the Parliament. As Philip Willan noted in *Puppetmasters: The Use of Political Terrorism in Italy* (London: Constable, 1991), 104, "Pazienza claimed that only the Americans could provide the Italians with sophisticated poisons capable of killing people without leaving any suspicious traces that might be detected at an autopsy."

23. Spiazzi, *Il Mistero della Rosa dei Venti,* 189.

24. Quotation in "Oltranzismo atlantico," Commissione Stragi, Proposal of Relation by Senator Giovanni Pellegrino, chapter 8, section 7. On the FBI, see Willan, *Puppetmasters,* 348, reporting the D'Amato statement. It should be remembered that he was at Reagan's inauguration. However, the connection with the FBI, in our opinion, is unlikely. It is more likely one of the other U.S. agencies, not the CIA or FBI.

25. Willan, *Puppetmasters,* 95.

26. "Sentenza-ordinanza del giudice istruttore Guido Salvini of 18 March 1995," 337–340. When questioned by the prosecutor, Gelli said he had "nothing to say."

27. Salvini, 572.

28. The Pike Report, presented in January 1976 to the U.S. House of Representatives, concludes that the CIA only executed orders coming from "parties outside the CIA." Quoted from Noam Chomsky, *Radical Priorities* (Montreal: Black Rose Books, 1981), 169.

29. Salvini, 573–575.

30. Vincenzo Vinciguerra, "L'albero caduto," in "Sentenza-ordinanza del giudice istruttore Guido Salvini of 18 March 1995."

31. One son now lives in Australia.

32. Bale, *The "Black" Terrorist International*, 296.

33. Colonel Terence Taylor, ed., *The Military Balance, 1999–2000* (London: IISS, 1999), 63.

ABBREVIATIONS AND RANKS

ABBREVIATIONS

AA Anti-aircraft

AN Avanguardia Nazionale (National Advanced Guard). A sister right-wing organization to the FN.

AUSSMM Archivio Ufficio Storico Stato Maggiore Marina (Italian Naval Archives).

BA-MA Bundesarchiv-Militärarchiv (Federal Archives of Germany, Military Branch). Located at Freiburg im Breisgau.

CLN Committee of National Liberation

DC Democrazia Cristiana, or Christian Democrats

FN Fronte Nazionale (National Front). Borghese's 1968 organization.

GC&CS Government Code & Cypher School. Located during World War II at Bletchley Park in England.

Kg Kilogram.

Km Kilometer.

MA Motoscafo Assalto (assault motorboat). The first name given to the explosive boat in 1936, though documents also mention MTA.

MAS Motoscafo Anti Sommergibile (antisubmarine motorboat). Though the small craft were originally intended to hunt submarines, the term became idiomatic. The X Flotilla MAS, for example, is often called the 10th Light Flotilla in English works.

MI6 The British Secret Intelligence Service (we use MI6 instead of SIS to avoid confusion with the Italian Navy's SIS).

MT Motoscafo Turismo (touring motorboat). In the 1936 design, this acronym was given to the first two series produced in 1938 and 1939, of six and twelve boats, respectively.

MTA Motoscafo Turismo Aviotrasportato (air-transported touring motorboat). Also called MAs.

MTL Motoscafo Turismo Lento (slow motorboat).

MTM Motoscafo Turismo Modificato (modified touring motorboat). A development of the MT; some fifty were built.

MTR Motoscafo Turismo Ridotto (reduced motorboat).

MTS Motoscafo Turismo Silurante (touring torpedo motorboat). A small motor torpedo boat that was a failure.

MTSM Motoscafo Turismo Silurante Modificato (modified torpedo touring motorboat). A development of the MTM weighing about 4.5 tons. They were capable of carrying a short version of the 17.7-inch torpedo.

MTSMA Motoscafo Turismo Silurante Modificato Allargato (modified, enlarged touring torpedo motorboat). An MTM capable of carrying a torpedo, powered by two Alfa-Romeo 2500 hp engines, modified from the failed MTS. It was initially built in 1943 and was also referred to as the SMA. The "M" originally stood for "Marino" to emphasize the craft's seagoing capabilities.

NP Nuotatoi Paracadutisti or swimmers and paratroopers. A unit formed from paratroopers of the *Folgore* and *Nembo* divisions and swimmers trained in special operations from a special *San Marco* marine unit.

OSS Office of Strategic Services, United States.

OTO Odero-Terni-Orlando was one of the two main shipbuilders in Italy. The other was Ansaldo.

PCI Partido Comunista Italiano (Italian Communist Party).

PRO Public Record Office, Kew, London.

RSI Repubblica Sociale Italiana (Italian Social Republic). Mussolini's rump state, 1943–1945, sometimes called the Salò Republic for Mussolini's residence in Salò, Lake Garda, Italy.

SIA Servizio Informazioni Aeronautica (Air Force Intelligence Service).

SID Servizio Informazioni Difesa (Defense Intelligence Service). The Italian CIA/FBI at the time of the 1970 coup attempt.

SIFAR Servizio Informazioni Forze Armate (Armed Forces Intelligence Service).

SIM Servizio Informazioni Militari (Military Intelligence Service).

SIS Servizio Informazioni Segrete (Secret Intelligence Service). The navy secret service organization.

SISDE Servizio Informazioni Sicurezza Democratica (Intelligence Service for Democratic Security). Italy's domestic intelligence agency since 1977.

SLC Siluro a Lenta Corsa (low-speed torpedo). The Chariot and the "pig" are examples.

TSR Torpedine Semovente Rossetti

USSMM Ufficio Storico Stato Maggiore Marina (publisher of Italian official histories)

RANKS

Comando Supremo—Italy's supreme command
Supermarina—Italian naval high command
Grande Ammiraglio—Admiral of the Fleet
Ammiraglio di Armata—Admiral*
Ammiraglio di Squadra (A.S.)—Vice Admiral
Ammiraglio di Divisione (A.D.)—Rear Admiral
Contrammiraglio di Divisione (C.A.)—Rear Admiral (lower half, and we refer to them as Divisional Admirals)
Capitano di Vascello (C.V.)—Captain
Capitano di Fregata (C.F.)—Commander
Capitano di Corvetta (C.C.)—Lieutenant Commander
Tenente di Vascello (T.V.)—Lieutenant

---

*There was also an Ammiraglio Designato di Armata that would be a high-ranking vice admiral. The list is drawn from *La X Flottiglia Mas: La sua leggenda perché i giovani sappiano . . .* , edited by Press Office of the X MAS, privately printed in 1993 by the X MAS veterans association.

APPENDIX

DECIMA FLOTILLA MAS UNITS

HQ
HQ Decima Division

Barbarigo battalion
Lupo battalion
NP battalion
Fulmine battalion
Valanga battalion
Saggittario battalion
Colleoni artillery battalion
Da Giussano artillery battalion
San Giorgio artillery battalion
Freccia battalion
Castagnacci battalion
Servizio ausiliario femminile (women auxiliary service)
Ardimento Group
Longobardo battalion
Pegaso battalion
Antiaircraft artillery battalion
Risoluti battalion
San Giusto battalion
Scirè battalion
Serenissima battalion
Vega battalion
Cumero detachment
Milano detachment

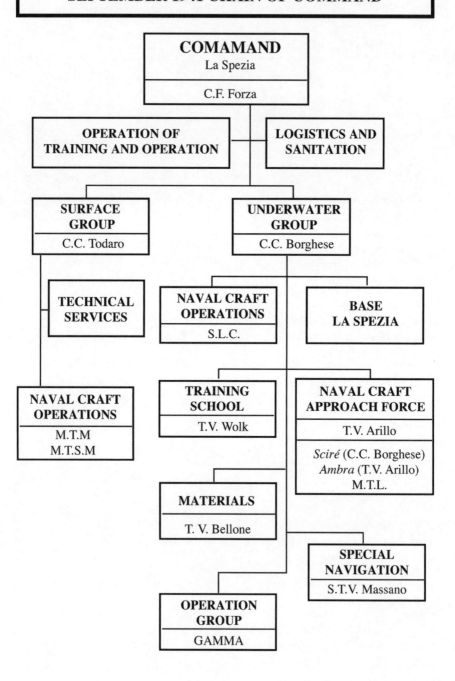

SEPTEMBER 1941 CHAIN OF COMMAND

COMAMAND
La Spezia

C.F. Forza

OPERATION OF TRAINING AND OPERATION

LOGISTICS AND SANITATION

SURFACE GROUP
C.C. Todaro

UNDERWATER GROUP
C.C. Borghese

TECHNICAL SERVICES

NAVAL CRAFT OPERATIONS
S.L.C.

BASE LA SPEZIA

NAVAL CRAFT OPERATIONS
M.T.M
M.T.S.M

TRAINING SCHOOL
T.V. Wolk

NAVAL CRAFT APPROACH FORCE
T.V. Arillo

Sciré (C.C. Borghese)
Ambra (T.V. Arillo)
M.T.L.

MATERIALS
T. V. Bellone

SPECIAL NAVIGATION
S.T.V. Massano

OPERATION GROUP
GAMMA

SELECTED BIBLIOGRAPHY

ARCHIVES

Archivio Centrale dello Stato, Rome
b. 73 fasc. 10, 11, 11C 12F
b. 49 fasc. 581
b.48 fasc. 544, 546

Archivio di Stato, Vicenza
CLNP, bundle 11

Bundesarchiv Militärarchiv –Freiburg i.Br.
RM7/952–RM7/237
RM7/233
PG33969

Carlo Alfredo Panzarasa, personal collection

Decima MAS Archive, copy at Museo della Guerra di Rovereto (Trento)

Modern Military Records Division, Nuremberg, Interrogation of Karl Wolff
RG 238, M-1019, roll 80
RG 226, Entry 119A, Folder 1824, Box 71, OSS London-X-2-PTS-35

National Archives and Record Service
Records of the German Navy
T1022 Roll 3015
Records of the German Army
T311, roll 10
765.00/9-1950

PRO, Kew Garden, London
ADM 223/460
ADM 11872
ADM 116/3534
ADM 116/4555
WO 204/7031–39706

BOOKS AND ARTICLES

Algardi, Zara. *Processi ai fascisti* (Firenze: Parenti, 1973).

Arena, Nino. *Bandiera di combattimento* (Rome: CEN, 1974).

Bagnasco, Erminio. *Submarines of World War Two* (Annapolis, Md.: Naval Institute Press, 1977).

_____. *M.A.S. e mezzi d'assalto di superficie italiani,* 2d ed. (Rome: Ussmm, 1996).

Bale, Jeffrey McKenzie. *The "Black" Terrorist International: Neo-Fascist Paramilitary Networks and the "Strategy of Tension" in Italy, 1968–1974* (Ph.D. dissertation, UC–Berkeley, 1994).

Bandini, Franco. *Vita e morte segreta di Mussolini* (Milan: Mondadori, 1978).

Barca, Luciano. *Buscando per mare con la decima Mas* (Rome: Editori Riuniti, 2001).

Bargoni, Franco. *L'impegno navale italiano durante la guerra civile spagnola (1936–1939)* (Rome: Ussmm, 1992).

Battaglione Fulmine X Flottiglia MAS, 1944–1945: Documenti ed immagini, a cura di Maurizio Gamberini e Riccardo Maculan (Bologna: Lo Scarabeo, 1994).

Battistelli, Paolo. "Il 'buco nero' nella storia della RSI: Analisi storiografica dell'apparato militare della repubblica di Salò," *Storia contemporanea* 26 (February 1995), 101–132.

Bertoldi, Silvio. *La guerra parallela (8 settembre 1943–25 aprile 1945). Le voci delle due Italie a confronto* (Milan: 1966).

_____. *Contro Salò* (Milan: Bompiani, 1984).

Bertucci, Aldo. *Guerra segreta dietro le linee: I "Nuotatori paracadutisti" del gruppo Ceccacci (1943–45)* (Milan: Mursia, 2001).

Boatti, Giorgio. *Spie imperfette* (Milan: Rizzoli, 1987).

Boccazzi, Cino. *Missione Col di Luna* (Milan: Rusconi, 1977).

Bonvicini, Guido. *Battaglione Lupo, X Flottiglia Mas (1943–1945)* (Rome: Ed. del Senio, 1973).

_____. *Decima marinai! Decima Comandante* (Milan: Mursia, 1988).

Bordogna, Mario, ed. *Junio Valerio Borghese e la X Flottiglia Mas: Dall'8 settembre 1943 al 26 aprile 1945* (Milan: Mursia, 1995).

Borghese, Junio Valerio. "Tecnica costruttiva dei mezzi d'assalto," *La scienza illustrata* (December 1950), 36–41.

_____. *Decima flottiglia Mas: Dalle origini all'armistizio* (Milan: Garzanti, 1950). English editions: *Sea Devils* (Chicago: Regency, 1954; 2d ed., Annapolis, Md.: Naval Institute Press, 1995).

Bravetta, Ettore. *La Grande Guerra sul mare,* 2 vols. (Milan: Mondadori, 1925).

Buttazzoni, Nino. *Solo per la bandiera: I nuotatori paracadutisti della marina* (Milan: Mursia, 2002).

Cadorna, Raffaele. *La riscossa* (Milan: Rizzoli, 1962).

Caputo, Livio. "Valerio Borghese ci serviva," *Epoca,* 11 February 1976.

Ceva, Lucio. "Aspetti militari della Resitenza (1943–1945)," in *Guerra mondiale: Strategie e industria bellica 1939–1945* (Milan: Franco Angeli, 2000), 214–244.

Conti, Giuseppe. "La RSI e l'attività del fascismo clandestino nell'Italia liberata dal settembre 1943 all'aprile 1945," *Storia contemporanea* 10, no. 4/5 (October 1979), 941–1013.

Corvo, Max. *The OSS in Italy, 1942–1945: A Personal Memoir* (New York: Praeger, 1990).

Deakin, Friedrich W. *The Brutal Friendship: Mussolini, Hitler and the Fall of Italian Fascism* (New York: Harper and Row, 1962).

Del Bono, Luigi. *Il mare nel bosco* (Rome: Volpe, 1980).

_____. *I giorni del furore: X flottiglia Mas, 1943–1945* (Savona: Ed. Liguria, 1986).

Della Volpe, Nicola. "La sorte dei soldati della RSI," in *L'Italia in guerra: Il sesto anno 1945* (Rome: Ussmm, 1996).

Del Pero, Mario. *La guerra fredda* (Rome: Carocci, 2001).

De Lutijs, Giuseppe. *Storia dei servizi segreti in Italia* (Rome: Ed. Riuniti, 1984).

_____. *Il lato oscuro del potere: Associazioni politiche e strutture paramilitari segrete dal 1946 a oggi* (Rome: Ed. Riuniti, 1996).

De Micheli, P., et al. *L'onore delle armi alla X Mas* (B.T. Brescia: Decima, 1989).

Dolfin, Giuseppe. *Con Mussolini nella tragedia* (Milan: Garzanti, 1950).

Donà, Enno. *Tra il Pasubio e gli altipiani: Ricordi della Resistenza* (Rovereto: Museo storico italiano della Guerra–Memorie 4, 1995).

Fasanella, Giovanni, and Claudio Sestieri, with Giovanni Pellegrino. *Segreto di stato: La verità da Gladio al caso Moro* (Turin: Einaudi, 2000).

Ferrante, Ezio. *La Grande Guerra in Adriatico nel LXX anniversario della vittoria* (Rome: Ussmm, 1987).

Franzinelli, Mimmo. *I tentacoli dell'Ovra* (Turin: Bollati Boringhieri, 1999).

_____. *Delatori. Spie e confidenti anonimi: l'arma segreta del regime fascista* (Milan: Mondadori, 2000).

Fucci, Franco. *Spie per la libertà* (Milan: Mursia, 1983).

Garland, Albert N., and Howard McGaw Smith. *Sicily and the Surrender of Italy: U.S. Army in World War II* (Washington, D.C.: Office of the Chief of Military History, 1965).

Gatti, Claudio. *Rimanga tra noi: L'America, l'Italia e la "questione comunista": I segreti di 50 anni di storia* (Milan: Leonardo, 1990).

Giorgerini, Giorgio. *Uomini sul fondo: Storia del sommergibilismo italiano dalle origini a oggi* (Milan: Mondadori, 1994).

Greene, Jack, and Alessandro Massignani. *Ironclads at War* (Conshohocken: Combined Books, 1997).

_____. *The Naval War in the Mediterranean, 1940–1943* (London: Chatham, 2002, pbk).

Greger, René. *Austro-Hungarian Warships of World War I* (London: Ian Allan, 1976).

Grossi, Enzo. *Dal Barbarigo a Dongo* (Rome-Trieste: 1959).

Gurrey, Donald. *Across the Lines: Axis Intelligence and Sabotage Operations in Italy, 1943–45* (Tunbridge Wells, V.K.: Parapress, 1994).

Ilari, Virgilio. *Il generale col monocolo: Giovanni De Lorenzo 1907–19* (Ancona: Nuove Ricerche, 1994).

_____. *Storia militare della prima repubblica, 1943–1993* (Ancona: Nuove Ricerche, 1994).

_____. "L'impiego delle forze armate della RSI in territorio nazionale," in *L'Italia in guerra: Il quinto anno 1944* (Rome: Ussmm, 1995), 172–229.

Inzerillli, Paolo. *Gladio: La verità negata* (Bologna: Analisi, 1995).

Kemp, Paul. *Underwater Warriors* (London: Arms and Armour, 1996).

Lanfranchi, F. *La resa degli ottocentomila* (Milan: Rizzoli, 1948).

Lau, Manfred. *Schoffssterben vor Algier, Kampfschwimmer, Torpedoreiter und Marine-Einsatzkommando im Mittelmeer, 1942–1945* (Stuttgart: Motorbuch, 2001).

Mallett, Robert. *The Italian Navy and Fascist Expansionism, 1935–1940* (London: Frank Cass, 1998).

Maugeri, Franco. *From the Ashes of Disgrace* (New York: Reynal and Hitchcock, 1948).

Le missioni militari alleat e la resistenza nel Veneto: La rete di Pietro Ferraro dell'OSS, ed. Chiara Saonara (Venice: Marsilio, 1990).

Murgia, P. G. *Il vento del nord: Storia e cronaca del fascismo dopo la Resistenza (1945–1959)* (Milan: n.p., 1975).

Nesi, Sergio. *Decima flottiglia nostra . . . I mezzi d'assalto della marina italiana al sud e al nord dopo l'armistizio* (Milan: Mursia, 1986).

_____. *Un Alcione dalle Ali Spezzate,* 3 vols. (Bologna: Arti grafiche Elleci, 1989).

O'Neill, R. *Suicide Squads* (London: Landsdowne Press, 1981).

Pansa, Giampaolo. *L'esercito di Salò* (Milan: Mondadori, 1970).

_____. *Borghese mi ha detto* (Milan: Palazzi, 1971).

Perissinotto, Marino. *Duri a morire: Storia del battaglione fanteria di marina Barbarigo, Decima Flottiglia Mas, 1943–1945* (Parma: Albertelli, 1997).

Pisanò, Giorgio. *Storia della guerra civile in Italia 1943–1945,* 3 vols. (Milan: FPE, 1965–1967).

_____. *Gli ultimi in giorgioverde Storia delle forze armate della Repubblica sociale italiana,* 3 vols. (Milan: FPE, 1967–1969).

Po, Guido. *La guerra marittima* (Milan: Corbaccio, 1934).

Prados, John. *President's Secret Wars: CIA and Pentagon Covert Operations from World War II Through the Persian Gulf* (Chicago: Ivan R. Dee, 1996).

Ricciotti, Lazzero. *La Decima Mas: La compagnia di ventura del principe nero* (Milan: Rizzoli, 1984).

Riservato a Mussolini: Notiziari giornalieri della Guardia nazionale repubblicana, Novembre 1943–giugno 1944, with an introduction by Natale Verdina (Milan: Feltrinelli, 1974).

Rochet, Giorgio. "La questione militare della Resistenza," in *Ufficiali e soldati: L'esercito italiano dalla prima alla seconda guerra mondiale* (Udine: Gaspari, 2000), 189–198.

Rohwer, J. *Axis Submarine Successes of World War Two* (London: Greenhill Books, 1999).

Sadkovich, James J. *The Italian Navy in World War II* (Westport, Conn.: Greenwood Press, 1994).

Santoni, Alberto, and Francesco Mattesini. *La partecipazione tedesca alla guerra aeronavale nel Mediterraneo* (Rome: Bizzarri, 1980).

Savorgnan, Alvise. "La Resitenza osovana nel Basso Friuli: sulla via di Trieste," in *La Resistenza in Friuli,* convegno di studi promosso dall'Istituto friulano per la Storia del movimento di liberazione (Udine: Maggio, 1970).

Setta, Sandro. "Borghese, Junio Valerio," in *Dizionario biografico degli italiani,* vol. 34, 1st Supplement, A–C (Rome: Istituto della Enciclopedia italiana, 1988).

Simpson, Michael, ed., *The Somerville Papers* (Aldershot: Naval Records Society, 1995).

_____. *The Cunningham Papers,* vol. 1 (Aldershot: Naval Records Society, 1999).

Sogno, Edgardo, with Aldo Cazzullo. *Testamento di un anticomunista: Dalla Resistenza al "golpe bianco"* (Milan: Mondadori, 2000).

Spampanato, Bruno. *L'ultimo Mussolini (Contromemoriale),* vol. 2 (Bologna: 1964), 187, 243–244, 271, 279, 281–284.

Spertini, Marco, and Erminio Bagnasco. *I mezzi d'assalto della X Flottiglia Mas, 1940–1945* (Parma: Albertelli, 1991).

Spiazzi, Amos. *Il mistero della Rosa dei Venti* (Verona: Centro Studi Carlomagno, 1995).

Taviani, Paolo Emilio. *I giorni di Trieste: Diario, 1953–1954* (Bologna: Il Mulino, 1998).

_____. *Politica a memoria d'uomo* (Bologna: Il Mulino, 2002).

Valentini, Norberto. *La notte della Madonna* (Rome: 1978).

Viviani, Ambrogio. *I Servizi segreti italiani, 1815–1985* (Rome: Adn Kronos, 1985).

Wade, Frank. *A Midshipman's War* (Vancouver: Cordillera, 1994).

Zarotti, Armando. *I Nuotatori paracadustisti: Nord Sud* (Milan: Auriga, n.d. [1991]).

Zeloni, S. *Il battaglione "Lupo" sulla linea Gotica* (Udine: Fiamma sociale, 1970).

INDEX